The proceeds from the sale of this book will be used to support the mission of Library of America, a nonprofit organization that champions the nation's cultural heritage by publishing America's greatest writing in authoritative new editions and providing resources for readers to explore this rich, living legacy

THE MAD FILES

THE MAD FILES

WRITERS AND CARTOONISTS ON THE MAGAZINE THAT WARPED AMERICA'S BRAIN

David Mikics, Editor

LIBRARY OF AMERICA

The* MAD *Files:
Writers and Cartoonists on the Magazine That Warped America's Brain

Published in the United States by Library of America.
Visit our website at www.loa.org.

Distributed to the trade in the United States by Penguin Random House Inc.
and in Canada by Penguin Random House Canada Ltd.

Library of Congress Control Number: 2024936101
ISBN 978–1–59853–792–5

1 3 5 7 9 10 8 6 4 2

Printed in the United States of America

contents

David Mikics
Introduction   xiii

Mary Fleener
Growing Up *MAD*   3

Ivan Cohen
The Golden Age Is Twelve Dept.   9

Geoffrey O'Brien
Stark Raving *MAD*   19

Roz Chast
A *MAD* Childhood   31

Tim Kreider
The World According to *MAD* Magazine   32

Peter Kuper
H. Kurtzman   37

Grady Hendrix
Cahiers du Ciné*MAD*   43

R. Crumb
MAD and Me   51

Art Spiegelman
MAD Love   52

Frank Jacobs
Preface to Gaines   54

R. Sikoryak
What a Load of Craft!   61

Liel Leibovitz
High Holy *MAD*   64

Mary-Lou Weisman
Reverse Immigrant   73

Leah Garrett
Jaffee in Yiddish   81

Michael Benson
*MAD*ness in Anatolia   89

Daniel Bronstein
Brueghel of the Bronx   98

Nathan Abrams
MAD's Jewish America   108

David Hajdu
With a Little Bit of Ecch: *MAD* and the Movie Musical   117

Clifford Thompson
MAD and the Insurrectionists   125

Bonnie Altucher
"Spy vs Spy" vs. Prohías   132

Sarah Boxer
Mind the Gap   138

Max Andersson
Normal   146

Adam Gopnik
MAD, the '50s, and the '60s: A (Slightly) Dissident View   155

Rachel Shteir
The "Obscure and Awesome" Women Cartoonists
of *MAD*   162

Chris Ware
To Antarctica and Back   172

Jonathan Lethem and Mark Allen
Here We Go With Our Own Execrable Simulacrum:
MAD Fold-In   183

Contributors   185
Sources and Acknowledgments   195

Introduction

David Mikics

I DON'T REMEMBER when I picked up my first issue of
MAD. But by the time I was ten years old, in 1971, I was
a rabid fan, waiting religiously for each new issue. The
peak of my MADness coincided with the magazine's greatest success.
Its bestselling issue ever, #161 (September 1973), was one of my prize
possessions: the cover, a spoof of *The Poseidon Adventure*, showed a
drowning Alfred E. Neuman with his skinny legs sticking out of a life
preserver. MAD taught me all about pubescent snark, but also about
hippies, beatniks, advertising executives, the military-industrial complex, sex, pollution, politics, and other grown-up subjects. Most of
all, it showed me that wisecracking could be a royal road to cultural
literacy. (Cartoonist Alan Moore recalls that, after discovering MAD
as an eight-year-old in the early '60s, he astonished his parents with
his banter about Caroline Kennedy, Fidel Castro, and Jimmy Hoffa.)
MAD's cackling satire was aimed in every direction, including its own
writers and artists—known as the Usual Gang of Idiots—as well as its
snot-nosed readers, who were mostly kids like me.

Before MAD there were the funny papers, with their well-worn
jokesters: Dagwood and Blondie, Archie and Jughead, Little Orphan
Annie. The funnies were calculated to make you smile or (rarely) crack
you up, but not to dangle you upside down and show you the sheer

dimwitted lunacy of life itself. For that, comics reader, you had to wait for the advent of *MAD*, whose Usual Gang of Idiots poked smirking fun at cows both sacred and profane. Proudly unfurling its adolescent gibes, *MAD* was kin to wild-card TV comedy like the Smothers Brothers and *Laugh-In*. Small visual doodads festooned its pages, and there were tiny, snide jokes strewn about like buried treasure. This was a device to make young readers pore over each panel repeatedly, while picking their noses and ignoring calls to come to the dinner table. *MAD*'s densely textured comic vibe inspired the Firesign Theatre, along with Dr. Demento, Monty Python, Second City, *Saturday Night Live*, *The Simpsons*, *The Onion*, and on and on—a comic Valhalla.

  MAD's history is as richly encrusted with oddities as one of Al Jaffee's Fold-Ins. Submitted for your approval, then, a tour through the decades, with pauses to admire landmarks along the way—the way-out movie parodies of Mort Drucker, Don Martin's knuckleheaded Foneboniana, Dave Berg's eye-rolling teens and übergrouchy suburban dads, Sergio Aragonés's skittering nitwits, Antonio Prohías's sleekly designed spy duels, and more.

The '50s

It all began in the late summer of 1952, when the first issue of *MAD*—then a comic book, not yet a magazine—hit the newsstands. The initial spur came from publisher William M. Gaines, who wanted to give the artist Harvey Kurtzman something to do besides his elaborately researched war comics. Kurtzman's counterpart, Al Feldstein, was doing yeoman's work on the EC horror line, turning out seven comics at a time compared to Kurtzman's two. Kurtzman wanted to up his salary, and so Gaines decided to let him try his hand at a satirical comic.

Bill Gaines's father, Max, was the man who invented the comic book. In 1934 he started binding together newspaper comic strips and selling the books for ten cents. Max, a crazed disciplinarian who was the terror of his family, died in a freak boating accident in 1947. Twenty-five-year-old Bill, whom the elder Gaines had always considered a ne'er-do-well, was now in charge of Max's company, EC. The initials stood for Educational Comics, but Bill would change the name to the more apropos Entertaining Comics.

EC was renowned for its spine-chilling horror comics, so replete with gore that a national scandal ensued. (One infamous panel depicted a game of midnight baseball where the dead villain's organs were used as bases, connected by his intestines.) In 1954 a psychologist named Fredric Wertham published *Seduction of the Innocent*, which railed against comic books' purported effects on young minds. Gaines had to testify in front of a Senate committee to try to save his horror comics from charges of depravity. The upshot was that censorship came to the comics industry. EC horror was finished. *MAD*, to escape the bowdlerizing steamroller, was transformed from a comic into a magazine, so it couldn't be censored. From spring 1955 onward (issue #24), *MAD* the magazine was shielded from the persecutory fingers of government.

Kurtzman wound up turning out only five more issues. Hugh Hefner offered him a sweet deal to edit *Trump*, a lavishly produced imitation of *MAD*. Kurtzman, who was at odds with Gaines, took Hefner's offer and brought with him two *MAD* stalwarts: Will Elder and Jack Davis.

Gaines was in a tizzy. How would *MAD* survive without Kurtzman, Elder, and Davis? His first move was to appoint the rock-solid Al Feldstein as his editor. Over the next eight years, Feldstein and Gaines hired a panoply of persnickety smart alecks, including artists Mort

Drucker, Bob Clarke, George Woodbridge, Paul Coker Jr., and Jack Rickard. Writers Dick DeBartolo, Frank Jacobs, Nick Meglin, Larry Siegel, Stan Hart, and Lou Silverstone kept the *MAD* zaniness in top form. Gaines also relied on Wally Wood and Joe Orlando, stalwart artists from the old EC days.

Don Martin, with his slovenly lunatic characters and his unique goofball vocabulary (Shplik! Blort! Farp!), joined the *MAD* crew. Antonio Prohías, a refugee from Castro's Cuba who spoke no English—but didn't need any for his wordless "Spy vs Spy"—came, too, and a few years later, Sergio Aragonés, known as the fastest cartoonist in the business, began splattering *MAD*'s margins with furious miniature comics. Al Jaffee, a member of Kurtzman's stable, became maestro of the Fold-In. Angelo Torres arrived in the late '60s to draw TV parodies, and Jack Davis returned to the *MAD* fold.

It was Feldstein who made the shop run, getting out an issue every forty-five days. Gaines sometimes commented on the cover choice but otherwise didn't interfere with the magazine's content. That was Feldstein's territory. (Feldstein, who was *MAD*'s editor until 1985, was succeeded by John Ficarra and, for a time, Nick Meglin.)

MAD wouldn't be *MAD* without its poster boy, Alfred E. Neuman. The gap-toothed idiot savant appeared on the cover for the first time in 1956 (#30). The dapper Norman Mingo, who looked like the millionaire from the Monopoly board, originated *MAD*'s Neuman cover. The moronically grinning boy with jug ears and one eye lower than the other dates from the late nineteenth century, and had been used to advertise everything from soda pop to "painless dentistry." Mingo gave him a makeover and, as Alfred E. Neuman, he went on over the years to impersonate a string of celebrities, including the Maharishi, Uncle Sam, Superman, Yoda, and Michael Jackson.

Fifties *MAD* made elaborate fun of social climbing through hipsterish snootiness. "How to Be Smart," from April 1956 (#27), announced, "On the following pages we will show you in a matter of minutes, how you can look and act so that everyone will think you are smart, making you, in effect, smart." Among the suggestions are some still very much au courant: Wear "heavy black eyeglasses" and a "strange textured jacket." Use words like "fabulous" and "darling" (even at the meat market!). And don't forget to remark, with a "withering sneer," "Who watches (yech) television?" ("Practice this sneer, try it on your friends.") Among your home furnishings you will want an indoor firepit rather than a fireplace, and of course a ferociously abstract painting.

Also from the late '50s (#48), the "*MAD* Treasury of Unknown Poetry" spotlighted some choice lines from "The Cantilever Tales" by Melvin Chaucer:

> Whon thot Aprille swithen potrzebie,
> The burgid prilly gives one heebie jeebie.
> Do pairdish kanzas sittie harrie truman
> Though brillig to the schlepper alfred neuman.

"Potrzebie" was one of *MAD*'s signature nonsense words, along with "furshlugginer" (which sounds just like a Yiddish expletive), both ideally to be pronounced with a thick Eastern European accent. And as for Melvin Chaucer . . . prior to Alfred, the shape-shifting Melvin— sometimes a child, sometimes an adult, always a nebbish—was *MAD*'s all-purpose mascot.

"Only *MAD* non-conformists achieve genuine originality," the magazine explained in June 1959. Not the beatniks but the "bravely idiotic *MAD* readers" were the true rebels. Beatniks sported jeans, sandals, and "scratchy beards," and raised outré pets like "ocelots, minks, deodorized skunks and rhesus monkeys." But vastly cooler *MAD* non-conformists wore "smart-looking *MAD* straight jackets" (a real item briefly marketed by the magazine!) and "light-weight pith helmets." For pets they raised "falcons, leeches, octopi, anchovies, water buffaloes and performing fleas."

In spite of such nose-thumbing, *MAD* also doted on the beatniks, recognizing a kinship between their daffy rhythms and the magazine's penchant for absurdity. *MAD* caught some flak for rewriting Lincoln's Gettysburg Address in hipster-speak à la Lord Buckley: "Fourscore and like seven years ago our old daddies came on in this scene with a new group, grooved in free kicks, and hip to the Jazz that all cats make it the same. Now we're real hung up in a crazy big hassle, digging whether that group, or any group so grooved and so hip can keep on swinging."

MAD made fun of celebrity gossip magazines too. A fearless exposé, "Was Snow White Really Snow White?"—after demonstrating that "these seven dwarfs are imposters"—called on readers to "Act! Form groups! Write your congressman! But mainly, go kill yourself!"

My favorite *MAD* one-page parody from the '50s is "Reader's Disgust" (#33, April 1957), a pitch-perfect takeoff on the *Reader's Digest* table of contents, drawn from various lifestyle magazines. Featured are "I Can't Wiggle My Ears" from the *American Journal of Psychiatry*, "Locksmiths Are Lousy Lovers?" from *Hardware Annual*, and "Renovate Your Bathysphere" from *House and Aquarium*.

The '60s

By 1960 *MAD* had conquered the teenage market. According to some estimates, it was read by most American college students and almost half the country's high school students (at least the male ones). Believe it or not, *MAD* would become even more popular in the next dozen years.

As the '60s dawned *MAD* continued its fond mockery of rebellious youth, notably in "Tomorrow's Parents," drawn by the superb Wally Wood, where two aging juvenile delinquents discover to their horror that their children are growing up square. Upon learning that her son wants to be a doctor, the bobby-soxed mother cries, "Like, I have no son!" In "My Fair Ad-Man," *MAD*'s *My Fair Lady* spoof, a beatnik shaves his goatee and becomes a Madison Avenue exec.

The '60s were the golden era of *MAD* movie parodies. They were drawn by Mort Drucker, whose characters sported spindly twining legs and fleshy faces, and their sources were instantly recognizable. My favorite among Drucker's parodies is "Flawrence of Arabia" (written by Larry Siegel), a merciless skewering of David Lean's epic. When Flawrence first puts on the typical Islamic male's white robes and headdress, he bursts out in song: "I Feel Pretty" by Sondheim and Bernstein. A conflicted soul, he laments to General Allenbuzz, "I mean, I know I'm great—but I think I'm a fraud! I like killing—but then again I hate it! I'm a show-off—but I'm really shy! What should I do?" He then winds up on a psychoanalyst's couch. The shrink, playing the Jewish mother role, suggests, "Why don't you find yourself a nice Egyptian girl and settle down." But uh-oh: the girl turns out to be Liz Taylor as Cleopatra, and Flawrence's troubles are just getting started.

MAD also delivered expert television spoofs like "Bats-Man," by Drucker and Lou Silverstone. Sparrow the boy wonder wants to be a normal teenager who goes out on dates ("Holy Kinsey Report! I've got a date with a girl"), only to be told by Bats-Man, "What's wrong with you kids today? Your date will have to wait until evil and injustice have been erased from Gotham City! And after that, we've got problems in Asia!" Many decades later, I still remember being shocked by

Sparrow's evil scheme to kill Bats-Man. With "Bats-Man" *MAD* managed the unlikely—making fun of a show that made fun of itself.

A much easier target was Stanley Kubrick's *2001: A Space Odyssey*. In "201 Min. of a Space Idiocy," by Drucker and DeBartolo, Dr. Haywire, using the video phone from the space station, catches his wife and the milkman in flagrante delicto. Unruffled, she asks him, "On the way home from the moon, will you pick up a loaf of bread, Dear?" On the Jupiter mission the astronauts treat themselves to a glass of steak and a glass of potatoes, followed by a glass of pie. Best of all are the apes dancing around the monolith. Is it "a Prehistoric Handball Court," they wonder? The massive monolith orbiting Jupiter resembles "the box the United Nations building came in." So much for Kubrickian sublimity.

I cherish "*MAD*'s Peek Behind the Scenes at a Hospital," by Al Jaffee and Larry Siegel, in which an orderly tells a hapless patient, "What do you mean you want us to *change your room*? The pairing off of people in Semi-Private rooms is a *highly specialized science!*" Jaffee's art is a busy cartwheel of doctors, nurses, and patients, all being slowly devoured by mindless medical snafus.

Antonio Prohías, a Cuban émigré who had the barest sliver of English, brought "Spy vs Spy" to *MAD*. To Prohías the Cold War was a zero-sum contest in which each side was at its wit's end but still hopeful that some new bit of ingenuity would reduce the enemy to a poof of black or white smoke. Prohías's spies, always outsmarting themselves, had the ageless tenacity of Wile E. Coyote and were every bit as luckless. With no identifying marks except that one was black and the other white, they were perfect mirrors of each other. "Spy vs Spy," with its mind-bending puzzle-like format, resembled the diagram of a joke rather than the joke itself.

The '60s was the era of the great advertising slogans, each one an unforgettable bit of poetry: "Put a Tiger in Your Tank," "I'd Walk a

Mile for a Camel," "Let Your Fingers Do the Walking," "I'd Rather Fight than Switch." *MAD* relentlessly spoofed these classic ads, saving special ire for cigarette-makers (whose product, they insisted, would lead you straight to the graveyard).

Arnie Kogen's celebrity wallets were a highlight, particularly his Howard Hughes, whose home address was listed on his ID card as "Texas, Las Vegas, The Bahamas, Nicaragua, a car parked somewhere in the Western Hemisphere, a treehouse in Brazil, and a summer home in Atlantic City, N.J." An accomplished prankster, Kogen once placed a Situations Wanted ad in *The New York Times* that read: "Shepherd, Experienced. Will not cry wolf." When a *Times* staffer asked Kogen about the phrase "Will not cry wolf," he explained, "It's a familiar line in the trade. A man who won't cry wolf is one who'll stick to his job and watch over his flock."

In the April 1968 issue (#118), the *MAD*sters introduced readers to the magazine "Hippie," with its priceless headline "Is Free Love Worth It?" But their greatest hippie satire was "'Uptight' Is a Dry Sugar Cube," using *Peanuts* characters. Here were the *Peanuts* crew, grimy and bedraggled, smoking pot, turning on and dropping out. *MAD* explained that "Uptight is . . ."—among other things—"taking an LSD Trip and seeing 'The Mormon Tabernacle Choir.'" The illustration showed a slumped-over, shaggy-haired Linus surrounded by dozens of Charlie Brown heads, all singing piously.

Dave Berg was the house square at *MAD*. He was a religious Jew and, like Al Jaffee, later contributed drawings to the *Moshiach Times*, a Lubavitcher publication. Berg's "Lighter Side" was always worth a chuckle as he lambasted the foibles of teens and their parents. Dad would blow his top while Junior snickered and guffawed. This was a throwback to an older, more mainstream style of comedy, but Berg pulled it off in style.

Sergio Aragonés's humans were tiny pullulating figures rushing around the page, usually at the margins of a bigger *MAD* story. Aragonés did a vast splash panel depicting Woodstock as a takeoff on Brueghel's *Children's Games*, with oodles of hippies doing their separate things: grinning, strumming, tripping, chasing pigs, dancing, stripping, sitting in trees, doing handstands, and finally dissolving at the horizon into a swath of unwashed, jammed-together concertgoers.

"*MAD*'s Great Moments in Politics" for January 1968 (#116) was a bombshell. There was LBJ in the famous photo showing his appendix scar to reporters—but artist Max Brandel had laid a map of Vietnam over the president's stomach. Another bold '60s satire was *MAD*'s Dr. Seuss book for grown-ups, "The Cats Are All Bats," in which a potbellied Seussian Hawk "wants to blow / a great big hole / into the Earth / from Pole to Pole"—"It's the Army's answer to birth control."

MAD was playing with countercultural fire. As early as 1958 they suggested that readers write to J. Edgar Hoover for official government-issued draft-dodger cards. So many did that Hoover, fuming about his name appearing in the magazine, sent FBI men to the *MAD* offices to interrogate Feldstein.

But *MAD* never picked a side. The magazine found long-haired revolutionaries just as ludicrous as establishment fat cats, both too earnest to be taken seriously. Both the Left and the Right were unable to take a joke, and so were a perfect match for each other.

The '70s

By the early '70s Bill Gaines, increasingly rotund, was sporting long hair and a beard, though he was no fan of the hippies (he canceled his membership in the ACLU when he found out they defended people who had damaged government property). Gaines was a wine connois-

seur, gourmet, outspoken atheist, collector of *King Kong* memora-
bilia, and compulsive neatnik with many obsessive habits. He was also
a member of the Lighter than Air Society, for zeppelin fans. Gaines
led *MAD* staffers on a number of junkets to exotic locations. In 1969
the Usual Gang traveled to Kenya, Tanzania, and Athens; in 1970 to
Japan, Thailand, and Hong Kong; and in 1971 to London, Copenhagen, Amsterdam, Leningrad, and Moscow, where locals told Gaines
he looked like Karl Marx. The number of bearded *MAD* men on the
tours, someone jested, made them resemble Benjamin Harrison's
cabinet.

The *MAD* trips led to a memorable series of drawings by the gang.
Gaines appears as Copenhagen's Little Mermaid in one, holding a mug
of beer; in another, by Don Martin, he is a goofy pear-shaped Snow
Queen in the Leningrad Ballet. Cartoonist Paul Peter Porges, after
sharing a Paris hotel room with Gaines, depicted the bug-eyed hirsute
publisher yelling into the phone: "Room Service!! Send up some liv-
erwurst with paté foie gras and a side order of braunschweiger with a
gallon of wonton soup, extra kreplach, and a bottle of Chateau Lafitte
Spätlese, and make sure the umlauts are inside, not outside the label!
Lotsa onion rolls and poach me a goyim in sherry for later and reserve
me a table at the Café le Puique for twenty and where is my tarte aux
midgets I ordered . . ."

Richard Nixon was a popular target for '70s *MAD*, along with disco,
the Me Decade, and, as always, the nonstop lies produced by the ad
industry. *MAD* also explored the peaks of high culture with features
like "A *MAD* Treasury of Shakespeare's Lesser Known Quotations" (a
sample: "Women, Mercutio, are the itch we gladly scratch"; "A tragic
tale is best for winter. In summer, 'tis off to the beach"). The magazine
itself was just as suitable for wrapping fish as it ever was.

The '80s and Beyond

MAD published new content until 2019, but starting in the '80s it began what many have viewed as a long slow decline. There were still lots of standout moments—who could forget the full-page poster from August 2008, where candidate Barack Obama, in boxing trunks and gloves, towered over the knocked-out Hillary Clinton like Ali over Sonny Liston, with an astounded Bill Clinton gaping from front row ringside? A withering satire of TV's *Mad Men* from 2011, by Arnie Kogen and artist Tom Richmond, was worthy of *MAD*'s golden age. And Dick DeBartolo's finest hour might have been in 1997, with his endless list of side effects for a miracle drug called Stoppa-da-Sneezin, all in tiny print. The admirable Peter Kuper inherited "Spy vs Spy." A platoon of new artists and writers came to the magazine in its last years. *MAD* lost some of its dash and zing, but it went out in a properly nutty and daft manner.

MAD was, for all its cynicism, too determinedly silly to be cool, much less superior. The magazine never took on self-righteous airs and never shared in the mean-spirited snarkiness that drives our current politically correct mud wrestling. "What, me worry?" was the slogan of a holy fool, wiser than the know-it-alls, and forever young.

A Little—Yecch—Bibliography

Since my mother threw away my copies of *MAD* a little over forty years ago, I have relied on the excellent anthologies compiled by Grant Geissman: MAD *About the Fifties*, MAD *About the Sixties*, and so on through the decades. The invaluable Doug Gilford has digitized many issues of *MAD* at https://madcoversite.com/covers.html. And for all things *MAD*, don't forget the unofficial fan site www.MADTrash

.com. Every *MAD* scholar happily dotes on Maria Reidelbach's excellent history *Completely* MAD, as well as Frank Jacobs's piquant *The MAD World of William M. Gaines*. There's also *Inside* MAD, edited by John Ficarra—and of course the host of pocket-sized paperback reprints from *MAD*, if you can find them, or still have the stack that you acquired as a kid.

Needless to say, the book you hold in your hands is an even better guide to *MAD* than any of these others. (That's why you bought it or, as the case may be, stole it from your friend's bathroom.) Our unusual gang of contributors will take you on a trip down memory alley. Distinguished graphic artists Art Spiegelman, Max Andersson, Roz Chast, R. Sikoryak, Drew Friedman, Mary Fleener, Tim Kreider, Chris Ware, and Peter Kuper are all here—even R. Crumb, the daddy of underground comics! Liel Leibovitz, Ivan Cohen, Clifford Thompson, and Michael Benson summon the moments when *MAD* bonked their childish heads like Newton's apple. Rachel Shteir celebrates *MAD's* unsung woman cartoonists. Mary-Lou Weisman and Leah Garrett delve into Al Jaffee, the late Frank Jacobs looks at Bill Gaines, Daniel Bronstein studies Will Elder, and Nathan Abrams examines the Jewish dimensions of *MAD*. Geoffrey O'Brien surveys *MAD's* early years as a comic book. Bonnie Altucher salutes Prohías, and David Hajdu fondly describes *MAD's* musical parodies. Grady Hendrix recalls *MAD* at the movies. Adam Gopnik and Sarah Boxer take a few potshots at the *MAD Weltanschauung*. What more could you ask? Okay, a Fold-In— et voilà—here's one by Jonathan Lethem and Mark Allen. May the yucks, and the yecchs, be with you.

tHe MAD fiLes

GROWING up MAD

Mary Fleener

'LL NEVER forget the day my older brother told me to meet him on the side of our house that was hidden by overgrown bushes and out of parental view. It was a kid hangout, not obvious, but a place we went when we wanted to escape adult scrutiny. "I have something to show you," he said with a sly grin. "It's better than *Playboy*!" My dad had a stack of *Playboy*s next to his side of the bed, carefully hidden under several *Life* magazines, but we knew they were there and would sneak into the room when our parents weren't around and look at the naked ladies. But what really got my attention were the full-page single-panel cartoons. Those cartoons were glorious. To me, that was art!

That day, my brother showed me a few copies of *MAD* that a friend had given him. They were well-read, beat-up, creased, and falling apart. The first one was #11, May 1954, the Basil Wolverton cover. "The Beautiful Girl of the Month" was creepy, audacious, and the coolest drawing I'd ever seen. She was absolutely hideous, eyeing the reader lasciviously, with her animal snout adorned with warts and sores, her drooping tongue, jagged teeth, and spaghetti-strand hair. That image torpedoed into my eight-year-old cranium and never left.

I asked, "What's 'Humor in a Jugular Vein' mean?" My brother laughed. "The jugular is this huge vein in your neck, and if you cut it, you'll bleed to death!!" "Why is that funny?" I asked. "Aw, yer too young to 'get it.' Open it up and look inside!" As I turned the pages, I felt like what I was looking at was so wrong yet it was exactly what I wanted to see in comics. I couldn't believe they could get away with this! Everyone was sleazy and rotten and I loved it!

Our parents would probably kill us if they saw this stuff, we thought. That was my first look at *MAD*, but in just that short time, I was ruined for life!

I was already a fan of cartoons. Even though we didn't have many comic books in our home, we had the daily funnies, and the glorious twenty-four-page Sunday comic section in the LA *Herald Examiner* that I drooled over and studied for hours, so I knew what the good stuff looked like. To me, there were categories: (1) "Realistic," like *Mary Worth* and *Rex Morgan*; (2) "Adventure"—that was *Tarzan* and *Prince Valiant*; (3) "Funny Families," like *Li'l Abner* and *Blondie*; (4) "Minimalistic," such as *The Little King* and *Nancy*; and (5) "Good Guys vs Bad Guys," like *Dick Tracy* and *Rick O'Shay*. When I opened that issue of *MAD*, I was overwhelmed by the drawings, which didn't look like anything I had seen in the funny papers. Pages and pages of insanely detailed, beautifully rendered panels of grotesque faces, sexy ladies with exaggerated figures, oddballs of all shapes and sizes, ugly people with scars and pimples, monsters, goofy expressions—and it all seemed so crazy, and so irresistible. I now had a new category for these *MAD* graphics: "Wild and Weird."

Two years later, we moved to Vancouver, Canada. I was ten years old and got a small allowance for doing chores around the house. I bought *MAD* faithfully every month. It shaped my way of dealing with the world, and it influenced my sense of humor. I became fond of Mort Drucker, who had the gift of portraiture, and I even liked Dave Berg.

Though he came off as a blunt, nasty old coot, Berg's stuff was very funny, and I loved it when he made fun of beatniks and hippies. A lot of his barbs were "right on." I realized that everything could be and should be criticized, poked fun at, and not taken too seriously, and that was a tall order for 1961. The Adult Problems that I saw on TV and heard on the radio were, to me, just excuses for making more rules, and the fear factor motivated normal people to do all kinds of stupid things. Everything wrong with society could be blamed on the Boogie Man, and the biggest one was the Commies! They were coming to kill us all and kidnap all the children! They could drop a bomb on us at any minute! They were a gang of thugs who didn't believe in Religion! They were going to take us children away from our parents and send us to indoctrination camps!!

Even fashion was uptight and constrictive. Women wore gloves, heels, hats, bullet bras, and girdles; slept with rollers in their hair; and inhaled hairspray on a daily basis. Men wore pressed trousers, ties, hats, undershirts, black shiny shoes, and garters on their calves to hold up their socks. Kids were expected to dress like little adults. Your hair couldn't be too long or too short. Girls wore skirts and boys wore trousers; no jeans allowed. It seemed that people decided that if they just had the right house, the right figure, the right job, the right number of kids, the right car, and the right deodorant, then every-one would live happily ever after. As we all know, it didn't quite work out that way. People still got divorced, became alcoholics, and spent money foolishly.

MAD magazine busted this fantasy and stripped the veneer of mindless conformity that the advertisers of products convinced us we needed to have, as they lined their pockets with money from gullible consumers thirsty for "the good life," which didn't provide real satis-faction. The elusive conformist goal of "fitting in" and "being normal" was a joke.

The movies and TV shows that *MAD* made fun of were propaganda machines under the guise of "entertainment," and *MAD* savagely mocked their purpose: to make money off people too trusting and worried about their place in the world. But *MAD*'s writers and artists were self-mocking too.

MAD said, "When you get right down to it, we're all slobs, whether you like it or not!"

When I was about twelve, I went to a bookstore and found a dozen *MAD* paperbacks for five cents each. I bought them all. Here were those wild stories again, and now I could read them at leisure! "Starchie" stands out to me as one of the most subversive things ever published in *MAD*. *Archie* comics were really popular, and I read them but found them pretty boring, so when I could finally comprehend the gags in "Starchie," it sent my brain reeling again. The whole cast as juvenile delinquents and a dirty old man for a high school principal: this was genius! Everything about it made me uncomfortable, but I realized that was what it was *supposed* to do. I just loved the cards, cigarettes, pills, and hypodermic needle flying out of "Biddy's" purse. After reading all the books, I decided Will Elder was my favorite.

Naturally, my parents were concerned that I loved *MAD* magazine. I don't think I knew one kid whose parents weren't mystified by our devotion to *MAD*. They found the humor disrespectful, and the message was ignored, just like when Lenny Bruce's critics chose to focus only on his swearwords. Some of my friends had their *MAD*s confiscated because the women were drawn "too dirty," which was laughable when you consider all the T&A in the Sunday funnies, not to mention the almost daily Hollywood gossip that fixated on the silhouettes of Marilyn Monroe, Jayne Mansfield, Sophia Loren, Brigitte Bardot, and Elizabeth Taylor, to name a few.

When it came to political stuff, most of *MAD*'s gags went over people's heads, which is probably why they got away with it. But making fun of Commies wasn't funny; that was a serious National Emergency, not something to giggle about. I had a few issues "disappear" because my parents just didn't understand.

The term "generation gap" was never so apparent as it was during that time. Young people were supposed to play the same game that their parents did, but they wound up rejecting instead of respecting the game because it was a hollow quest for something the middle class wasn't quite able to define, and a lot of it was soul-crushing and superficial. People weren't satisfied with what they had and they always wanted more, a desire that advertisers took full advantage of. I called it the "You're-Not-Good-Enough Syndrome." You're too fat. You're too skinny. You need a bigger house, a bigger loan, a bigger car, a diet, and on and on. *MAD* magazine made fun of this consumer addiction with relish. And let's not forget the draft and the never-ending Vietnam War that served absolutely no purpose except to make billions of dollars for the military-industrial complex. People, especially young people, were sick of The Big Lie, and *MAD* magazine was there to help make sense of a world gone . . . well, *MAD*!

All this satire and mockery fermented a deep distrust of authority that I proudly have to this day. No one gets my respect unless they earn it, and that includes teachers, bosses, mayors, presidents, and popes. I learned from satire that, often, those who seek leadership are compensating for a deficiency they believe they possess, and instead of working toward a common good, they just try to pile up wealth and power. It's the oldest story of mankind, utterly predictable and fodder for ridicule—and that's what *MAD* did best.

Humor can educate and change a person's thinking way more effectively than ranting and screaming and using fear to gain control. That's also why many older people detested *MAD*. They didn't want us youngsters to question authority and challenge the status quo. Many have said the antiwar sentiment and counterculture movement were influenced by *MAD* magazine, and I agree. When one can see the absurdity in a situation, a truth emerges that is more powerful than confrontation, and if you can use humor you have more power than the guy with the bigger fists.

When I started college, I worked in the school's art gallery, and I'd often bring the *MAD* pocket books with me. So many people never saw them the first time around, and twenty years later the humor was just as fresh and original as it was in the '50s. I don't have those paperbacks anymore. All were "borrowed" or stolen. I had a shady group of friends, and when I used to have wild parties, I would hide all my jazz and blues records because we knew a lot of vinyl collectors and they wouldn't think twice about lifting some of your LPs for their hoard. Books suffered the same fate.

I was thrilled when Russ Cochran reprinted *MAD* in 1986, and I bought them all. What fun to see the pages in color and the proper size.

The great colorist Marie Severin, who passed away in 2018, is the biggest influence on my color palette, and she did some of her best work for *MAD*. Her nontraditional, clashing hues, and the way she used opposites, were very psychedelic. "Ping Pong" is the one that made me rethink how color could be used. A yellow sky, purple wood, and a blue gorilla? Why the heck not? As Marie once told me: "My goal was clarity, and if I needed to use a wacky color combo, I did it."

MAD was the first underground comic, and *MAD* influenced *everything.*

THE GOLDEN AGE IS TWELVE dept.

Ivan Cohen

HE FIRST issue of *MAD* I ever bought wasn't my first issue. Not even close.

As the youngest of four kids in a house that seems absurdly large in my middle-aged memory, I was constantly finding artifacts left behind by my older siblings in closets and on finished-basement shelves—books, toys, and records that didn't make the cut for dorm rooms and first apartments. As a result, my early childhood in the bicentennial decade was spent reading stories of adventures on dude ranches, speculative nonfiction about what wonders we might discover should astronauts ever make it to the moon, and cutting-edge satire about the antics of LBJ and Nikita Khrushchev in the pages of *MAD*.

Luckily, to a ten-year-old, everything that smacks of being grown-up is mysterious and fascinating. Just as I stayed up late to sneak peeks at NBC's *Saturday Night Live* and did my best to figure out what the jokes were about, I pored over those inherited *MAD*s and strove to keep up, looking for context clues to follow what was going on. It was even somewhat educational: I discovered songs I'd never heard in parodies of movies I thought I'd never see.[1]

---

1. In those pre-streaming, pre-VCR days, it seemed like there were only about a half-

MAD was a primer for the world I'd be inheriting soon, although of course I didn't know that at the time.

But being ten doesn't last forever, and soon those dog-eared, folded-in *MAD*s wouldn't be enough to satisfy me. I wanted my own things, things that would speak more directly to *me* because *I* chose them.

It brings to mind a saying that started with science fiction[2] before being adapted to comic books, the aforementioned *Saturday Night Live*, and pretty much anything else that lasts long enough to span generations:

"The golden age of _____ is twelve."

Taken broadly, it means that whatever a twelve-year-old spends their own money on is an experience they consider *theirs*. And when grown-ups—whether they're critics, fans, or casual consumers—argue about which era of a particular thing was the "best," deep inside they're still weighing the contenders against the things they treasure most, sometimes beyond all reason . . . the things they discovered at twelve.

So as a child born in the late '60s, even though Charles Schulz's *Peanuts* was certainly darker and richer in the 1950s strips I'd appreciate years later, the more mass-appealing strips of the late '70s and early '80s established, for me, the baseline of what *Peanuts* was, despite there being more time spent with Snoopy's brother (!) than on the challenges of, well, being a kid.

---

dozen movies you could reliably count on seeing on the "Big Three" TV networks, and after *The Wizard of Oz* it was pretty rough sledding. (If you think *Gone With the Wind* is tolerable, even despite its baked-in racism, you've never seen it bloated with commercials and spread over two nights.)

2. Comic book writer, publisher, and historian Paul Levitz credits science-fiction fan Sam Moskowitz with the expression, while the Quote Investigator website (quoteinves tigator.com) discusses other SF fans and professionals who might be the originator.

"My" *Saturday Night Live* was the one without Lorne Michaels at the helm, the one that introduced Eddie Murphy and Joe Piscopo among an otherwise forgettable cast. A season that remains by far the biggest outlier of that show's multidecade run is, in my lizard brain, what other seasons are judged against.

Were earlier and later seasons of *SNL* superior to '80–'81? More memorable? Was *Peanuts* better when Snoopy wasn't a part-time salesman for insurance and "Happiness Is . . ." slogans? Unquestionably.

Could anyone beat the 1981 New York Mets? Their fifth-place division finish answers that pretty decisively. But I was twelve, and they were *mine*.

My personal golden age started in fall of 1980. Adults then probably thought it was no weirder a time than any other, certainly not as tumultuous as the years of political unrest and assassinations that had just ended. The fire hydrants' bicentennial colors were chipping away with no one in any rush to repaint them, there was an ongoing US hostage crisis in a country many of us didn't know anything about. . . . Luckily, the ex-governor of California, a former movie actor whose starring roles were barely remembered—and when they were remembered, only as a punchline—had been elected president, and *that* was going to fix everything, unless he or the Russians started World War III first.

So late at night, sheets drawn up, flashlight in hand, I staved off fears of the coming apocalypse with a steady diet of comic books, science-fiction novels, and, of course, *MAD*. Not the *MAD*s in the closet, but rather the *MAD*s I bought for myself.

I recently looked back at those issues from 1980 to 1981. The one word that comes most readily to mind?

Blecch.

(Hey, at least it's a very *MAD* word.)

The first issue to come out after I turned twelve[3] didn't even have beloved(?) mascot Alfred E. Neuman on the cover, just a Don Martin gag with a fireman watering flowers during a blaze. Inside, in addition to more fireman comedy, there were parodies of two movies I *still* haven't seen (*Little Darlings* and *Coal Miner's Daughter*), and a fairly reactionary bit of humor called "If We Ever Have Real Equal Rights Laws," which includes among its examples an ABC series called "Chubby's Angels," and an "Equal Rights for Ugly Guys Amendment" that would make it a violation for "girls" to "date desireable [*sic*] men exclusively." Not exactly high points in comedy.

Wrapping things up was the best bit of the issue, "The Dopes of Haphazzard," which parodied my beloved[4, 5] *The Dukes of Hazzard*. While it scores some solid jokes about the level of destruction and mayhem and short-shorts-wearing that fueled the series, it disappointingly goes in lockstep with the viewing audience by paying no attention to the TV show's *heroes* driving a car with the Confederate flag on its roof, alongside the iconic car's name: the General Lee.

Yep.

While the first issue that came out in my golden age was a mixed bag, the second was so in my wheelhouse, I can't imagine being a *MAD* fan without it.

That issue has Alfred on the cover. And not just Alfred—Alfred as *Yoda*. To a twelve-year-old *Star Wars* fan in 1980, hard-pressed to find a surer sell you'd be. While the issue included a typical TV send-up

3. Issue #219. That issue's frontmatter explains that *MAD* was "published monthly except February, May, August and November." For those not great at math, that would mean eight issues a year, with the skipped months featuring all-reprint *MAD Super Special* magazines.
4. Reminder: I was twelve.
5. No, it's not much of an excuse.

THE GOLDEN AGE IS TWELVE DEPT.

(of the *CSI*–before–*CSI Quincy, M.E.*) and a four-page parody of a
. . . school-supply catalog ("Amalgamated School Supply," helpfully
abbreviated as "A.S.S."), it was the issue's take on the already beloved
The Empire Strikes Back that I remember as if it were brand new.

"Star Bores: The Empire Strikes Out" had a terrific grip on the film
concepts and characters—several months had passed[6] between the
film's release and the parody's publication, so presumably everyone
involved had seen the furshlugginer thing—including spot-on dialogue, like this exchange between the *MAD* versions of Han Solo and
C-3PO:

> HAM YOYO: Hey, this is the Aluminum Falcon! This baby's
> still got a lot of surprises left in her!
> CREEPIO: Sir! The entire control panel just shorted out!
> HAM YOYO: See! There's one surprise already!

On the other hand, enough time had elapsed that they might have
reconsidered the introduction, whose view that "this sequel . . . doesn't
compare to the original" had certainly already been contradicted by
box-office grosses and fan reactions. More in line with fans to come
was the writer's exasperation—which would echo in fan conversa-
tions for nearly twenty years[7]—about how the second movie in the
series wasn't "*Star Wars II*, but instead *Episode V*," making the previous movie retroactively a IV, and so on.

---

6. *Empire* was released on May 21, 1980. *MAD* #220 (January 1981) appeared on newsstands in December of that year.

7. Once the prequels began coming out (with 1999's *The Phantom Menace* being "Episode I"), the frustration largely shifted to complaints about the quality of the movies,
not the numbering scheme—though some of us found it possible to complain about
both aspects.

MAD's potshots at *Empire* were just my first experience of one of the most valuable lessons *MAD* teaches twelve-year-olds of any era: that just because something is popular doesn't mean you can't make fun of it. And if that popular thing is something you yourself love, so much the better. *Superman II* was another favorite of mine, and *MAD*'s "Superduperman II"[8] helped me reconcile loving it with, among other silliness, Superman's newfound ability to kiss away his girlfriend's memories.

The topics that year's *MAD*s took on were wide-ranging, with equally mixed results: a parody of *The Shining*, describing the movie as "giving the book and all past horror movies a black eye," is another verdict that hasn't aged well, but an anti–secondhand smoke *MAD* Fold-In has. "That's Really Incredible, People" mixes two different reality shows (*Real People* and *That's Incredible*) into one, in a way almost identical to that of a sketch nearly a year earlier[9] on *Saturday Night Live* ("Real Incredible People"). In this case *SNL* and *MAD* both caught the tokenism of the source material with one of the "real incredible people" on the TV sketch making the cut by being "a guest whose skin is *very* dark brown!" while *MAD* had *Real People*'s one African American cohost introduce himself with "I'm Byron Allen, and I feel like I don't belong here!"

Whether one believes this was plagiarism or just a case of great minds thinking alike, *Saturday Night Live* and *MAD* covering similar ground—with *SNL* getting the joke out faster—was just one example

8. It's hard not to appreciate *MAD*'s editors for maintaining a sense of history. The magazine's first Superman parody, "Superduperman!," appeared in 1953's *MAD* #4, and they kept using the awkward, not-exactly-a-pun title on *Superman* satires for thirty years, breaking the streak with 1983's "Stuporman ZZZ."
9. The *Saturday Night Live* episode aired May 17, 1980. *MAD* #222 appeared on newsstands in March 1981.

of the mass culture starting to make *MAD* redundant, if not irrele-vant. *MAD* and TV series like *The Ernie Kovacs Show* and *Your Show of Shows* launched out of the same post–World War II "sick" humor tradition, but as those TV series dropped away and mainstream cul-ture tacked back to a blander, more uniform aesthetic, *MAD* stayed edgy well into the '60s. In the 1970s and 1980s, however, the aftermath of Watergate and the Vietnam War found mainstream pop culture starting to incorporate the style of *MAD* (as well as the more adult—though not necessarily more mature—humor found in *National Lam-poon*), and it never really turned back.

In addition to *Saturday Night Live* (which premiered in 1975), the 1974 box-office hits *Blazing Saddles* and *Young Frankenstein* had already been doing the *MAD* movie satires one better by going after whole genres; by the 1980s, broader parody movies like *Airplane!* and *Top Secret!*[10] stuffed as many jokes as possible into the "margins" of the screen, seeming even more like *MAD* than their predecessors. (It's arguable that the advent of home video and the ability to pause and rewind made this kind of joke overload more commercial than it might have been a decade earlier.) In other media, radio personalities like Howard Stern were beginning to find commercial success with "shock" antics and a no-sacred-cows approach that included parodies of songs, TV, and movies. Comedian-turned-talk-show-host David Letterman and his writers were mixing the snark of "Snappy Answers to Stupid Questions" and the traditions of Johnny Carson's *Tonight*

10. A 2020 article on the website Rotten Tomatoes (https://editorial.rottentomatoes .com/article/why-airplanes-title-is-one-of-the-classic-comedys-best-jokes/) argues that the exclamation points in these titles were an homage to the 1957 movie *Zero Hour!* (on which *Airplane!* is based), but I find it hard to ignore the similarity to 1950s *MAD* parodies ("Superduperman!," "Melvin of the Apes!," etc.).

Show, first as an unsuccessful morning TV show, then as *Late Night with David Letterman*, changing the late-night television landscape for the next thirty years.

But while *MAD*'s glory days of the '50s and '60s underpinned much of this newer wave of humor, *MAD* itself was getting repetitive and was very much showing its age. A parody of *Tiger Beat* devoted to classical music and a repurposing of Shakespeare quotes to serve as movie reviews seem aimed at a more erudite audience than *MAD* had attracted in decades, if ever. *MAD* Fold-Ins,[11] "Lighter Side of . . ." strips, "Spy vs Spy" and Sergio Aragonés's "marginals" (cartoons so small my middle-aged eyes need a magnifying glass to read them) kept going with so much mechanical efficiency they could have been reprints and readers would likely never notice. While one of *MAD*'s best efforts, "Raving Bully," was spot-on in highlighting *Raging Bull*'s theme of violence-as-substitute-for-sex, its strongest gags were a cameo by Sylvester Stallone as his *Rocky* character ("He's got at least five more 'fight pictures' in him!")[12] and, at the magazine's most meta, a ringside debate over how times had changed in how *MAD* handled swearing.[13]

When you're a humor magazine whose freshest jokes are about your own struggle to stay relevant, you have a problem.

If recognizing that some of the things you love aren't necessarily all

---

11. One lesson *MAD* failed to teach me was that things you liked could stay good with their back covers folded up. A comic book collector at the same time I was mainlining *MAD*, I'd carefully roll the Fold-In so I could make out the punchline without mangling the magazine.

12. As of this writing, Sylvester Stallone has played Rocky Balboa in six films since 1979's *Rocky II*.

13. I'm a grawlixes—punctuation marks used to replace @!##@??% profanity—man myself, though the "modern" *MAD* leaned heavily on "friggin.'"

that great is a sign of maturity, then realizing that you don't need to keep buying them out of habit is another. Somewhere between adolescence and renting my first apartment, I stopped buying *MAD*.

I don't remember any one specific tipping point. Maybe *Spy* magazine[14] (and later, *The Onion*[15]) and Letterman and Stern had all my needs for irreverence and snark covered, or because (no "maybe" about this) entry-level publishing jobs didn't pay nearly enough to finance all my pop culture needs.

But whatever the last issue of *MAD* I ever bought was, well, it wasn't my last. Not even close.

By the late '90s, I was on staff at DC Comics, then the publisher of *MAD*, with free copies of every new issue as a perk. And while some of my older colleagues—whose personal "golden ages" were probably more golden than mine—decried the current iteration as doing little more than keeping the lights on, unfairly ignoring a generation of talented writers and artists, I was more forgiving. Late '90s *MAD* wasn't anything to be ashamed of.

After all, I'd seen worse.

When I left DC a decade or so later, *MAD* was in full color (like other magazines—great!) and ran actual paid advertisements (like other magazines—booooooo!). Soon after, *MAD*'s offices would move from its birthplace of New York to Los Angeles, and a corporate focus on leveraging original, corporate-owned "IP" into other media left *MAD* fitting in about as well as the forty-fourth player on a Squamish

---

14. Launched in 1986, *Spy* took a highbrow approach to *MAD*-level humor as it reported on the real-life antics of New Yorkers like Donald Trump and Rudy Giuliani.
15. A Wisconsin-based humor newspaper launched in 1988, *The Onion* would win acclaim (and a Peabody Award) as a free national weekly publication that combined snarky news parody with arts and culture reviews.

team.[16] Even a comics-style relaunch (a new #1, a revamped "classic" logo), new features by new creators, and a bigger digital presence[17] couldn't make *MAD* what its owners needed it to be, and it now exists almost entirely as a series of reprint collections.

But, for those of us whose golden ages overlapped any part of *MAD*'s tenure—at this writing, anyone from their mid-teens to their early eighties—*MAD*'s not gone at all. We know that the most popular things are the most ready to be taken down a peg, that what we love isn't perfect, and that stupid questions always deserve snappy answers. Generations of fans-turned-creators have made sure *MAD* lives on in the books we read, the podcasts we listen to, the comedies we frankly wish were at least a little bit funnier, even the social media platforms we're constantly trying to quit.

People may one day forget the name, but *MAD*'s never going away.

The former twelve-year-olds won't let it.

16. One of the most celebrated features of 1960s *MAD*—and thus sneakily part of my golden age by way of paperback reprint collections I either tracked down for myself or got handed down from siblings' hand-me-down copies of *MAD Strikes Back!* and *The Portable MAD*—1965's much-beloved "43-Man Squamish" introduced a sport whose elaborate rules place it somewhere on the spectrum between baseball's infield fly rule and Quidditch from the *Harry Potter* series.

17. Full disclosure: I even got paid—though, in the parlance of *MAD* covers for decades, the rate was "Super Cheap!"—as a freelancer writing jokes for that final iteration of *MAD*'s Twitter feed. I consider it an uncredited badge of honor.

stark raving MAD

Geoffrey O'Brien

W E LIVE in strange days: within a floodlit mausoleum of show business, the hours are measured by the anniversaries of music festivals and movie premieres, by the birth of Mickey Mouse and the death of Elvis. All that was once disposable is frozen into monumentality—and in the age of mechanical reproduction, that makes for more monuments than even the previous century had to contend with. One might well wonder how we got here. A major piece of the story can be found in *The Complete MAD*: itself a monument but a welcome one, twelve pounds of budding media awareness, a guided tour of early '50s image glut conducted in a mood far removed from today's mournful nostalgia.

Who would have imagined, when *MAD* began publication in October 1952, that thirty-seven years later we would have its first twenty-three issues preserved for us in this boxed, hardbound, full-color facsimile, annotated with Talmudic devotion? Certainly not *MAD*'s creator, Harvey Kurtzman, or the extraordinary artists who helped realize his vision of American pop culture; it would have been an altogether different magazine if they had. "We were working by the seat of our pants," Kurtzman remarks in an interview in *The Complete MAD*. "I didn't really know what the hell I was doing. All I was doing was 'funny.' Funny. Gotta make it funny, gotta make me laugh, gotta tickle myself." The out-of-control things that happened in the pages of the early *MAD* were of the sort that occur when people are not erecting monuments. "When you're desperate to fill space, you think of outrageous things."

MAD was engaged in an elaborate practical joke at the expense of the available culture, covering billboards and movie posters and comic strip pages with graffiti that were more entertaining than what they defaced. Today's *MAD*—the black-and-white magazine that has carefully replicated the same formulas for the past thirty years—is so much a part of the landscape that it is hard to re-create the impact of Kurtzman's original color comic book version. Without venturing into obscenity, blasphemy, or revolutionary sloganeering, it managed to anticipate all the assaults on public taste that were to follow. (Kurtzman himself left *MAD* in 1956, following a dispute over financial control, and was replaced by Al Feldstein; the magazine was never quite the same, and Kurtzman's own later ventures, though often brilliant, never achieved such popularity.)

In this boxed form, *MAD* stands revealed as a perfect postmodern epic, decentered, multireferential, inextricable from the particulars of its place and time. To read it adequately we would in theory have to re-create its original circumstances, watch the same television shows, listen to the same jukeboxes (for a hundredth chorus of "How Much Is That Doggie in the Window"), scan the same comic strips. Intertextuality can go no further. *MAD*'s guiding principle was spillover: the TV programs on neighboring channels blended, the separate comic strips on a page began communicating among themselves. Everything got thrown into the soup. No figure was allowed to dominate a space for long: the foreground action was forever being upstaged by clusters of microscopic idiots grimacing or waving absurd placards, like bystanders grinning at the camera on TV news. It was an aesthetic of interruption and intrusion. *MAD*'s panels retained the classicism of traditional comics only to subject it to remorseless pummeling. The foursquare frame persisted, with Superduperman poised heroically in its center, but the walls and floors could be seen collapsing all around him.

In 1952, American culture was a parody waiting to happen. It was an era of oddly unconscious abeyance and dereliction. Not long before, popular art had gone through a series of more or less concurrent golden ages: of the movies, of jazz and the big bands, of radio, of the pulps and the comics. But a slow unraveling had begun. The forms that had seen the country through depression and world war seemed to have lost the effortless confidence that had given them the air of a national religion, a precarious unity of spirit encompassing swing records, Jack Benny, and *Terry and the Pirates*.

The postwar period's most brilliant manifestations—bebop, film noir—were already marginal. At center stage a warped stiffness seemed to have taken over. The Red Scare generated such movies as *My Son John*, *I Was a Communist for the FBI*, and *Red Planet Mars*, gibbering studies in deception and religiosity whose every frame seemed grotesquely off-key. The bestseller list alternated between billowing clouds of spiritual comfort (*The Silver Chalice*, *The Gown of Glory*, *A Man Called Peter*, *The Power of Positive Thinking*, *This I Believe*) and the sustained paranoid outbursts of Mickey Spillane's *Kiss Me Deadly*. Television was exemplified by variety and quiz shows of trancelike somnolence (*The Arthur Murray Show*, *Arthur Godfrey's Talent Scouts*, *I've Got a Secret*, *You Asked for It*) and transplanted radio serials like *Gangbusters* and *The Lone Ranger*. As for Hollywood, it offered little beyond Martin and Lewis, Abbott and Costello, the desperate grandiosity of 3-D and Cinerama, and, for the Saturday afternoon crowd, cheapo adventure flicks like *Son of Ali Baba* and *The*

Battle at Apache Pass. The comic strips, in the meantime, persisted without change, as *Skeezix*, *Dick Tracy*, and *Orphan Annie* lived on in a world where nobody ever got older.

In that strange era before the dawn of media self-consciousness, evidence of mental fatigue was everywhere. Humor consisted of Jack Benny and Bob Hope recycling their old routines or Donald O'Connor locked in conversation with a talking mule. The real humor, however, was in all the places it wasn't supposed to be: in the lurid solemnity of movie posters, in the sanctimonious hucksterism of advertising, in the unquestioned formulas that governed comic book plots. Plainly people had gotten so used to grinding the stuff out that it had been a while since anyone actually looked at it.

MAD was like the lone giggle that subverts a hitherto respect-ful audience into uncontrolled laughter. Well, not exactly lone. The Warner Brothers cartoonists had created a parodistic parallel world throughout the '40s, and since 1950 Sid Caesar and Imogene Coca had been broadcasting *Your Show of Shows*, to be joined in 1952 by *The Ernie Kovacs Show* and Steve Allen on *Tonight*. More remotely, there was the lingering influence of the Marx Brothers and of S. J. Perel-man's fantasias on the themes of pulp fiction and advertising. Before long Stan Freberg would bring another medium into the picture with recorded parodies like "St. George and the Dragonet" and an echo-ridden "Heartbreak Hotel." None of these could top *MAD*'s secret weapon: its explosive visual presence. You might not find it funny, but you couldn't take your eyes off it; its graphics changed the tone of a room just by being there.

By adopting the form of a comic book, *MAD* had the advantage of surprise, like a sniper firing from an unsuspected position. Comic books until then had fed the same material over and over to an audi-ence limited in age and influence, rarely reaching anyone outside that

audience except for crusading congressmen, psychologists, and cler-
gymen. No comics were more targeted than those of *MAD*'s parent
company, EC (Educational Comics), creator of the most morbidly
explicit horror tales, the most inventively apocalyptic science fiction,
and the most harrowing and socially conscious crime stories, all of
them written and edited by the brilliant and astonishingly prolific Al
Feldstein. When Harvey Kurtzman joined EC, he had the advantage
of working with a staff that had already mastered the sharp and savage
tactics of *The Vault of Horror* and *Shock SuspenStories*.

Kurtzman, a Brooklyn-born journeyman gag cartoonist in his late
twenties, was remarkable for his combined mastery of writing and
drawing. A perfectionist in matters of detail, he habitually sketched
out each story frame by frame, allowing artists small leeway in inter-
preting his layouts. Initially he edited a pair of war comics, *Two-Fisted
Tales* and *Frontline Combat,* notable for their sober restraint and mor-
ally serious tone in contrast to EC's usual sardonic Grand Guignol.
The Civil War issues (reprinted as part of Russ Cochran's EC Classics
series) demonstrate an eye obsessed with fusing swarms of historical
detail into impeccably harmonious sequences of frames; if Kurtzman
had not been a great humorist he could clearly have been a great pro-
pagandist. The distinctive styles of his artists (Wallace Wood, Will
Elder, Jack Davis, John Severin) are, although still apparent, carefully
held in check. Kurtzman's directorial control of his comics' overall
look was unchallenged although sometimes resented.

MAD started routinely enough, with farcical variations on standard comic book plots, hit its stride with the "Superduperman!" and
"Shadow!" features in the fourth issue, and grew steadily more experimental as long as it was under Kurtzman's editorship. In the meantime
it became a success of cultlike intensity, trailed by a pack of imitations—including EC's own *Panic,* which featured the same artists as

MAD but under the guidance of Al Feldstein. Judging from the issues reprinted by Cochran, *Panic* had a rougher edge than *MAD*; the violence in its Mike Hammer and *This Is Your Life* takeoffs is almost on a par with one of Feldstein's horror comics. There is not a trace, however, of Kurtzman's flair for fantasy and pure nonsense, or of his capacity for bending the comic book form into unexpected shapes.

Kurtzman didn't have to invent his humor—it was already there. "I was always surprised at how people living and working in different places around the city would be thinking the same thing. We were a product of our Jewish backgrounds in New York; we were in the same city living in different boroughs, yet we were having the same experiences. It was bizarre that at Music and Art in the lunch room we'd carry on and do our satire parodies. . . . I remember specifically sitting around in the lunch room doing the 'operating scene,' or better still, doing the 'airplane scene,' the German ace going down in the Fokker in flames. . . . You'd see a movie, and you'd make fun of it, and twenty other guys who saw the same movie, and who had the same kind of Jewish direction of thinking would come up with the same scene."

However familiar its tone was on the streets of Manhattan or Brooklyn, for most of its readers *MAD* was a new noise: noise about noise, about the noise that had been going on in every form of public entertainment and information but had never been labeled, an encyclopedia of what had been bombarding people's eyes and ears. Reading *MAD* was like watching a documentary about how it felt to be on the receiving end of everything that had not yet been named the media. To children growing up in the '50s, *MAD* provided the reassurance that someone else was watching, someone else had seen what it looked like. The specific content of its satire was not as important as the simple acknowledgment that we were all soaked in mass-produced words and images.

Whether parodying comic strips ("Prince Violent," "Manduck the Magician"), movies ("From Eternity Back to Here!" "Under the Waterfront"), or TV shows ("The Lone Stranger," "Howdy Dooit"), Kurtzman reiterated a single point: just because this stuff was everywhere didn't mean it was real or normal. He got off on the sheer oddness of, for instance, comic strip conventions: that Mickey Mouse wore white gloves or that the characters in *Gasoline Alley* aged at drastically different rates. For a '50s child, who unlike Kurtzman and company had not been reading the same comics since the '30s, the most anachronistic aspect of *MAD* was its loving assault on the funny papers. By 1954 who knew or cared about *Smilin' Jack, Gasoline Alley, Mandrake the Magician*, or even *Flash Gordon* or *Little Orphan Annie*? For *MAD*'s makers, however, this was home base, the root of their aesthetic education.

Television was a more alien presence for them; it's fascinating to see how they render the actual retinal impact of the TV image, complete with wavering horizontal lines, reception problems, and the test patterns that persisted before and after the shows. *MAD*'s TV parodies almost invariably ran in black-and-white, because that denoted television: TV was still visible as something other, a rackety and unsightly intrusion.

When all else failed, *MAD* relied on a repertoire of instant laughgetters. These included a select list of words ("furshlugginer," "potrzebie," "halvah," "blintzes"), names (Melvin Coznowski, Alfred E. Neuman), expletives (of which "Hoo-hah!" and "Yech!" were early favorites), and a few standard syntactical ploys. Kurtzman relied heavily on the "but mainly" construction, as in: "We are giving special attention to T.V. because we believe it has become an integral part of living . . . a powerful influence in shaping the future . . . but mainly we are giving attention because we just got a new T.V. set," or "Once more I go to fight for law and order . . . for justice . . . but mainly for adding the sadistic element that is such a vital part of comic books!" With slight variations the cadence was good for a thousand gags, as in Flesh Garden's declaration: "That's the trouble with us earthlings! We always assume that alien creatures are hostile! I refuse to kill said alien creature in the belief it is hostile! I will kill it just for fun!"

That this was Jewish humor was a well-kept secret; to most of *MAD*'s readers, judging from the letters' pages, "halvah" and "blintzes" were nonsense words springing from nowhere. (The "bop talk" intervals and passing references to Charlie Parker must have been equally arcane to many.) As Kurtzman has noted, however, the in-jokes underwent a peculiar alchemy in their passage to the outside world: "Of course these names come out of the artist's, the author's experience. But when they turn into things like furshlugginer or potrzebie they take on an air of mystery. . . . These were personal real things to us that we were talking about, and private in a sense, and so they imparted a sense of intrigue; the audience would be touched by this mysterious arrangement of sounds." A new in-group was forged, with "furshlugginer" and "potrzebie" as its shibboleths.

Kurtzman's *MAD* had one underlying joke: What if the hero turned out to be a jerk? All the heroes, whether Superduperman or Flesh Garden or the Lone Stranger, were the same, lecherous, avaricious cowards, betraying every ideal to stay on top and most of the time losing. If they won, it was in demonic fashion: Bat Boy in *Bat Boy and Rubin* turned out to be a vampire bat, and Teddy of *Teddy and the Pirates* ended up operating an opium smuggling ring with his fellow pirates.

Although much has been made of *MAD*'s satirical bent, its jibes tended to be quite mild; Kurtzman's takes on the hypocrisies of television, advertising, and the funny papers would not have stirred controversy if couched as essays in *The Saturday Review*. His rare forays into politics—notably the routine in which Senator McCarthy became a panelist on *What's My Shine?*—were significant not so much for what they said as for raising the subject at all. Kurtzman's humor was less satire than formalist delirium; much of the funniest stuff, the send-ups of such items as picture puzzles or *Ripley's Believe It or Not!*, had no real point beyond a pleasure in their own gratuitousness. He loved particularly to parody print media; through his work small children unconsciously absorbed lessons in typography and layout, and beyond that the underlying lesson that format is content. The formats he played with included the *Daily News*, *The Racing Form*, movie ads, the posters for the Miss Rheingold contest, 3-D comics, fill-in-the-dots and "What's Wrong With This Picture?" puzzles, the ads in the back of comic books. The tiniest visual details were significant: changes in typeface, the spacing between letters, the relative size of different elements on the page.

MAD had an air of chaos just barely held at bay. Crazed as it might appear, there was always the implication that things might get much worse. In every frame the forces of coherence fought a losing battle against entropy. The jokes stepped on each other's toes, one gag shoved another out of the way, voices drowned each other out in violently escalating shouting matches. In the final frames of the *Julius Caesar* lampoon—intended as a self-referential commentary on *MAD*'s own methods—Marlon Brando as Mark Antony and James Mason as Brutus metamorphose rapidly into Dick Tracy, Fearless Fosdick, and Rip Kirby, while Marilyn Monroe rips apart the frame to reveal Donald Duck and Goofy underneath ("Here everyone whips off rubber masks and you find out the hero really isn't the hero . . . the villain really isn't the villain . . . I'm not really your *MAD* writer . . . matter of fact, this *MAD* comic book isn't really a *MAD* comic book . . ."). In "3-Dimensions!," a dazzling exploration of the double vision and general disorientation produced by 3-D comics leads into more basic questions of perspective and reality. Holes are ripped in the frame, one page collapses onto another, and the last page of all is an empty white space.

No two people will agree on just how funny *MAD* was, but it always hummed with energy and it always looked great. *The Complete MAD* presents the splendors of Elder, Wood, Davis, and company as they have never been seen before, to such effect that the humor is almost swamped by the magnificence of the drawing. (In particular, the love-it-or-hate-it all-out ugliness of Basil Wolverton's monstrous candidates for Miss Potgold take on terrifying proportions.) While Wallace Wood and Jack Davis executed Kurtzman's ideas with wonderful fluency and humor, Will Elder was *MAD*'s other guiding genius. Elder's eerie ability to appropriate the style of other cartoonists is amply displayed in his parodies of *Gasoline Alley*, *Bringing Up Father*, *The Katzenjammer Kids*, and *Archie*, but beyond mere mimicry there's a blast of wildly destructive humor. If Kurtzman was the satirist, Elder was the anarchist: "I always wanted to shock people . . . I was the Manson of the zanies." Elder's vision of Archie and Jughead as sullen juvenile delinquents becomes genuinely ominous, while his transformation of Mickey Mouse into the vengeful, stubble-faced Mickey Rodent cut too close for the "Walt Dizzy" people, who threatened legal action.

The Kurtzman-Elder collaboration can be seen at its best in "Howdy Dooit," with its commercials for Bupgoo ("Bupgoo makes a glass of milk look exactly like a glass of beer!") and Skwushy's Sliced White-Bread ("If it's good bread—it's a wonder!") and its maniacal contingent of children in the "Peewee Gallery," an underage mob ready to overwhelm the repellent "Buffalo Bill." When Buffalo Bill asks one sinister-looking youngster what he wants to be when he grows up ("A police chief? A fireman? A Indian? Or, [hot dog], maybe a jet-fighter

pilot? Huh?") the boy replies: "Please, Buffalo Bill, don't be juvenile!
. . . If one had the choice, it would probably be soundest to get into a
white-collar occupation such as an investment broker or some-such!
Of course . . . advertising and entertainment are lucrative fields if one
hits the top brackets . . . much like Howdy Dooit has! In other words
. . . what I want to do when I grow up, is to be a hustler like Howdy
Dooit!" To which Bill replies: "But child . . . Howdy Dooit is no hustler! . . . Howdy Dooit is a happy wooden marionette, manipulated by
strings! Howdy Dooit, child, is no mercenary, money grubbing hustler
. . . I, Buffalo Bill, am the mercenary, money grubbing hustler!" Seizing
a pair of scissors, the child cuts Buffalo Bill's invisible strings. As Bill
falls limp and vacant-eyed to the studio floor, a raging Howdy Dooit
screams for the cameras to cut.

The humor to a large degree was about the uncanny skill of the artists. Their ability to summon up the "real" figures of television, movies, and comic strips and force them to do outrageous things provoked
a manic glee. It was the revenge of the cartoonists, and every reader
got a jolt of subversive satisfaction from it. That Mickey Mouse and
Archie were not really the targets even a child could begin to grasp.
MAD made it clear that all the images and characters were made by
people—and that what was made could also be unmade. They took
them apart before our eyes, put mustaches on them, made them speak
Yiddish or pig latin.

The world *MAD* caricatured no longer exists, but the *MAD* of the
'50s still seems remarkably current. After all, the age of parody that
it helped kick off—the age that extended through Lenny Bruce, *The
Realist, Zap Comix, Blazing Saddles*, and *Saturday Night Live*—ended
only recently. It ended when the potential targets of parody, from
Ronald Reagan and Joe Isuzu on down, finally worked out how to
short-circuit the process by deliberately making themselves parodies

in advance: precaricatured, as jeans are preshunk. Presumably some future Kurtzman is working on the problem right now.

The problem of distinguishing parodies from the real world had been broached from the beginning in the pages of *MAD*. It was another unusual, perhaps unintended dimension of that reading experience. For me, as for many of *MAD*'s youngest readers, the objects of parody were altogether unknown. Although I could follow them when it came to Captain Video, the Lone Ranger, and Howdy Doody, I was at sea on everything else, and besides, no one had explained what a parody was. Slowly, by a painstaking archaeological process, I divined that something else was being referred to, but it was no easy matter to reconstruct the unknown referent, to re-create, say, Little Orphan Annie from "Little Orphan Melvin" or the McCarthy hearings from *MAD*'s conversion of them into the quiz show *What's My Shine?* It was a peculiar education, learning about the world from the image it cast in *MAD*'s deforming mirrors. It was also an education from which one never quite recovered, for by the time those original models were at last revealed, they had acquired in the uncovering a haunting and perpetual aura of incongruity.

(1989)

A MAD CHILDHOOD

My favorite cousin subscribed to MAD. I'm pretty sure that's where I first saw it.

It was love at first sight. MAD made fun of stuff that I thought needed to be made fun of.

I had a vague sense that it was a magazine for boys, but I didn't care. I was used to being kind of a weirdo.

MAD made me laugh like a bat. I loved Don Martin, Dave Berg, the ad and TV and movie parodies... all of it.

It was one of my first inklings that there were other people out there who found the world as ridiculous as I did. And if I was the only girl, big deal.

Better to be a weirdo than a stupid, humorless robot !!!

When I was sixteen, I wrote a letter to the Editors which was actually published.

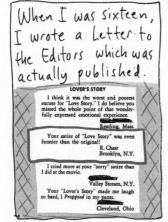

This was probably the high point of my youth.

Oh, well. As Alfred would have said: WHAT, ME WORRY?

R. Chast

тHE WORLD ACCORDing to MAD magazinE

Tim Kreider

HERE'S A photo, taken in 1936, of Al Jaffee and Wolf Eisenberg, a.k.a. Will Elder, goofing around in the cafeteria of the High School of Music and Art in New York, where they were students.

They're mugging for the camera, their faces pulled into the kinds of caricatures they would later draw—Jaffee grimacing with his eyes squinched up and nose twisted to one side while shoving a whole sandwich in his mouth, Elder making a cross-eyed Quasimodo face and tipping a milk bottle toward his protruding lips and tongue, their hands clawed and gesticulating—basically acting like wiseass teenagers of any era. But these boys grew up to become two of "the Usual Gang of Idiots"—the stable of artists for *MAD* magazine, who turned teenage wiseassery into an art form and an institution, and eventually turned all America into one big high school cafeteria.

The announcement last week that *MAD* would cease monthly publication of new material made me sad in the far-off way you feel when you hear that a celebrity you didn't know was still alive has died. I was a regular reader of *MAD* in the 1970s, when the magazine was at the height of its popularity and influence. I learned many things from *MAD*: who Spiro Agnew was, the plots of R-rated movies like *Coma* and show tunes like "I Got Plenty o' Nuttin,'" which the writers of *MAD* evidently assumed would be familiar enough to ten-year-olds of the '70s to parody—"I Got Plenty of Muslims," sung by a Black militant. I also learned about Black militants.

I also learned from *MAD* that politicians were corrupt and deceitful, that Hollywood and Madison Avenue pushed insulting junk, that religion was more invested in respectability than compassion, that school was mostly about teaching you to obey arbitrary rules and submit to dingbats and martinets—that it was, in short, all BS. Grownups who worried that *MAD* was a subversive influence, undermining the youth of America's respect for their elders and faith in our hallowed institutions, were 100 percent correct.

I never wrote or drew for *MAD* (though I have several friends who did), but my own cartooning was deeply influenced by its artists, from Mort Drucker's obsessive perfectionism for the most inconspicuous detail to Don Martin's wild, spontaneous precision. I learned from *MAD* that a line could be funny: not just a face but the cock of an eyebrow, the sploosh of a bowl of soup. Certain expressions drawn by Harry North, Esq.—a vacationing veteran's hollow-eyed paranoia at the lying smiles of the Japanese all around him, a guy realizing what he should've said to the jerk who cut him off in traffic earlier that day—have become engraved as the dictionary illustrations in my brain for "xenophobia" and "l'esprit d'escalier."

Even Dave Berg, ostensibly the squarest of *MAD*'s artists, is a kind of elbow-patched George Grosz in retrospect. "Berg's characters grin with sickening expressions," Austin English wrote in *The Comics Journal*, and "appear constipated and on the verge of tears even when at rest." *MAD*'s roster of talent was too idiosyncratic to have a house style, but it was all *loud*: kinetic, expressive, a brand of caricature that's out of fashion these days, when an amateurish DIY aesthetic or dreary minimalism is de rigueur.

But *MAD*'s influence went deeper than aesthetics; it had a comedic sensibility, a view of the world as a hilarious cavalcade of hypocrisy and folly—an attitude embodied by the insolent simpleton's grin of Alfred E. Neuman, a figure whose origins are untraceable, that seems to have arisen from the collective moronic American unconscious.

By the time most of us hit adolescence and learn that the world is unfair, exploitative and brutal, and that most people in it live in shocking poverty and squalor, and that we're all somehow implicated in this even though it wasn't our idea, plus there's no God and we're all going to die and the grown-ups have been secretly having sex the whole time, you feel ripped off. You feel lied to.

So you turn to art that rips the facades off everything, exposing adults and their institutions as swinish and rotten. Humor is adolescents' reflexive defense against all the unpleasantness they're confronting for the first time. It's a distinctively adolescent form of humor we now call "snark"—irony, sarcasm, satire, and parody—whose agenda is to mock and tear down and caper gleefully upon the grave of everything sacred and respectable.

It's no coincidence that *MAD* reached its highest circulation in the era of the Vietnam War, Watergate, and the "credibility gap"—the collapse of public faith in the integrity and honesty of our government. It was a healthy antidote to earlier generations' automatic deference to an authority that too seldom deserved it.

It's hard to believe now that there was really a time when people trusted their elected officials to act in the best interest of the country or had reverence for the presidency: they seem, to us, like a race of credulous children. But the '60s and '70s were America's adolescence. I still have a *MAD* article by Larry Siegel called "Those Wonderful

'70s!" that serves as a bracing antidote to any Gen Y or Z illusions that it was a simpler time—it's an extended piece of mock-nostalgic reminiscence, from the future year 2000, about political scandals, nuclear accidents, gas lines, hijackings, death cults, and really bad TV.

"How we laughed and sang and danced," he wrote, "as we wiped up the ground with each other and blew up our cities and destroyed our land and wildlife and polluted our air and ruined our water and did a thousand other loony things."

Adolescents are also scarily passionate absolutists, and there is, behind all parody and satire, a moral agenda; people like Jon Stewart and Stephen Colbert aren't America haters but closet patriots and true believers. *MAD*'s ethos was essentially conservative: its all-fronts, iconoclastic assault on bigotry and hypocrisy was a tacit appeal to good old-fashioned decency and integrity. *MAD* made good enemies: the Ku Klux Klan once demanded an apology and threatened to sue over what it considered a libel against its organization.

Even in 2018, *MAD* hadn't lost its edge: a parody of Edward Gorey's droll *The Gashlycrumb Tinies*, called "The Ghastlygun Tinies," showed wan tots alternately practicing the cello or cowering under their desks, accompanied by rhymes like "Q is for Quinn, whose life had just begun/R is for Reid, valued less than a gun."

But this Swiftian bitterness was mostly disguised with huge dollops of the stupidest, most puerile humor imaginable. I once misguidedly tried to console a friend after a breakup by showing her an enormous treasury of Don Martin cartoons—this was well into adulthood—and ended up laughing so uncontrollably that she eventually excused herself and went home. By contrast, *New Yorker* cartoons are humor for grown-ups, for people who have forgotten how actual out-loud, can't-breathe, ten-year-olds-on-a-sleepover laughter felt, the same way *Fifty Shades of Grey* is erotica for people who don't remember orgasms.

In a way, the eulogies for *MAD* are coming late. The magazine was dead to me the day it started accepting advertisements—real ads, as opposed to the countless fake ones it had always run to parody the stratagems of advertising. Even though I was no longer a reader by then, it felt like a betrayal. That magazine had been an agenda-free zone, one place where grown-ups who hadn't quite gone over to the other side would tell you the truth.

MAD's influence is ubiquitous now. The glut of satire and subversive comedy we all now consume daily is created by kids who grew up on *MAD* or on humor inspired by it: *Saturday Night Live*, *The Simpsons*, *The Daily Show*, *The Colbert Report*, and *The Onion* are all in one way or another the spawn of *MAD*. But in the end, the magazine largely obviated itself as a cultural force by becoming the dominant mode of humor in America. The languages of advertising, PR, and even politics have all appropriated the snark and irony of *MAD*. Even The Man wants to be a wiseass now.

(2019)

H. Kurtz

HARVEY KURTZMAN, THE COMIC GENIUS BEHIND SOME OF THE GREATEST HUMOR PUBLICATIONS EVER CREATED, WAS ALSO THE FIRST ARTIST TO ADDRESS THE COMPLEXITIES OF WAR IN COMIC BOOKS. AS EDITOR, WRITER, AND OFTEN ARTIST, HE CREATED STORIES THAT BLAZED NEW TRAILS IN THE MEDIUM, INCLUDING MASTERPIECES LIKE...

CORPSE ON THE IMJIN!

THOUGH HE PASSED AWAY IN 1993, KURTZMAN HAS LEFT A LEGACY THAT WILL LIVE ON IN THE LEGIONS HE INFLUENCED.

FROM THE UNDERGROUND COMIX MOVEMENT TO THE DAILY SHOW, KURTZMAN'S BRAND OF HUMOR HAS BEEN THE GUIDING LIGHT.

WITHOUT HARVEY KURTZMAN WE WOULD NOT HAVE...

KUPER

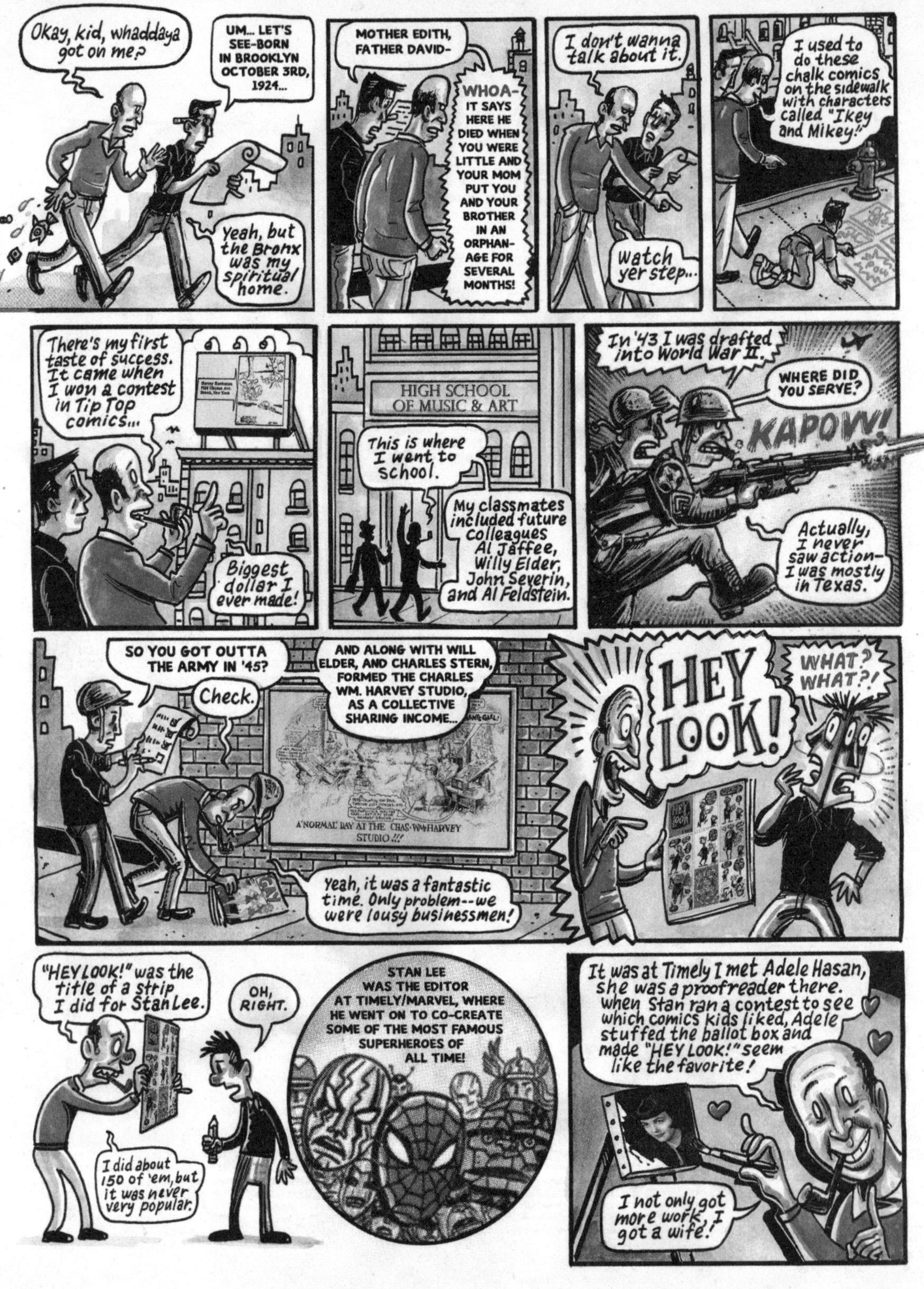

Okay, kid, whaddaya got on me?
UM... LET'S SEE–BORN IN BROOKLYN OCTOBER 3RD, 1924...
Yeah, but the Bronx was my spiritual home.
MOTHER EDITH, FATHER DAVID–
WHOA– IT SAYS HERE HE DIED WHEN YOU WERE LITTLE AND YOUR MOM PUT YOU AND YOUR BROTHER IN AN ORPHANAGE FOR SEVERAL MONTHS!
I don't wanna talk about it.
Watch yer step...
I used to do these chalk comics on the sidewalk with characters called "Ikey and Mikey."
There's my first taste of success. It came when I won a contest in Tip Top comics...
Biggest dollar I ever made!
HIGH SCHOOL OF MUSIC & ART
This is where I went to school.
My classmates included future colleagues Al Jaffee, Willy Elder, John Severin, and Al Feldstein.
In '43 I was drafted into World War II.
WHERE DID YOU SERVE?
KAPOW!
Actually, I never saw action– I was mostly in Texas.
SO YOU GOT OUTTA THE ARMY IN '45?
Check.
AND ALONG WITH WILL ELDER, AND CHARLES STERN, FORMED THE CHARLES WM. HARVEY STUDIO, AS A COLLECTIVE SHARING INCOME...
A 'NORMAL' DAY AT THE CHAS-WM-HARVEY STUDIO !!!
Yeah, it was a fantastic time. Only problem--we were lousy businessmen!
HEY LOOK!
WHAT? WHAT?!
"HEY LOOK!" was the title of a strip I did for Stan Lee.
OH, RIGHT.
I did about 150 of 'em, but it was never very popular.
STAN LEE WAS THE EDITOR AT TIMELY/MARVEL, WHERE HE WENT ON TO CO-CREATE SOME OF THE MOST FAMOUS SUPERHEROES OF ALL TIME!
It was at Timely I met Adele Hasan, she was a proofreader there. When Stan ran a contest to see which comics kids liked, Adele stuffed the ballot box and made "HEY LOOK!" seem like the favorite!
I not only got more work, I got a wife!

OVER THE NEXT FEW YEARS, HARVEY TOOK WHATEVER COMIC BOOK WORK HE COULD FIND, THEN IN 1949 HE BROUGHT HIS PORTFOLIO TO E.C. PUBLICATIONS...

PUBLISHER BILL GAINES LOVED THE "HEY LOOK!" STRIP AND GAVE HARVEY A SHOT...

HAHAHA

KURTZMAN DREW EDUCATIONAL COMICS, SCI-FI, CRIME AND EVEN HORROR COMICS, (WHICH HE HATED), BUT HE LONGED FOR MORE...

Control.

I need more control over the content.

SO HARVEY PROPOSED A NEW CONCEPT TO GAINES: WAR BOOKS HE WOULD WRITE, LAYOUT AND OFTEN DRAW...

FRONTLINE COMBAT

TWO-FISTED TALES

UP TO THIS POINT, WAR COMICS ALWAYS GLORIFIED WAR AND DEMONIZED THE ENEMY...

POW

TAKE THAT, YOU SLANT-EYE NAZI-JAP!

KURTZMAN INTRODUCED COMPLEX TALES EXAMINING THE STRUGGLES AND MORAL AMBIGUITIES IN BATTLE.

IF THE EVER A TRU HELL O EARTH IT WAS HERE

IWO

HE'D SPEND COUNTLESS HOURS METICULOUSLY RESEARCHING EACH STORY, DOWN TO THE FINEST DETAILS...

NY PUBLIC LIBRARY

THEN HE'D PRODUCE EXACTING LAYOUTS AND DEMANDED HIS ARTISTS FOLLOW THEM PRECISELY.

HARVEY WOULD EVEN ACT OUT EACH SCENE FOR THEM, RIGHT DOWN TO THE SOUND EFFECTS...

...then the cannon goes—

BWAM!

BILL ELDER

SEVERIN

BUT THIS PROCESS TOOK TIME, AND HIS PAY SHRANK WITH EVERY EXTRA HOUR...

WHEN HE TOOK HIS CONCERNS TO GAINES, THE PUBLISHER SIMPLY SUGGESTED:

Why don't you come up with a book that's not so labor intensive?

THEY SAY NECESSITY IS THE MOTHER OF INVENTION-- IN KURTZMAN'S CASE IT WAS THE MOTHER LODE!

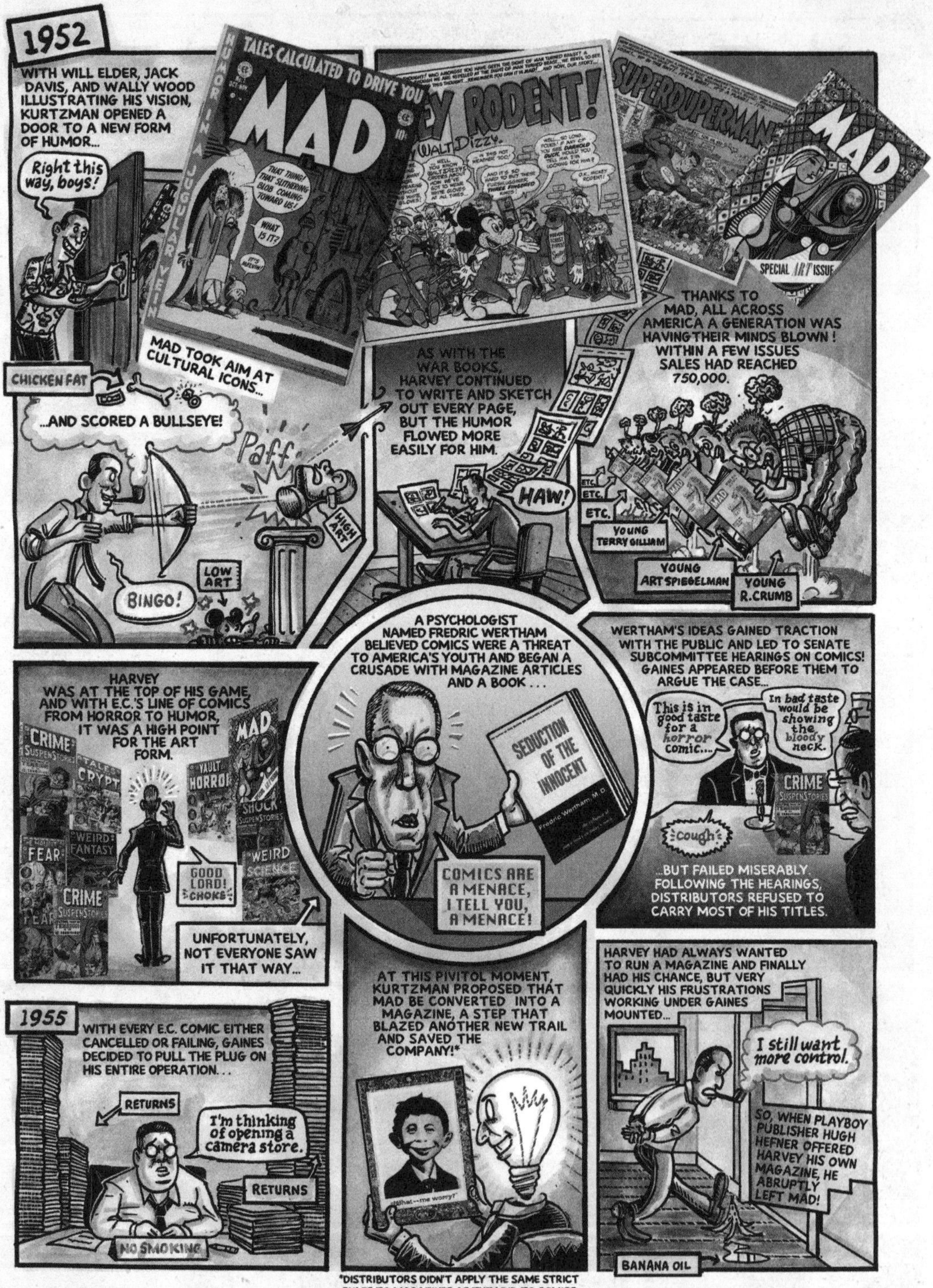

1952
WITH WILL ELDER, JACK DAVIS, AND WALLY WOOD ILLUSTRATING HIS VISION, KURTZMAN OPENED A DOOR TO A NEW FORM OF HUMOR...
Right this way, boys!
TALES CALCULATED TO DRIVE YOU MAD
HUMOR IN A JUGULAR VEIN
RODENT!
SUPERDUPERMAN
MAD
SPECIAL ART ISSUE
MAD TOOK AIM AT CULTURAL ICONS...
CHICKEN FAT
...AND SCORED A BULLSEYE!
Paff
HIGH ART
LOW ART
BINGO!
AS WITH THE WAR BOOKS, HARVEY CONTINUED TO WRITE AND SKETCH OUT EVERY PAGE, BUT THE HUMOR FLOWED MORE EASILY FOR HIM.
HAW!
THANKS TO MAD, ALL ACROSS AMERICA A GENERATION WAS HAVING THEIR MINDS BLOWN! WITHIN A FEW ISSUES SALES HAD REACHED 750,000.
ETC.
ETC.
ETC.
YOUNG TERRY GILLIAM
YOUNG ART SPIEGELMAN
YOUNG R.CRUMB
HARVEY WAS AT THE TOP OF HIS GAME, AND WITH E.C.'S LINE OF COMICS FROM HORROR TO HUMOR, IT WAS A HIGH POINT FOR THE ART FORM.
CRIME SUSPENSTORIES
TALES FROM THE CRYPT
VAULT OF HORROR
MAD
SHOCK SUSPENSTORIES
WEIRD FANTASY
FEAR
WEIRD SCIENCE
CRIME SUSPENSTORIES
GOOD LORD! CHOKE
UNFORTUNATELY, NOT EVERYONE SAW IT THAT WAY...
A PSYCHOLOGIST NAMED FREDRIC WERTHAM BELIEVED COMICS WERE A THREAT TO AMERICA'S YOUTH AND BEGAN A CRUSADE WITH MAGAZINE ARTICLES AND A BOOK . . .
SEDUCTION OF THE INNOCENT
Fredric Wertham, M.D.
COMICS ARE A MENACE, I TELL YOU, A MENACE!
WERTHAM'S IDEAS GAINED TRACTION WITH THE PUBLIC AND LED TO SENATE SUBCOMMITTEE HEARINGS ON COMICS! GAINES APPEARED BEFORE THEM TO ARGUE THE CASE...
This is in good taste for a horror comic....
In bad taste would be showing the bloody neck.
CRIME SUSPENSTORIES
cough
...BUT FAILED MISERABLY. FOLLOWING THE HEARINGS, DISTRIBUTORS REFUSED TO CARRY MOST OF HIS TITLES.
1955
WITH EVERY E.C. COMIC EITHER CANCELLED OR FAILING, GAINES DECIDED TO PULL THE PLUG ON HIS ENTIRE OPERATION. . .
RETURNS
I'm thinking of opening a camera store.
RETURNS
NO SMOKING
AT THIS PIVITOL MOMENT, KURTZMAN PROPOSED THAT MAD BE CONVERTED INTO A MAGAZINE, A STEP THAT BLAZED ANOTHER NEW TRAIL AND SAVED THE COMPANY!*
What--me worry?
HARVEY HAD ALWAYS WANTED TO RUN A MAGAZINE AND FINALLY HAD HIS CHANCE, BUT VERY QUICKLY HIS FRUSTRATIONS WORKING UNDER GAINES MOUNTED...
I still want more control.
SO, WHEN PLAYBOY PUBLISHER HUGH HEFNER OFFERED HARVEY HIS OWN MAGAZINE, HE ABRUPTLY LEFT MAD!
BANANA OIL

*DISTRIBUTORS DIDN'T APPLY THE SAME STRICT RULES TO MAGAZINES AS THEY DID TO COMICS.

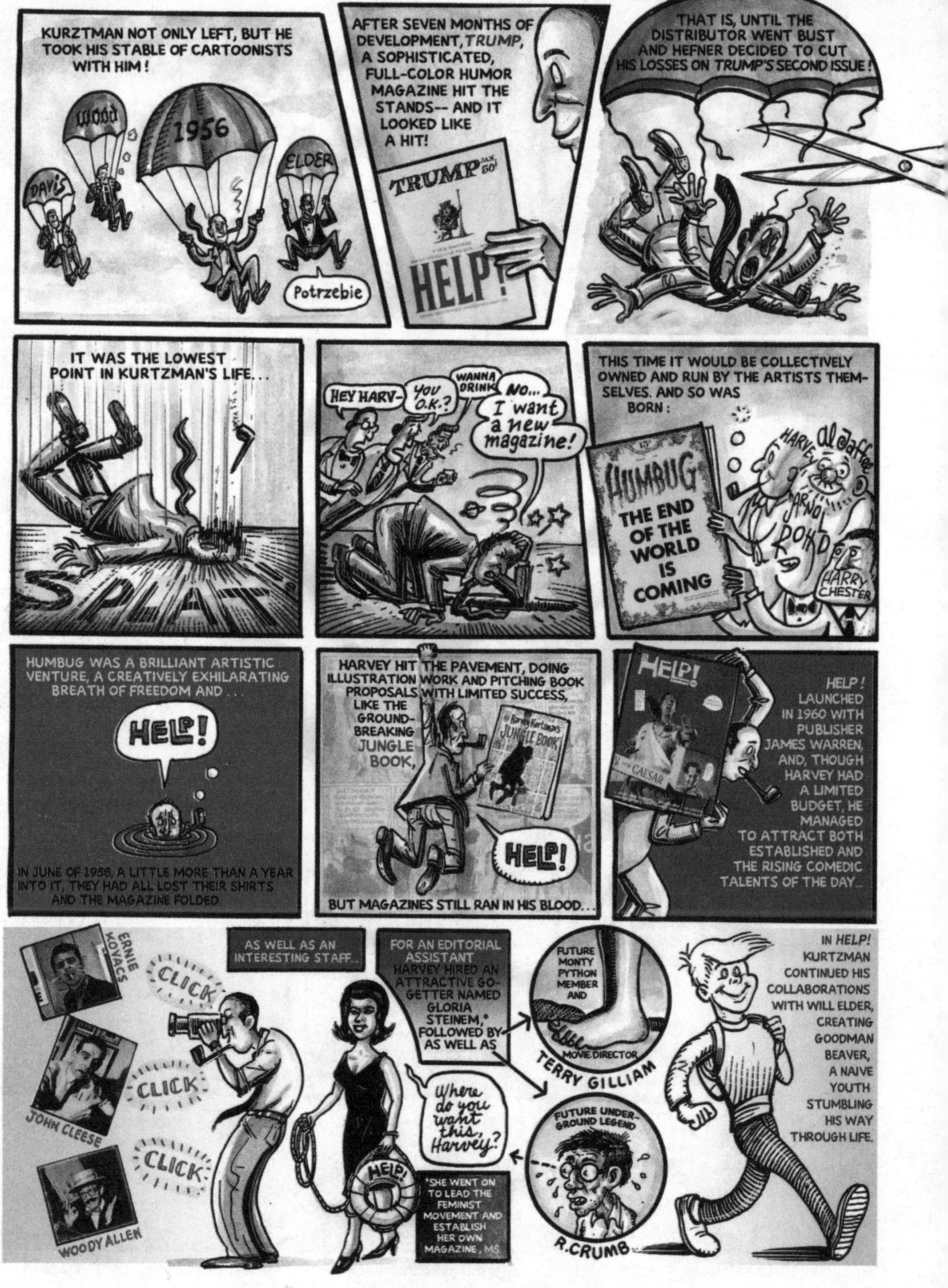
KURTZMAN NOT ONLY LEFT, BUT HE TOOK HIS STABLE OF CARTOONISTS WITH HIM!
DAVIS
WOOD
1956
ELDER
Potrzebie
AFTER SEVEN MONTHS OF DEVELOPMENT, TRUMP, A SOPHISTICATED, FULL-COLOR HUMOR MAGAZINE HIT THE STANDS-- AND IT LOOKED LIKE A HIT!
TRUMP JAN 50¢
HELP!
THAT IS, UNTIL THE DISTRIBUTOR WENT BUST AND HEFNER DECIDED TO CUT HIS LOSSES ON TRUMP'S SECOND ISSUE!
IT WAS THE LOWEST POINT IN KURTZMAN'S LIFE...
SPLAT
HEY HARV-
YOU O.K.?
WANNA DRINK
NO... I want a new magazine!
THIS TIME IT WOULD BE COLLECTIVELY OWNED AND RUN BY THE ARTISTS THEMSELVES. AND SO WAS BORN:
HUMBUG
THE END OF THE WORLD IS COMING
HARVEY
al Jaffee
ARNOLD ROTH
HARRY CHESTER
HUMBUG WAS A BRILLIANT ARTISTIC VENTURE, A CREATIVELY EXHILARATING BREATH OF FREEDOM AND . . .
HELP!
IN JUNE OF 1958, A LITTLE MORE THAN A YEAR INTO IT, THEY HAD ALL LOST THEIR SHIRTS AND THE MAGAZINE FOLDED.
HARVEY HIT THE PAVEMENT, DOING ILLUSTRATION WORK AND PITCHING BOOK PROPOSALS WITH LIMITED SUCCESS, LIKE THE GROUND-BREAKING JUNGLE BOOK,
Harvey Kurtzman's JUNGLE BOOK
HELP!
BUT MAGAZINES STILL RAN IN HIS BLOOD...
HELP!
HELP! LAUNCHED IN 1960 WITH PUBLISHER JAMES WARREN, AND, THOUGH HARVEY HAD A LIMITED BUDGET, HE MANAGED TO ATTRACT BOTH ESTABLISHED AND THE RISING COMEDIC TALENTS OF THE DAY...
ERNIE KOVACS
CLICK
JOHN CLEESE
CLICK
WOODY ALLEN
CLICK
AS WELL AS AN INTERESTING STAFF...
FOR AN EDITORIAL ASSISTANT HARVEY HIRED AN ATTRACTIVE GO-GETTER NAMED GLORIA STEINEM,* FOLLOWED BY AS WELL AS
FUTURE MONTY PYTHON MEMBER AND MOVIE DIRECTOR
TERRY GILLIAM
FUTURE UNDERGROUND LEGEND
R.CRUMB
Where do you want this, Harvey?
HELP!
*SHE WENT ON TO LEAD THE FEMINIST MOVEMENT AND ESTABLISH HER OWN MAGAZINE, MS.
IN HELP! KURTZMAN CONTINUED HIS COLLABORATIONS WITH WILL ELDER, CREATING GOODMAN BEAVER, A NAIVE YOUTH STUMBLING HIS WAY THROUGH LIFE.

THOUGH *HELP!* LASTED FOR FIVE YEARS, AS EARLY AS 1962 HARVEY COULD READ THE WRITING ON THE WALL AND BEGAN MAKING MOVES BACK TO HIS OLD BENEFACTOR, HUGH HEFNER.

THE IDEA HARVEY PROPOSED TO PLAYBOY WAS TO TAKE HIS GOODMAN BEAVER CHARACTER AND FLIP GENDERS...

UNFORTUNATELY, HEFNER WAS NOTORIOUS FOR HIS HEAVY EDITORIAL HAND.

THE FINAL TWENTY-SIX YEARS IN HARVEY KURTZMAN'S CAREER BECAME DEVOTED TO *LITTLE ANNIE FANNY.*

AND TRYING TO PLEASE HEFNER WITH ENORMOUS COMPROMISES, ENORMOUS CHANGES...

AND... ENORMOUS BREASTS.

SADLY, THE BRILLIANT ARTIST BEHIND SO MANY GROUNDBREAKING INNOVATIONS WAS REDUCED TO—

Why, you little pissant!

WHA?!

You really think you can sum my life up in a few pages??

You never even mentioned my my work for—

Esquire or Parade or my teaching...

Or the fact that Adele and I raised four amazing children—

Or the struggles we faced with an autistic son!

Sure, I made mistakes and some financial blunders...

whatta you expect?

I'm a GOD-DAMN ARTIST—

Not a Furslugginer businessman!

I gave every job 200%!

Ahh, forget it—

Pearls before swine.

HE'S RIGHT. THERE'S NO WAY TO EXAMINE THE VALUE OF HIS LIFE IN SIX PAGES...

LET ALONE SIX HUNDRED!

THANK YOU HARVEY, THANK YOU.

AS LIGHTNING FLASHES ON THE RAIN-SWOLLEN IMJIN, A CARTOONIST FLOATS OUT TO SEA.

cahiers du cinéMAD

Grady Hendrix

OR MANY of us, the first exposure to classic films wasn't on film at all, it was in print. It was in black and white even if the films were in color, it was printed on cheap paper, and it was full of some of the worst puns known to man. We thrilled to Francis Ford Coppola's "The Oddfather," Arthur Penn's revisionist western "Little Dull Man," the sophisticated sex comedy "Shampooped," and Stanley Kubrick's groundbreaking "201 Min. of a Space Idiocy." For us, *Casablanca* was cast with professional wrestlers, *My Fair Lady* featured women's libbers trying to reform a male chauvinist Burt Reynolds, and *The Exorcist* ended with Satan demanding a six-film deal.

Rude, irreverent, and with fifty-eight years of history now behind them, *MAD* magazine's movie satires gave some of us our first encounters with the modern cinematic canon. Always happy to aim over the heads of its target audience of teenaged boys (issue #28 featured a guide to IRS form 1040), *MAD* was parodying movies like *Barry Lyndon* ("Borey Lyndon") and *Blow-Up* ("Throw Up") to a readership with little awareness of these movies beyond their newspaper ads. Long before most kids were old enough to see R- and X-rated movies like *Dressed to Kill*, *Altered States*, and *Midnight Cowboy*, they were familiar with "Undressed to Kill," "Assaulted State," and "Midnight Wowboy." While film studies majors gasp over the deconstruction of genre in the works of David Lynch and the meta-movies of Charlie Kaufman, "the Usual Gang of Idiots" over at *MAD* have been deconstructing, meta-narrativing, and postmodernizing motion pictures since the very first movie parody ("Hah! Noon!") appeared in 1954.

Four hundred and eighty-two parodies later, the *MAD* movie send-up has become an institution. Filmmakers like J. J. Abrams and Steven Spielberg buy the original cover art featuring parodies of their films, and back in 1973 Jack Davis, one of the kings of the *MAD* movie parody, was hired by United Artists to design a poster for Robert Altman's *The Long Goodbye* done in the exact same style as *MAD*'s trademark splash page, complete with word balloons. The *MAD* movie satires drew the blueprint for all motion picture parodies to come.

Before *MAD*, audiences looking for movie parodies had to be content with Britain's relatively toothless *Carry On* films, Bob Hope's gentle genre ribbing, or Abbott and Costello's goofy send-ups. But *MAD* was out for blood. Deeply meta and full of in-jokes, it constantly conflated characters with the actors playing them (lancing Brando's foppish accent in *Mutiny on the Bounty* a.k.a. "Mutiny on the Bouncy," one character says, "Don't worry, Trevar! He pulled a stupid Southern accent on me in *Sayonara* and I still won an Oscar!") and gleefully pointed out plot holes. When Roy Scheider is fatally stabbed in *Marathon Man*, he manages to make it back to his brother's apartment, over sixty blocks away. "Good Lord! What happened to you?" Dustin Hoffman gasps in "Marathon Mess." "I was stabbed in Lincoln Center, so I dragged myself to Broadway, caught an uptown bus to 72nd Street and got a crosstown bus to Riverside Drive, grabbed a No. 4 bus to 116th street . . . walked up the hill . . . and here I am . . ." Scheider replies.

Prior to the '70s and the advent of Monty Python, Mel Brooks's film send-ups, and the team of Zucker-Abrahams-Zucker, *MAD* contributors were the only people parodying Hollywood sanctimony on a regular basis. Jack Clayton's glossy version of *The Great Gatsby* might have been a profitable vehicle for Robert Redford, and it might have won two Academy Awards, but *MAD* saw right through it. Calling it "The Great Gasbag," they lambasted its lacquered artificiality ("Gasbag thought of everything!" Nick Carrawayseed remarks at a supposedly wild party. "He even had the dancing choreographed!"), bemoaned its monotony ("Why . . . ? Why?!?" screams Nick after Myrtle is run over by a car. "Why didn't they *FILM* the only scene with any action in this entire movie?!"), and revealed that Gatsby's mysterious absences were due to the fact that Robert Redford is having secret meetings with his agent, begging to get out of the picture before it ruins his box-office clout.

But when *MAD* switched from black and white to color and began running ads in 2001 (it had been ad-free since 1957), it coincided with the decline of the movie-satire golden age. In the eighteen years between 1984 and 2002 they published one hundred eighty of them, but between 2002 and 2012 there were only forty. The spoofs used to average seven pages each; now they average five, and sometimes even four. But this decline has more to do with movie industry practices than the quality of the satires themselves, and the parodies are too much a part of the magazine's DNA to disappear completely. They've also shown a remarkable continuity. Over the past fifty years, four editors (Harvey Kurtzman, Al Feldstein, Nick Meglin, and John Ficarra), and the same five writers (Dick DeBartolo, Stan Hart, Arnie Kogen, Larry Siegel, and Desmond Devlin) and five artists (Mort Drucker, Angelo Torres, Jack Davis, Tom Richmond, and Hermann Mejia) have been responsible for 87 percent of them, and the format has remained remarkably consistent.

Since the '60s, the parodies always opened with a two-page (or occasionally one-page) splash in which the characters introduce themselves to the reader ("I'm Appalled Neuman! In my new movie

The Color of Monotony, I take the corn I usually pop and put it on-screen!"). After the chaos of the opening spread, the borderless panels are laid out in simple grids and the dialogue is "copy cast," which means that all of the distinctively rectangular word balloons start at the same height to ensure ease of reading. Each row of panels can fit 108 characters across and word balloons are never allowed to run more than eight lines deep in order to leave some real estate for the artist, although that's loosened up in the last twenty years with the advent of digital technology. As visually chaotic as the panels get, this layout ensures that they scan quickly from left to right, flowing from joke to joke.

A familiarity with the films is assumed and the parodies play like greatest-hits albums, leaping from highlight to highlight. In "Midnight Wowboy" Joe Buck is seen getting turned down for a date by a dowager in one panel and having pillow talk in bed with a woman in the next, leaving all that narrative connective tissue on the drafting-room floor. There's also a talking-back-to-the-screen quality, as in "The Empire Strikes Out" when Ham Yoyo says to Princess Laidup, "Princess, sometimes I think you forgot how to be a woman!" "Oh? What makes you say that?" she replies. "Well . . . for openers you have your bra on backwards!" he says, sounding like a movie-theater smartass.

Ever since the second satire ("From Eternity Back to Here!"), sending up the marketing was also part of the program. In 1989's "Battyman" a bystander asks why Battyman needs exotic planes and cars to fight crime. "Actually, he doesn't!" someone explains. "Toy manufacturers do." In "Home A-Groan" they skewer product placement when Kelvin says, "The producers realize that audiences do not like to watch commercials on the screen before the movie starts. So they solved the problem by putting the commercials right into the movie itself!" *MAD*'s send-up of *Ghostbusters II* justifies the sequel by applying "the

Sly Stallone philosophy: If at first you *DO* succeed, do it over and over and over again!"

Even though the format became fixed in the late '60s, it took a long time to get there. When *MAD* debuted in 1952, it was a far cry from the *MAD* magazine of today. It wasn't even a magazine. A comic book for its first twenty-three issues, *MAD* started off parodying the same crime, war, science fiction, and horror comics its parent company, EC Comics, published. But as early as issue #2, it ventured into movie parodies, sending up *Tarzan* and jungle films as a genre (at the time there were twenty-four *Tarzan* movies to eviscerate). Issue #3 saw the first skewering of what would become a favorite target, television, kicking then-popular series *Dragnet* in the seat of the pants, while also poking fun at *The Lone Ranger*, another television mainstay.

Issue #9's first specific movie parody, "Hah! Noon!," was *MAD*'s fourth send-up of the western genre and it was published under the auspices of the "Western Dept." Soon after, in issue #12, the first non-western movie parody appeared under the "Movie Dept." rubric: "From Eternity Back to Here!" by comics master Bernie Krigstein. This was the first parody to caricature the actors as well as their roles, portraying a Montgomery Clift who stutters and stammers through his part, taking five word balloons to deliver a single line. It was more meta than a Tarantino film, with everyone referring to the kissing-in-the-surf scene as constantly as the studio's marketing department pushed it in ads—and, thanks to Krigstein's innovative touch, it was graphically experimental. The beach kiss is represented by a photo cutout of the characters taken from a still of the movie, locked in their sandy clinch, and it's repeated in one panel per page for five pages as the waves slowly engulf and drown them.

While it was still feeling around for a format, these early parodies unleashed a wave of visual innovation at *MAD*. A send-up of *The Wild*

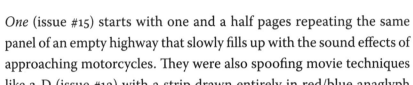

One (issue #15) starts with one and a half pages repeating the same panel of an empty highway that slowly fills up with the sound effects of approaching motorcycles. They were also spoofing movie techniques like 3-D (issue #12) with a strip drawn entirely in red/blue anaglyph style, that ended with the artist and writer creating a voluptuous 3-D dame so realistic that they tore the panels to shreds trying to get at her, leaving the entire last page a blank white void.

In July 1955, with issue #24, *MAD* abandoned the comic book format and became the black-and-white magazine we know today, complete with a parody of Robert Aldrich's *Vera Cruz*. Totally free of word balloons, it played out its satire in captioned pictures, more like illustrations in a magazine than cartooning. This remained the format for several years. Gradually, this captioned illustration approach was supplanted by true cartooning from Wood, a brilliant, hard-drinking draftsman, and a southerner named Jack Davis, who went on to design one-sheet posters for films like *The Bad News Bears*, Woody Allen's *Bananas*, and *It's a Mad, Mad, Mad, Mad World*. Both men were aided and abetted by the founding editor, Harvey Kurtzman, who sometimes even dictated figure composition and panel layout.

But the arrival of Mort Drucker in 1957 changed everything. Initially no one saw Drucker's talent. Then in 1959 he drew the television parody "The Night Perry Masonite Lost a Case," and the basic movie parody format for the next forty-four years was born. Opening with a splash panel that took up two-thirds of the page, it was all cartooning, used square word balloons, and the dialogue was copy cast. Playing to Drucker's strengths, "The Night Perry Masonite Lost a Case" opted for an extremely tame design, mandated by art directors John Putnam and Leonard Brenner, who gave Drucker his panel layouts. The panels were mostly two-shots and medium shots, usually showing the characters from the waist up. The comedy came from Drucker's uncanny ability to capture the likeness of an actor and then blow it up to the point where it started to deform but didn't quite tip over into caricature. The cartoonist's equivalent of an actor's director, Drucker was a master of drawing hands, faces, and body language, and his approach (he wound up creating 238 movie satires) became the house style. The layout innovations of Davis and Wallace Wood were things of the past, replaced by Drucker's less spectacular gifts. In recent years, artists like Tom Richmond and art director Sam Viviano have brought more visual flair to their parodies—for instance, Richmond's *Traffic* send-up ("Traff-eccch!") echoed the movie's shifting color palette (a joke only possible after *MAD*'s return to color printing in 2001), but for the most part it's Drucker's straightforward, actor-based style that carries the day.

The format is bulletproof, and it still works. Today's decline has less to do with the parodies themselves and more to do with changing film distribution patterns. When *Star Wars* came out in May 1977, *MAD*'s editors waited a few weeks to ensure it would be a hit before sending the writers to see it, and although the issue hit newsstands in January 1978, the movie was still playing eight months after its release. These days, movies are in theaters for three weeks or less. Since it takes up to three months to commission and draw a parody, the magazine is now in a constant race against time.

MAD's editors are now obliged to go after the biggest blockbusters that have the most expensive ad campaigns and splashiest home video releases to ensure that the source material for their parodies remains in the public consciousness. Back in the day, they did send-ups of everything from *Bunny Lake Is Missing* ("Bubba Lake Missed by a Mile") to *Is Paris Burning?* ("Is Paris Boring?"). In 2011, the only movie parodies they published were *Harry Potter and the Deathly Hallows: Part 1*, *Green Lantern*, and *Harry Potter and the Deathly Hallows: Part*

2. Early access to set photos and plot synopses would alleviate this problem, but studios have never cooperated with *MAD*, even going so far as to deny them press kits. Even Warner Bros., *MAD*'s parent company, refuses to give them advance access to movie materials. To get their Harry Potter parodies out on time, writer Desmond Devlin based his scripts on the books, not the movies, trusting that the filmmakers wouldn't deviate too far from J. K. Rowling's original stories.

There's also the issue of the magazine's own success. With over sixty years of history, it's hard for *MAD* to avoid repeating itself, especially when they've been so merciless from day one. In its first decade, *MAD* skewered everything from 3-D (1954) to celebrity magazines ("Anyone for Wrist Slashing?" in 1955) to bloated running times (1961's on-set visit of John Wayne's *The Alamo* depicts the extras murdering the star for making a three-and-a-half-hour movie)—and they even parodied their own parodies. In issue #17 their takedown of Joseph L. Mankiewicz's *Julius Caesar* featured a guide to the shortcuts and cheap tricks the artists and writers were using for comic effect.

But their satire still seems to sting, even though it's usually publicists and studio drones who get angry, not filmmakers. *MAD* has never been successfully sued, but that hasn't stopped people from trying. The magazine once received a letter from Lucasfilm's legal department after their *Empire Strikes Back* parody, demanding that they recall all printed copies of the issue and destroy them. *MAD* replied by sending a copy of another letter they had received the previous month—from George Lucas, offering to buy the original artwork for the *Empire* parody and comparing Mort Drucker to Leonardo da Vinci and the parody's writer, Dick DeBartolo, to Mark Twain. They never heard from Lucasfilm's legal department again.

(2013)

MAD and me

R. Crumb

AD WAS extremely influential on me in my teens. I was obsessed with it and constantly searching for old back issues, going back to the beginning, when it was a comic book. I finally got together a complete collection of the Kurtzman *MAD* comics and magazines, for it was really Kurtzman's vision that I found so strong, unique, inspiring. I also loved *Humbug* magazine, Kurtzman's last great satire work. Feldstein's *MAD* was less interesting, though he used some of the same artists. I *LOVED* the work of Wally Wood, Will Elder, and Jack Davis when they worked with Kurtzman. His ideas inspired these artists to do their very best work. It's tragic what happened to Kurtzman after *Humbug*. He got chewed up by the system, ended up having to take orders from Hugh Hefner, who fancied himself a genius of some sort and relentlessly meddled in the comics (Little Annie Fanny) that Kurtzman did for *Playboy*. It was a terrible thing to witness. I saw Kurtzman literally WEEPING over Hefner's interference, his blue-penciling of Kurtzman's roughs for Annie Fanny stories. I remember vowing to myself, "Don't let this happen to you."

Washington Heights, nyc. ca 1955

SPIEGELMAN [1972]

SHE LOOKED A BIT LIKE THE MONA LISA AND A BIT LIKE THOSE PICASSO WOMEN I'D LEARN TO LOVE YEARS LATER...

BUT SHE WAS THE MEATBALLS AND SPAGHETTI VERSION. SHE WAS "POST-MODERNISM" *AVANT LA LETTRE*...

SHE WAS BEAUTIFUL!

MAD WARPED A GENERATION. IN THE BLAND AMERICAN 1950s IT WAS SAYING SOMETHING NEW!

IT WAS SAYING: "THE MEDIA— THE WHOLE DAMN ADULT WORLD— IS *LYING* TO YOU... AND WE HERE AT MAD ARE PART OF THE MEDIA!"

BUT I WANNIT! I WANNIT! I *NEED* THIS!

OKAY, OKAY! JUST DON'T TELL DADDY I SPENT MY GROCERY MONEY ON IT!

LOOK, ARTIE— AMERICA!

I *STUDIED* MAD THE WAY SOME KIDS STUDIED THE TALMUD!

@&%?*! FURSHLUG-GINER KID!

I COULDN'T LEARN MUCH ABOUT AMERICA FROM MY REFUGEE IMMIGRANT PARENTS—BUT I LEARNED ALL ABOUT IT FROM MAD.,,,, AND I BEGAN TO THINK OF MAD AS AN ACRONYM FOR MOM AND DAD!

PREFACE to GAINES
Frank Jacobs

ONE DAY, so the story goes, a teenage reader wandered into the offices of *MAD* magazine and buttonholed the first person he saw.

"I want to talk to the publisher," the boy said.

"I am the publisher," said the person.

The boy blinked. The person he was talking to was a shaggy, rumpled hulk, dressed in a faded, pink sport shirt and baggy, unpressed trousers. Most of the bespectacled face was buried behind a hopelessly untrimmed beard. The rest of the head was enshrouded in a puzzle of hanging hair, styled only by the force of gravity.

"You've got to be kidding," the boy said.

No, it was true. The hulk was William Maxwell Gaines, publisher of *MAD*, millionaire, gourmet, wine expert, practical joker, *King Kong* fanatic, zeppelin enthusiast, hater of exercise, and one of the least probable men in the world.

"We all have our many sides," says his sister, Elaine, "but Bill seems to have so many more of them."

Gaines runs *MAD* on his own terms and would like to run the rest of his life the same way. Shortly after the magazine moved into its present offices at 485 Madison Avenue, he toddled down for a chat with the manager of the building's restaurant, Morgen's East.

Portrait of Bill Gaimes by Drew Friedman

"I'm going to be in this building for at least ten years and I'm going to eat in this restaurant, sometimes with guests, at least four times a week, forty to fifty weeks a year," Gaines said. "The only thing I wish is not to wear a tie. If you insist on my wearing a tie, you will lose a lot of business."

"I'm sorry," the manager said, "but we can't let anyone eat here without a tie."

"Okay," Gaines said, and left, crossing the place off his list. Several years later, the restaurant removed its ban and allowed guests to dine tieless. If Morgen's East thought Gaines would now become a patron, Morgen's East was mistaken. "There is no way I will ever set foot in the place," he says.

This is, in some ways, a pity, because Gaines likes comfort and convenience in his life, and the restaurant offers both. But, as he says, "There are some things you can't forgive."

If Gaines had his way, the outdoors would be air-conditioned in summer and heated in winter, and all stairs would be replaced by escalators. For the present, however, he must make do with the imperfect world he has been deposited in.

One night he and I were strolling to a restaurant.

"Frank, please," he objected.

"What's wrong?" I asked.

"You mustn't walk so fast. We are going *one degree uphill*."

Gaines's mind is a nest of compartments, each programmed to make day-to-day living easier. He has special routes for getting about New York and has been known to walk three blocks out of his way in order to avoid a short stretch of uphill climbing. Of course, these are one-way routes. When he leaves the *MAD* office to lunch at a place, say, five blocks downhill, he will return in a taxi.

One night he and I watched home movies taken during his boyhood. During a party sequence, he directed my attention to a young man jitterbugging. "Look at him," Gaines said.

"I'll have you know that he now wears a pacemaker in his heart. Can there be any doubt *why*?"

Gaines has danced twice—the first time when he took a lesson, the last time at a high school prom when he tried out the step he learned at the lesson. As a boy, he played softball once. He recalls getting one hit, which turned into a home run after the other team made four successive throwing errors. He might have played a second time, but someone told him that he threw "like a girl," which ended any dreams of sandlot glory.

Gaines has skied once. He gave it up after twenty minutes because of two handicaps: he couldn't bend over to fasten his skis, and when he finally got them on, he would soon fall and lie in the snow, like a beetle on its back, unable to right himself.

Gaines has aquaplaned once. Again there were physical problems. He required one hand to hold on to his horn-rimmed glasses (without them he can't see), and he required the other hand to keep his swim trunks from falling, which they did whenever the boat picked up speed. This left no remaining hand with which to hold on to the ropes.

But why dwell on one man's inadequacies? There are a number of things that Gaines does well—traveling, eating, wine-tasting, laughing, and, in between all these, publishing *MAD*.

"My staff and contributors create the magazine," he has said. "What I create is the atmosphere."

During *MAD*'s early years, Gaines employed a stockroom boy named Anthony, a well-behaved, industrious chap, who suffered from only one character flaw—extreme gullibility. One day Gaines revealed that he had a twin brother named Rex.

"Watch out for him, Anthony," Gaines warned. "Rex looks exactly like me except that he has a scar on his cheek and talks loud and mean and nasty. He doesn't have any money, so he steals from other people. If you see him, he'll be wearing my clothes because he stole them from me."

A few days later, Gaines walked out of the office, applied a rubber-cement scar to his face, and walked in as Rex. Anthony was appalled to see Rex stride through the office, shouting terrible oaths, bullying the employees, even rifling the petty cash box in Gaines's office. Anthony saw and Anthony believed.

Rex's visits continued. He would demand to see his twin brother, refusing to believe Anthony's explanation that William Gaines was out. Sometimes Rex had a scar on his right cheek, sometimes on his left—Gaines could never remember which he'd used the time before— but Anthony remained a believer.

Years passed, and Gaines feared that Anthony was catching on. One morning the phone rang in Gaines's office. "Anthony, it's for you," Gaines shouted. Anthony picked up the phone and, while Gaines looked on, heard Rex's voice, tape-recorded, on the other end: "Anthony, don't say a goddamn word—just listen!" The voice screamed on for thirty seconds, then hung up.

Gaines's mother visited the office and was cornered by Anthony.

"Mrs. Gaines, you wouldn't lie to me. Do you really have another son named Rex?"

"I'd rather not talk about it," she said.

Anthony was an aspiring playwright. After he left *MAD*, he wrote a play called "The Canary Cage" and sent it to Gaines to read. A few weeks later, Anthony phoned to get Gaines's reaction. Rex answered.

"Anthony, I just wantcha to know I'm producing a musical with Rodgers and Hammerstein called 'The Gilded Canary Cage.'"

Rex proceeded to describe the plot, which, of course, came from Anthony's script.

"That's my play!" Anthony protested.

"Yeah," growled Rex, "but can you prove it? I stole it from my brother when he wasn't here, and now it's mine and you can't do anything about it."

Anthony became so hysterical that someone in the office—Gaines never found out who—broke down and revealed the hoax for what it was. Gaines was sorry the gag was blown because he had been planning to end it himself in more appropriate fashion.

"We were going to kill Rex off, stage a funeral, and put up his tombstone in a cemetery, carved for real—'Rex Gaines, Born 1922–Died 1959.' It would have been the perfect ending."

More than a decade has passed, and *MAD* continues to be Gaines's private circus. Financially, the magazine is big business, bringing in a yearly profit in millions, but, unlike other publishing operations, there is a refreshing dearth of pomp and self-importance. This spirit was reflected on the cover of *MAD*'s centennial issue:

MAD PROUDLY PRESENTS

ITS

100th ISSUE

(Big deal!)

The staff works hard to sustain *MAD*'s worthless image. The magazine puts itself down as a cheap rag, containing trash, garbage, and other unworthy components. Gaines frets each time inflation forces the magazine to raise its newsstand price. For years *MAD* flaunted its price as "25¢—Cheap." But rising costs forced up the price to "30¢" (with the "Cheap" crossed out), then to "35¢—Highway Robbery." In 1971, *MAD* raised its price another nickel. For the next several issues, Gaines tried to placate his readers with these successive front-cover comments: "40¢—Ouch!" "40¢—Outrageous!" "40¢—No Laughing Matter" "40¢—Relatively cheap!" "40¢—Cheap (Considering!)" "40¢—Cheap?" and, finally, "40¢—Cheap."

This kind of self-deprecation is unusual for a magazine, but, then,

Gaines is not your usual kind of executive. Other publishers may insist their employees punch a time clock. Not Gaines, who lets his people come and go as they please. Other company heads may demand quiet and decorum. Not Gaines, who summons his staff with an interoffice shout and who once gleefully filled the office water cooler with five gallons of white wine and roared with laughter as the day rolled on and he and several of his staff got gloriously swacked.

Gaines's laugh is large and rolling and fills a room, but then so does he. "There is no more musical sound in the world than Bill Gaines laughing," says art director John Putnam. "Gaines has an infectious laugh, and if you stand too close to him you can catch a fat flu," says writer Larry Siegel. Even Gaines's ex-wife, Nancy, agrees that he is one of the greatest audiences in the world, although, reflecting on their stormy marriage, "I can't remember ever having done anything that amused him."

Gaines is not the marrying kind, although he has tried it twice. The closest thing in his life to a perfect union occurred when he began publishing *MAD*. Gaines and *MAD*, like a boy and his frog, are inseparable.

(1972)

WHAT A LOAD OF CRAFT!

©2023 R. Sikor

CREATOR *HARVEY KURTZMAN* WAS A PERFECTIONIST WITH HIS DETAILED SCRIPTS AND SKETCHES.

ARTISTS *JACK DAVIS, WILL ELDER,* AND *WALLY WOOD* ILLUSTRATED KURTZMAN'S LAYOUTS WITH FLAIR.

LETTERER *BEN ODA* AND COLORIST *MARIE SEVERIN* ADDED THEIR OWN STYLISH TOUCHES.

I NEVER CUT CORNERS. I NEVER KNEW HOW TO DO IT JUST FOR THE MONEY.

(HARVEY) HAS ALWAYS BEEN AHEAD OF A LOT OF US AND WAS DEMANDING... IT MADE ME WORK HARDER.

(HARVEY) WAS SO AUTOCRATIC... YOU DIDN'T MIND BECAUSE HE WAS JUST AS NUTTY AS YOU WERE!

KLAK KLAKETY KLAK

SCRITCH SCRITCHITY SCRITCH

DRIP DRIPPITY DRIP

QUOTES FROM *HARVEY KURTZMAN: THE MAN WHO CREATED MAD,* BY BILL SCHELLY.

I'M THE AUTHOR OF THIS ESSAY! AND HERE'S THE LESSON THAT *MAD* TAUGHT ME AS A CARTOONIST: YOU CAN ALWAYS QUESTION *AUTHORITY*, BUT YOU SHOULD NEVER QUESTION *CRAFT!*

LET'S *PEEL BACK* THE LAYERS OF THAT CRAFT, AND SEE HOW IT WORKS! ON THE SURFACE, THE CLASSIC COMIC BOOK *COLORS* ARE INVITING, ADDING CLARITY AND ENHANCING MOOD!

PRETTY!

SICK!

NEXT, THE *BLACK INKED LINES* FAITHFULLY REPLICATE THE SUBJECTS WITH DELICATE HATCHING AND SLICK STROKES!

I'M A *CARBON COPY!*

UNDER THAT, THE *TIGHT PENCIL DRAWINGS* PROVIDE ANATOMICAL SOLIDITY AND EXTRA VISUAL GAGS!

CHECK OUT MY *CANS!*

SPAM

BUT FIRST, THE *ROUGH DRAFTS* MAP OUT THE STORY AND CREATE RHYTHMS ACROSS PANELS!

EVERYTHING COMES IN *THREES!*

EVERY ELEMENT, DOWN TO THE *LETTERING*, WITH ITS FRIENDLY, CONSISTENT FORMS, CONTRIBUTES TO A SMOOTH, SATISFYING READING EXPERIENCE!

SLICK! HIP! COOL! CRAZY! DIG!

AND *ALL THE PIECES* ARE DESIGNED TO COME TOGETHER ON *EACH PAGE*, TO CREATE A LAYOUT WITH UNITY AND INTEGRITY!

ADD JOKES HERE

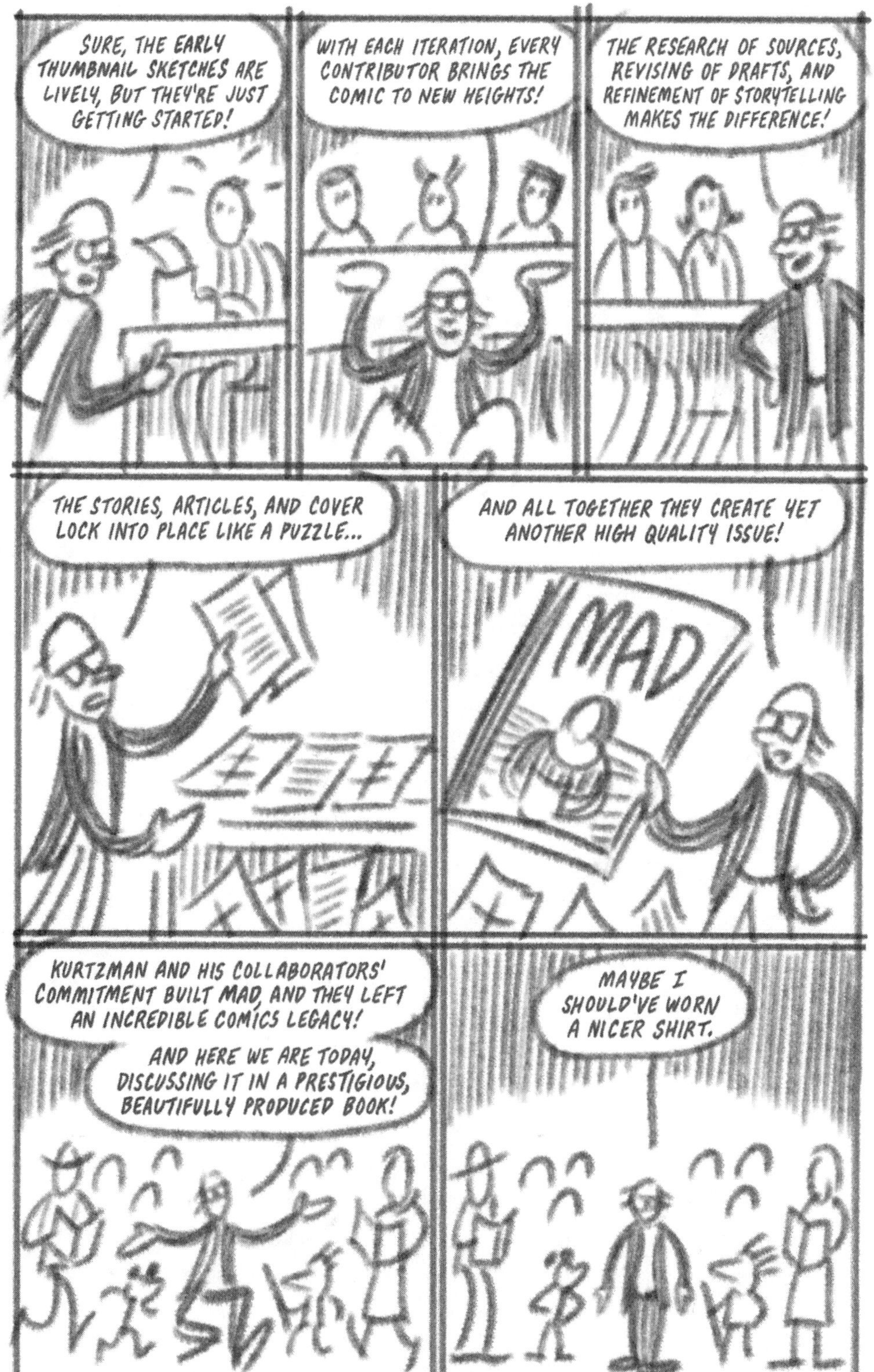
SURE, THE EARLY THUMBNAIL SKETCHES ARE LIVELY, BUT THEY'RE JUST GETTING STARTED!
WITH EACH ITERATION, EVERY CONTRIBUTOR BRINGS THE COMIC TO NEW HEIGHTS!
THE RESEARCH OF SOURCES, REVISING OF DRAFTS, AND REFINEMENT OF STORYTELLING MAKES THE DIFFERENCE!
THE STORIES, ARTICLES, AND COVER LOCK INTO PLACE LIKE A PUZZLE...
AND ALL TOGETHER THEY CREATE YET ANOTHER HIGH QUALITY ISSUE!
MAD
KURTZMAN AND HIS COLLABORATORS' COMMITMENT BUILT MAD, AND THEY LEFT AN INCREDIBLE COMICS LEGACY!
AND HERE WE ARE TODAY, DISCUSSING IT IN A PRESTIGIOUS, BEAUTIFULLY PRODUCED BOOK!
MAYBE I SHOULD'VE WORN A NICER SHIRT.

High Holy MAD

Liel Leibovitz

GROWING UP, I dreaded nothing more than Yom Kippur, the Jewish day of atonement. It wasn't because our rabbi informed us, in a tone that was as dark and knotted as his beard, that God, like a sadistic Santa, was busy making a list of all the people He intended to smite in the coming year, and that we had exactly one more day to repent extra hard and make sure our names weren't on it. Me, I feared a being far more wrathful than the Almighty: my mother, for whom Yom Kippur was an opportunity to put on a great display of piety and show the Lord that we were considerably more worthy of saving than anyone else on the block. With forty-eight hours to go before Judgment Day, she'd meticulously cut out toilet paper, carefully piling up one soft double-ply square on top of another so as to spare us the unforgivable sin of tearing TP on Yom Kippur, which apparently angered God and which also implied that the creator of all things made a habit of checking in on us even as we sat naked on that most intimate of thrones. Then, with two hours to go, she'd have us all slurp down chicken soup in preparation for our upcoming fast, ignoring any attempt at scientific reasoning that inhaling two quarts of salty broth wasn't the best way to prep for a day without drink. Finally, as the solemn occasion kicked in, my mother would remind me that for the next twenty-five hours, all pleasurable activities were strictly forbidden. There'd be no riding bicycles, no playing with friends, no watching TV. The only thing I was allowed to do on Yom Kippur was read.

Since rebellious boys are innately gifted at finding loopholes for mischief, I knew precisely what I had to do. As soon as we returned home from synagogue, I let my face grow long, and in a sorrowful voice informed my mother that I should now like to retire for the evening. Then I ran up to my room, closed the door, and broke out what I thought was the absolutely least appropriate thing a human being could read while waiting for God to pass His judgment: *MAD* magazine. As other Jews made their way solemnly through their prayer book, I snickered at Dave Berg's "The Lighter Side of . . . ," turned the page around and around to catch every detail of Sergio Aragonés's wild hieroglyphics, and, most blasphemous of all for a kid who wasn't even allowed to tear a bit of toilet paper, folded and refolded the back pages of each of my tattered copies to revel in Al Jaffee's genius.

It was more than just a fit of juvenile rebellion. In *MAD* magazine, I found something close to transcendence, not the airless faith of my forefathers with all its strictures but a rowdier religion that encouraged you to obey little and resist much and laugh at everything, particularly at those things that terrified you, like atomic mushroom clouds or natural disasters or the latest bit of Hollywood dreck. Which made perfect sense: you hardly had to be a Talmudic scholar to realize that Jaffee, Berg, Kurtzman, Feldstein et al. were all what my mother would call *unzereh*, our people. But unlike my literal people, my stern and mirthless relatives with their musty old sacred books whose pages wielded no jokes when folded, these Jews, the *MAD* Jews, had a much healthier relationship with the Big Guy in the Sky. My family taught me to think of God and be very afraid. The *MAD* Jews taught me to look heavenward and ask the ancient, resonant question us misfits and outcasts have posed since time immemorial: What, me worry?

If this were a story about any other magazine, it would end right here, a meek morality tale about a kid who makes his way from darkness into the blissful sunshine, from oppressive religion into the lively and life-affirming world of the arts. But the *MAD* Jews were never about feel-good moments; in each issue, they reminded you that the ninnies who pretended to be your intellectual and moral betters were all a bunch of morons and phonies, but they also reminded you that they themselves cheerfully belonged to the very same preposterous, useless class—they were, after all, the Usual Gang of Idiots, not some elevated cabal of enlightened thinkers. In other words, there was no escape—the whole world was a mess, and your only choice was whether to greet the torrents of stupid with a pout or with a prank.

And so it came to pass that I found myself, visiting my mother decades later, back in my childhood room. I was still a few cheeseburgers removed from the faith of my forebears, but, myself a father now, I'd begun immersing myself more attentively in Judaism. It was with the old-timey religion on my mind that I reached under that same old bed and pulled out those same old magazines that had once given me so many hours of subversive joy. What, I wondered distractedly, would *MAD* yield to the man that it hadn't revealed to the boy?

The first thing that struck me as I thumbed through the stack were the margins. There, on page after page, were Aragonés's wordless gags, crawling around corners, wrapping the layout like some savage climbing plant, daring you to take your eyes off the main attraction for a second and enjoy a quick giggle. If you did, sooner or later you noticed that story and side art weren't in competition for your attention; they were sharing it, weaving into each other to transform the way you read. To truly *get* a page of *MAD* you didn't just look at all the

pictures or read all the words, as you would with other, stodgy publications. Instead, you'd begin with a perfectly executed Mort Drucker
and Dick DeBartolo film spoof, say, then stop to see what Aragonés
was doing all the way on the upper right corner, maybe, then back to
the main piece, then turn the page and start over again. As your eyes
zigzagged like that, back and forth, you couldn't help but wonder what
it all meant. Was the tiny, zany nugget of art on the margins supposed
to be a commentary on the piece itself? Was it supposed to remind you
not to take the piece too seriously, because an irreverent *MAD* spoof
should never be consumed too literally? Or was it just a reminder that
MAD, like the cosmos, contained multitudes and mysteries you could
never hope to unlock?

As I pondered these questions, a realization sunk in, sending a
shiver down my spine. It wasn't only that I was now middle-aged and
in search of existential insights rather than puns and punchlines. It
was something more profound, something at once hilarious and terrifying: the text with the commentary in the margins; the constant
shifting of attention all over the page; the deconstructed, hyperlinked,
giddily nonlinear way of reading—I've seen it all before. In the Talmud.

Pick up a page of Judaism's seminal text—a collection of nearly
three thousand double-sided folios dating back at least fifteen hundred years and containing instructions, meditations, and conversa-
tions about every conceivable aspect of Jewish life and law—and the
first thing you'll notice is its structure. Right at the center, you've the
meat of the matter, the core paragraphs detailing the adjudications of
generations of scholars. Elsewhere, left and right and up and down
and all around, the Talmud's compilers included blocks and blocks of
commentaries, notes that sometimes illuminate and sometimes com-
plicate the main reading, inviting you to take nothing on faith. To read
the Talmud, then, isn't to be a passive imbiber of holy writ who merely

quietly follows instructions; it's to keep your eyes peeled and your mind sharp, because a provocation lies waiting everywhere you look, each one only barely concealing some nugget of insight. Which, if you think about it, isn't a bad way to describe the aesthetic sensibility of *MAD* magazine.

Or, for that matter, its emotional core. There's an old Hasidic story that tells of a poor man who goes to see his rabbi. "O wise one," the man weeps, "I can't take it any longer. We've no money! Our home is so small! We've so many kids! We barely have room!" The rabbi listens patiently before issuing a decree: the answer, he says, is procuring a goat and allowing it to live indoors with the family. The man is baffled by this strange advice, but, not wishing to disobey the wise rabbi, does as he was told. The following week, he goes to see the rabbi again. "Wise one!" he shouts, "things are even worse! The goat steals all my food. It even ate our couch!" The rabbi nods knowingly but does not change his mind. The goat, he says, must stay. Another week goes by, then two, and three, and four. The man returns again and again, each time complaining of the beast's insatiable appetite. Finally, the rabbi says it's time for the goat to go. The following week, the man comes back, smiling and relaxed. "Rabbi!" he says gleefully, "ever since that goat left us, our home feels so wonderfully spacious!"

It's a well-worn yarn, but it might as well have been written by Dave Berg. In one strip, his famous alter ego, the curmudgeonly Roger Kaputnik, goes to see his mustachioed physician. "Doctor," he quips, "I must really give you the credit for keeping me from possibly becoming an alcoholic!" The doctor, all prim and proper, says he was not aware that his patient suffered from such problems. "I don't!" Kaputnik quips, pipe in mouth. "Your prices are so high that I can't afford to buy liquor!" It's as good an introduction as any to Jewish theology, which promises you something like deliverance without the saccharine satisfaction of a savior. You want to be healthy? Save yourself, not by waiting for some sweet celestial grace but by following very earthly and commonsensical rules. The best God can do to lend a hand is making health insurance so darn expensive that you can't afford to indulge in any vice that might make you sick anyway.

When you're eleven, a joke like this makes you chuckle by virtue of its sheer, delightful absurdity. When you're forty-four, it makes you squeeze out a deeper kind of laughter, one that has more in common with relief than it does with carefree joy. In middle age, you appreciate Berg's take because, yourself now a Kaputnik of sorts, you know that the old man wasn't just trying to make you laugh; he was trying to teach you something.

What? That's easy: how to live when everything around you seems to be falling apart. *MAD* was first published in October 1952, just a few weeks before Operation Ivy announced the arrival of Mike, the world's first hydrogen bomb, 10.4 megatons of hellish fury. *MAD* flourished through Korea and Vietnam, the assassinations of MLK and RFK, the souring of the '60s, the oil crisis, the hostage crisis, and the Cold War. It began to wither only when the economy grew strong, the world peaceful, and its readers complacent. If it was ever anything, *MAD* was—to borrow a line from a Jewish poet, Leonard Cohen, who liked to refer to himself as the world's oldest teenager—a manual for living with defeat.

Which only means the *MAD* Jews—like Jesus Christ in an old zinger—were going into the family business. There's nothing more profoundly Jewish than ordering chaos by writing your way around your fractured reality. The Talmud itself came to be because the Romans destroyed the ancient Temple in Jerusalem, leaving Jews without the beating heart of their religion. What to do when you could no longer worship as your ancestors had done for hundreds of years?

How to live when life as you knew it suddenly burst into flames? The wise old rabbis had two radical ideas. First, they'd take their faith and put it in a book. Sure, there was no longer a Temple to go to, no altar on which to sacrifice rams, no priest wearing bejeweled breastplates to pray for you. But if you wrote an entire volume about what sacrifice, say, was like, and if you delved into each intricate detail—which knife was used? How was it held? How often was the ritual performed?—you'd somehow keep the whole experience alive. Books, unlike buildings, could be carried around, memorized, and internalized. Burn them, and their wisdom would still live on in the minds and the hearts of their readers.

But readers, the ancient rabbis knew, were fickle creatures. Readers wanted easy solutions, digestible revelations, bite-sized illuminations. They didn't want to work too hard or think too much. Give them a book, and they'd only look for reasons not to read it. "Oh, that old bit about the rams and the blood and the incense? Yeah, we drive Buicks now, so no need to worry about any of that primitive stuff." This led the rabbis to their second astonishing insight: Instead of just writing down all the rules of the religion, they wrote down their arguments. And, being Jews, they argued. *A lot*. About everything. To read the Talmud, then, isn't to be lectured to by lifeless scolds; it's to enter a room full of brilliant, crabby dudes who hurl insults (the treasury of Talmudic disses alone is well worth the trouble of learning Aramaic), tell ribald stories (ask me about the one with the farting prostitute; no, really), and make sense of the world by questioning every single assumption each and every one of them holds about all things earthly and divine.

One famous Talmudic passage, for example, tells of a famous rabbi named Rav who was making love to his wife one afternoon. As they indulge themselves on the bed, they hear someone squeaking under it. Rav takes a peek and is shocked to find his student, the esteemed and studious Rav Kahana, lying there, spying on his rabbi mid-coitus. When Rav demands an explanation, Rav Kahana smiles and shrugs his shoulders: sex, too, is divine, he tells Rav, and a student deserves a good teacher. Add a few garish '70s short-sleeve button-down shirts, and you've got a perfect Dave Berg strip, with Rav Kahana smirking triumphantly in the final panel while Rav stares directly at you, the reader, as if saying, "Can you believe this guy?"

The Jews who had been diligently studying the Talmud since it was compiled millennia ago weren't merely following the rules. They were questioning the rules, and the people who came up with the rules, and the very need to have rules in the first place. Their fierce dissent didn't lead to anarchy, or nihilism, or despair; it led to a deep-seated, heartfelt, and everlasting faith, which is to say, the only kind of faith worth having.

Did the *MAD* Jews inherit, by virtue of some mystical epigenetic intergenerational transmission, a bit or more of this spirit? You can argue that an artist like Berg—who held an honorary doctorate in theology, wrote for the religious Jewish publication *Moshiach Times*, and published a series of darkly humorous books about God—was more than a bit immersed in these ideas. But if you're looking for proof that the spirit of the Talmud was alive and well in 485 MADison Avenue, you need look no further than my favorite *MAD* anecdote. Each morning, the legend goes, Berg would greet Bill Gaines, the magazine's publisher and a proudly atheistic Jew, by smiling beatifically and saying "God bless you." And each morning, Gaines would smile right back and say "go to hell." It's hard to imagine a more astute, concise, and funnier conversation about religion.

The joke, then, had always been on me: I thought I was escaping my too-serious and too-stuffy tradition to hang out with the cool and brilliant minds of *MAD*, only to find out that those twisted geniuses were really only doing what our shared ancestors had done all along, that they got much of their zeal for questioning everything and everyone straight from the ancient source, and that the faith was never as fearful or as dreary as I ignorantly imagined it to be. Non-Jews too, of course, can enjoy their own version of this neat trick: here we all were thinking that we were sticking it to the Man by reading this wacky and rude and childlike magazine, whereas, behind our backs, *MAD* was teaching us the very lesson that high schools and universities, poets and professors and pundits and politicians, deacons and rabbis and Mom and Dad and Lord knows who else tried and failed to convey: how to think.

It worked. As I left my mother's house, my head still reeling, I left my stack of *MAD* magazines behind. They had taught me everything I needed to know. The following year, as I made my way to synagogue on Yom Kippur, my own bored children in tow, I remembered one of my favorite Dave Berg one-liners, a perfect distillation of what it means to live in an imperfect world and try to make sense of yourself and your faith and your God and everything and everyone around. "You don't have to be Jewish to be Jewish," Berg wrote, "but it helps."

rEVERSE IMMigRant

Mary-Lou Weisman

OR MORE than half a century, writer and cartoonist Al Jaffee gleefully put a premature end to the innocence of American youth in the pages of *MAD*, this country's first popular satiric magazine. Suddenly, parents were hypocrites, teachers were dummies, politicians were liars, life wasn't fair, and our culture was changed forever.

MAD ceased creating new material in 2019 after sixty-seven years, leaving millions of fans without *MAD*'s freckle-faced "What, me worry?" mascot, Alfred E. Neuman. Gone, too, were Al Jaffee's signature Fold-Ins—a spoof on *Playboy* magazine's foldouts, a marvel of artistic engineering that no one has been able to replicate. Missing, too, were his rudely hilarious "Snappy Answers to Stupid Questions." Happily, all of *MAD*'s five hundred fifty issues can be found online.

I met Al Jaffee and his wife, Joyce, in the early 1970s on Cape Cod, where, along with eight other families, we shared space in a repurposed nineteenth-century inn on Provincetown Bay. A common deck and laundry room made friendships inevitable.

One day while Al and I were walking on the flats at low tide, we came upon a veritable blanket of dead jellyfish. "Too bad we don't have any peanut butter," Al quipped, thus sealing a friendship between two silly people that lasts until this day. Of course, I knew him as a writer and cartoonist for *MAD* magazine, and as I got to know this shy man, he began to open up to me and tell me the story of his life as a "reverse immigrant."

Born in Savannah to parents who emigrated from Lithuania, he was effectively kidnapped at the age of six, along with his three younger brothers, by his mother, Mildred, an Orthodox Jew, who couldn't tolerate modern American life and yearned to return to Zarasai, a shtetl near the Latvian border. By contrast, her husband, Morris, had become an instant, enthusiastic American and soon landed a lucrative job as manager of Blumenthal's department store. Mildred told her husband that she was taking their four sons back to visit her parents for a month or so, but in fact she had no intention of returning.

The happiest times in Al's Savannah life had been Sundays, when he and his brother Harry would sprawl on the floor while his father read them the funnies. Morris had a unique artistic talent. He could draw exact copies of all the comic characters of the day, like Maggie and Jiggs and the Katzenjammer Kids. Before they left, a tearful Al made his father promise to send him the funnies. Over the next few years, the funnies would serve as a fragile lifeline between Al and his brothers, his father, and his native land.

The fearsome journey, which took them from the twentieth to the nineteenth century, consumed more than three weeks. They traveled by boat from New York to Hamburg, to Memel (known today as Klaipeda) to Kaunus (Kovno in Russian) and finally, 184 kilometers later, in a rickety bus on a gravel road, to Zarasai. At a time when Jews were fleeing Eastern Europe, Mildred Jaffee chose to return to Lithuania.

Al was in no mood to appreciate the beauty of hilly Zarasai, a town of about forty-two hundred people, which is located between two lakes and covered with birch and pine forests. Nor was he prepared for infestations of lice that feasted lavishly on his body, or the menacing wolves, the outhouses, the once-a-month communal baths, and winters that lasted from October to April, when temperatures often dropped to −20° Fahrenheit. Locals called Zarasai the "Siberia of Lithuania." (Today's tourists call it "the Switzerland of Lithuania.")

There was no formal ghetto in Zarasai. About one-third of the citizens were Jews, and the rest Poles, Germans, and Lithuanians, all of whom lived on separate streets. In 1928, when Al arrived, antisemitism in Lithuania was relatively benign compared to neighboring Poland. Nevertheless, Al was treated like a second-class citizen, much like the African Americans in his native Savannah.

Mildred's father, a relatively wealthy and prominent member of the Jewish community, was horrified when Mildred showed up, unannounced, with Al and his brothers, Harry, Bernard, and David, in tow. Only a crazy person, he assumed, would return from the United States, the land of promise, to primitive Zarasai. Still, Al and his brothers found a measure of stability and kindness with their mother's relatives, especially when they recognized that Mildred was a neglectful mother who abandoned her children and frequently failed to feed them when she went on religious retreats.

Al and Harry, the two eldest, had inherited their father's artistic talent that would eventually help them make friends in Zarasai. Al was teased and bullied when he first arrived, but after he quickly learned to speak Yiddish, they relished his stories of life in America.

Al's father was true to his promise. When the Sunday comics started to arrive and Al shared them with the other kids, the bullying stopped, and they included him in their ragamuffin gang of Jewish kids.

Al dazzled his new friends by drawing cartoon characters in the dirt with a stick. Paper was rare in Zarasai.

Al had been a curious, freelance hell-raiser in Savannah. He lit fires so he and his friends could watch the fire trucks arrive and put them out. He dove from the roof of his house into a palm tree to see if he could fly. He brought that same questionable talent to Zarasai.

With little parental guidance, Al, always hungry, learned to fend for himself. In the summertime he invented a fruit-stealing device that could reach over the farmers' high fences. He figured out how to tie reeds from the lake together so he and his pals could float in the lake. In wintertime, eager to careen down the hills and into the frozen lakes, he built sleds out of discarded lumber. Years later, his talent for invention would find its way into *MAD* magazine as "Al Jaffee's *MAD* Inventions."

(This childhood pleasure of making things from virtually nothing would turn Al into a lifelong scavenger and inventor who preferred homemade to store-bought. He would forever covet garbage. While other artists dipped their brushes into pots of paint, Al would use the tops of spent seltzer bottles.)

After a year in Zarasai, just when Al had adjusted to his new, primitive life, Morris Jaffee arrived to take his family home. He had been writing letters to his wife, pleading with her to come home. The lengthy two-way trip had cost him his job at Blumenthal's and left him penniless.

Mildred exacted a severe price for agreeing to leave. She insisted upon living in Far Rockaway, where Al imagined there must have been a lot of Orthodox synagogues; this, in spite of the fact that the only job Morris could find was in a cigar store in Charlotte, North Carolina. He commuted to his family on the weekends. Maybe it would have been different if he had returned to Savannah, but Al, bitterly disappointed, felt alienated from his father. Neglected once again by his mother, Al wandered the beaches, harvesting and smoking cigarette butts.

"I was longing for my friends and relatives in Zarasai. I felt that if there was anything in me that was worthwhile, it was beaten out of me. Rockaway was nearly a complete blank. Everything was temporary. I never knew how long anything would last. I kind of drifted through it all." Al was relieved when his mother, after a stay of about one year, saved up enough money to return to Zarasai.

On their return trip to Lithuania in 1929, when Al was eight years old, their mother rented a small cottage on the estate of twenty-one-year-old Karolka Mikutovistsch, a Polish Catholic man, and his three sisters. At a time when Al had given up all hope of ever seeing his father again, Karolka filled that emotional vacuum, serving as both father and big brother. Unlike most of the gentiles in Zarasai, Karolka harbored no antisemitic feelings. He took Al and Bernard spearfishing in the winters and fly-fishing in the summers. They relished a meal of *trayf* (nonkosher food) with his family. Al, a master adapter, had become a thoroughly primitive shtetl boy.

By 1933, when Hitler became chancellor of Germany, Morris Jaffee had been reduced to poverty by Mildred's constant requests for money. Antisemitism was on the rise throughout Eastern Europe. Fearing for the life of his family, Morris borrowed money from his American relatives and arrived in Kaunas, prepared to bring his family home. "Go tell your mother that I'm here and I'm going to take everyone back to America."

"After four years, there was my father. He was smoking a Lucky Strike. He reached his arms out. I moved reluctantly toward him. I didn't think this was going to be a particularly good turning point in my life either."

Mildred refused to leave. She would part with the three older boys but she insisted upon keeping six-year-old David, the youngest and her favorite, the child who, as a babe in arms in Savannah, had never really known his native land. However, she promised to "get her affairs in order" and return with David to America in six months.

Al's fear that returning to America might not be "a particularly good turning point" was realized in spades. Morris Jaffee now lived in New York and worked part-time as a mail sorter in Grand Central Station. The family was split up. He could not afford to hold them together. Al was separated from his two brothers who, in turn, were separated and farmed out to different relatives. Al would stay with his father, now a broken man, who could only afford to rent a single bedroom in a series of eight different households. (Because of the Depression, homeowners granted two months' free rent for a single bedroom, an inducement that kept Morris and Al constantly on the move.) For the rest of his life, Al suffered from terrible stomachaches when he had to change places.

If Al first had difficulty adjusting to life in Zarasai, life for a country boy in noisy, crowded New York was at least as awful. He arrived on what was now a foreign shore, an unschooled Lithuanian boy wearing cobbled boots and speaking his native English with a foreign accent.

He was twelve years old but he was placed in the third grade and bullied anew. "The kids called me 'greenhorn.'"

Ever the adapter, once again Al made himself at home. He made friends by drawing cartoon characters, this time in chalk on the sidewalks. Academically, he made up for lost time in P.S. 6 and, later, at the Herman Ridder junior high school. It was there that his art teachers, amazed by his artistic ability, chose him, along with several other talented students, to take a citywide test that might win these youngsters a coveted place at the High School of Music and Art, which had just been created by Mayor La Guardia.

Each student was given a blank piece of paper and instructed to draw something. Al drew the village square in Zarasai. The skinny freckle-faced boy in front of him drew a portrait of a peasant. Al caught a glimpse of it and thought to himself, "If everyone in this room is drawing as well as this twerp, then what am I doing here?"

After the drawings were collected and reviewed, the monitor announced, "Everybody is excused except Abraham Jaffee and Wolf Eisenberg." (In adulthood, they both changed their names. Abraham would be "Al"; Wolf became Will Elder.) They were told to report to the principal's office, two words that, spoken in conjunction, filled Al, still a major misbehaver, with dread.

While the chosen two were waiting outside the principal's office, Wolf turned to Al and said, in his thick Bronx accent, "I tink dere gunna send us to art school." Wolf was right.

The year was 1935. For a kid whose life had been dominated by disastrous turning points, Al's life took a radical and permanent turn for the better. He found his worth. He found lifelong friends. He found his career. It was at Music and Art that he and Will met another art student—Harvey Kurtzman. It didn't take long for the threesome to become close friends and recognize one another's comic talent. Even in high school, Kurtzman dreamed of someday starting a humorous magazine.

By 1939, Morris Jaffee worried that his wife would be murdered by the Nazis, along with David. He wrote to her, begging her to return with David to the States. She refused. "God will provide," she wrote back, prompting Morris to arrange for David's successful rescue through an American Jewish agency. At very long last, the family, with the exception of Mildred, who was murdered by the Nazis, with an enthusiastic assist from her Christian neighbors, was united at last.

For Al, it was a long, winding road to *MAD*. Al didn't arrive at his cartooning career until he impressed Will Eisner, then best known for his crime-fighting comic hero The Spirit. As Eisner flipped through

Al's portfolio he stopped at Al's depiction of Inferior Man, a satiric response to the wildly popular Superman. Inferior Man, an accountant by day and a skinny, failed superhero by night, would flit around in droopy socks and garters, dingy underwear and a cape, looking for crimes, but when the crime was more than he could handle, he'd retreat to a phone booth, change into street clothes, and fade into the crowd. For Al, Inferior Man was his first break. He was also Al's alter ego.

Years later, after all three had gone their separate artistic ways—by then Al was drawing Patsy Walker comic books—Kurtzman became the editor of *MAD* magazine and hired his high school pals Will Elder and Al Jaffee. Together they changed the face of cartooning and humor in America.

Al's mad childhood seems to have led him inevitably to satire and to *MAD*. For more than fifty years he spoke to the awkward social outcast and the nerd in every *MAD* reader. He knew their fears. He verified their suspicions. Adults *are* bluffing. Politicians *are* lying. He, of all people, understood their feelings of alienation. Jaffee was our man from Mars, by way of Lithuania.

Jaffee in Yiddish

Leah Garrett

ON A snowy February afternoon, Al Jaffee, my childhood hero, invited me into his well-lit studio in Midtown Manhattan. The walls were covered with his drawings, images from *MAD* magazine and a photo of Stephen Colbert's homage to Jaffee on his television show. I wanted to talk to Jaffee about the relationship between *MAD* and Jewish culture and I was struggling to contain my excitement. In the 1970s and 1980s, when I was growing up in Newton, Massachusetts, everyone I knew obsessively read, shared, and discussed *MAD*, and my brothers and I would always fight over who got to do the famous *MAD* Fold-In. Old copies of *MAD* were hoarded and new copies were bought at the newsagent in Newton Center. On Passover visits to our grandparents in Brooklyn, my brothers and I would use our *afikoman* money to rush down and buy the most recent copy from the magazine stand on Prospect Avenue. Yes, occasionally we would buy *Cracked* as well, but we always considered that to be a second-rate version of the original. When we read *MAD*, it seemed to speak directly to us in our own language, and it was a punchy alternative to boring suburban life.

As a kid, I was unaware that one reason *MAD* seemed so familiar was that most of the writers and cartoonists came from a demographic I knew well: New York, Jewish, left-wing. Today, teens have a vast assortment of online and print choices for satiric takes on current events, but for us, the choice was basically limited to *MAD* and comic books. For an entire generation, *MAD* was one of the most central factors in shaping our understanding of the "adult" world.

Jaffee is a sprightly ninety-four-year-old with sparkling eyes, a deep voice and the energy of someone twenty years younger. He still wakes his wife in the middle of the night with fresh ideas for covers or cartoons, and spends his days creating new pieces for *MAD*. Jaffee, who started working at *MAD* in 1955 and has been drawing the Fold-Ins on the final page for the last fifty-two years, is the magazine's longest-lasting and most important contributor. He has also created countless ridiculous inventions for things such as improved drink cans and cigarettes to help you stop smoking, as well as *MAD*'s "Snappy Answers to Stupid Questions."

"So what is it you want to know?" Jaffee asked me as I stood next to his big draftsman's table.

I explained that I was working on a book about *MAD* and Jewish culture, so my first question was the obvious one: Why was there so much Yiddish in *MAD*?

"Well, first of all, because I tend to think in Yiddish, and Yiddish conveys humor better than English."

"You still think in Yiddish then?" I asked.

"It's *narishkeit*, but I still do," he said with a chuckle.

As a child, Jaffee lived for seven years in a shtetl in Lithuania. He was born in America, but his homesick mother took her four sons back to Eastern Europe for most of 1927 through 1933, and during that time, he lived much of his daily life in Yiddish. Yet, as he explained, upon returning to New York at twelve, he switched back to English so his "intellectual Yiddish is only up to the age of twelve."

Jaffee explained to me that the two main architects of *MAD* during the first decade, the editor Harvey Kurtzman and the artist (and his best friend) Willie Elder, had both grown up in New York families where their parents spoke and argued in Yiddish. For them, Yiddish was the inherently funny language that their parents would use to tell secrets and swear. While Jaffee was fluent in Yiddish, Kurtzman and Willie were not. According to Jaffee, Willie "didn't know any Yiddish, and his parents would be arguing and all he would hear was a stream of funny words, and he would pick up the curse words his parents were throwing at each other in anger." As a result, the Yiddish Kurtzman and Elder used during *MAD's* first decade was based on finding the funniest-sounding words to evoke their parents' humorous cut-downs.

For example, the iconic *MAD* word "furshlugginer" was derived from the Yiddish word *shlogan* (to hit), while the meaning of the word "potrzebie" has been debated by *MAD* readers and academics for years. The word was first introduced in the Letters to the Editors section called "*MAD* Mumblings" in response to a query from a soldier (many if not most letters during the early 1950s were from men in the military): "Please tell me what in the world 'Furshlugginer' means.—Larry E. Lengle E.M.F.N—c/o F.P.O., New York, New York." The answer from the editors to this was "It means the same as Potrzebie.–ed."

The adamant refusal of the editors to explain the made-up word became a running joke. Today, *MAD* scholars theorize that "potrzebie" was in fact based on a Polish word that Kurtzman discovered on a jar of aspirin. According to Jaffee, though, this is not the case: "There was an expression in Lithuania when I was a kid—'putz-rebbe.' Harvey must have heard that. *Putz* is 'genitals,' and it is applied as an insult to the rebbe. It's like saying, 'Oh, that stupid teacher' or '*putz-rebbe.*'"

In fact, as Jaffee explained to me, much of the humor in *MAD* was deeply Jewish because it was based on satire created by a community that saw itself as not having much power and that used the jokes to take down those who "had it made"—that is, rabbis, parents, and, later, the rich and powerful. As he explained it, being a Jewish kid in the shtetl who was constantly hungry, "your only revenge is to expose and make fun of the frailties of the big shots and the 'better-than-thou' people. We made fun of our rabbis. Some of it was a bit raw and mean-spirited, especially the comments about the personal habits of the rabbi when he went to the outhouse and defecated all over the board. This is the stuff that makes you feel equal [to] or better than they are. So going after the wealthy is such a release when you are barely getting by."

Revisiting *MAD* as an adult, I was stunned to see the constant use of Yiddish, particularly during the first decade. In *MAD*'s first issue, there was a story entitled "Hoohah!" a transliterated Yiddish term for "a big to-do," and the Yiddish/Hebrew term *ganef* (thief) was employed in a satire of spy magazines. In nearly every issue of the first eight years of *MAD*, there was at least one Yiddish word, and in many cases more. Typically, the Yiddish words were used in mainstream settings, such as in the fourth issue of the magazine in a parody of Superman called "Superduperman!" Here, the supremely American iconic hero said the words "Shazoom? Vas ist das Shazoom?" For non-Yiddish-speaking readers, the comedy was based on the archetypal American hero uttering strange Jewish-intoned words. For the Yiddish-speaking reader, Clark Kent was hiding not only the fact that he was Superman but also that he was a Jew. It was a typical yet extraordinary moment of *MAD*'s writers suggesting that beneath the surface of even the most iconic American hero, there were Jewish roots, which of course there were.

MAD is famous for delivering pointed attacks on the powerful from a subversively left-wing perspective, and, according to Jaffee, this was because the first generation of *MAD*—Kurtzman, Elder, and Jaffee himself—came from Jewish traditions. All the founders had grown up in Yiddish-speaking New York homes and became close friends at the High School of Music and Art. Raised in a world of Jewish humor and Borscht Belt schtick, this group of talented young men brought that background to *MAD* and in so doing made it one of the most popular magazines in American history, reaching a pinnacle of two million circulation during the 1970s.

I asked Jaffee if he and the other writers, artists, and editors considered their non-Jewish readers when they were using so much Yiddish, and he recalled that Kurtzman, the first editor, "wanted funny meaningless words. Meaningless to the general reading public, but not meaningless to someone who grew up in a Jewish household." Overall, "Kurtzman's philosophy was 'why do I think it's funny? If I think it's funny, other people will too. Even if it is these throwaway words.'" For the readers who did not know the Yiddish words and jokes, Jaffee felt "the average reader in the country" wouldn't have "made a connection between these strange words and the fact that a lot of people working for *MAD* were Jewish." For them it would have been a jokey, funny, curse-like word. Yet over time, as non-Jewish readers learned the specific Yiddish language of *MAD*, even they began using Yiddish terms in their letters to the magazine.

During the magazine's first decade, the word "Jewish" was never used, even though the Jewishness constantly came through in varied ways, from such overt markers as Yiddishisms and foods associated with Jews to less obvious ones such as commentaries on postwar American indifference to the Holocaust, attacks on McCarthyism, subversive ideas about gender, and challenges to suburbanization. I knew that the avoidance of the term "Jewish" was a common aspect of postwar Jewish American comedy, from the Marx Brothers to Sid

Caesar's *Your Show of Shows*, and I wondered whether it was a conscious choice or if the creators of *MAD* determined that there was no need to say "Jewish" or even "Yiddish" since it was already so obvious.

Jaffee explained to me that his generation of Jewish artists was very sensitive to the fact that they were Jews in a non-Jewish world overshadowed by the Holocaust. In fact, the writers and artists of *MAD* used to joke "amongst ourselves about looking too Jewish. You know, if you walked with your portfolio into an advertising agency, if you looked too Jewish or had a name like Ginsberg, you were dead meat." Whenever possible, the men changed their names to make them sound less Jewish. (For example, Jaffee changed his name from Abraham "to something more American—Alan," although he said he would not have done so if he'd had to pay for it—it was a free service to GIs.) It was not necessarily that they were ashamed of their names, but they didn't want to be pigeonholed.

For Jaffee, the decision not to "advertise himself by wearing a Magen David" had more to do with his family history: when Jaffee's father brought him and his brothers back to the US in 1933, his mother remained in Lithuania. Jaffee never saw her again, and she disappeared with the countless other Jews of Lithuania during the Nazi invasion.

"I lived through a period when Jewish people were very nervous about flaunting their Jewishness," Jaffee said. "Even after the war, you were aware that there were people out there who wanted to kill you just because you were Jewish. And it's still around." So while *MAD* would have an intensely Jewish feel to it, the term would not be used.

Reaching mass new readerships and training them to laugh at and challenge broader trends, *MAD* can be seen as a central force destabilizing mainstream platforms, and at times doing so from a Jewish American perspective. And as Jaffee pointed out, not only were they writers and artists taking down the mainstream world, they were also "making fun of ourselves. We made fun of a certain kind of Yiddish-keit just by using these words. *Farshimmelt. Furshlugginer. Potrzebie.*" Yet in the act of satirizing both worlds, the magazine transformed itself into a mainstream American voice. And in its evolution, *MAD* taught its broad readership to be more comfortable with New York Jewish culture. By the 1970s and 1980s, the writers' rooms in virtually every sitcom on American TV were filled with men who had grown up reading *MAD*. If *Seinfeld* became the number-one show in subur-ban Texas or in Boise, Idaho, it was in part because *MAD* had paved the way.

The day I spent with Jaffee was one of the most exciting I've ever had, not only because I met a childhood hero but also because he was so generous and honest with me.

As an academic, I spend most of my days researching and writing about Jewish culture, and this was the first time I've had a chance to grill one of the subjects of my work. His answers to my questions, par-ticularly on the fear of antisemitism, suggest to me yet again that the postwar "golden age of American Jewry" perhaps was not as golden as we tend to think.

On the one hand, there was *MAD*, with its Jewish comedy having a huge impact on mainstream America. Yet at the same time, *MAD* and its writers evoked the deep stresses second-generation Jews felt about life in America during the postwar era. Toward the end of our din-ner, during which we spent three hours talking about Jaffee's extraor-dinary life as an artist who shared so much humor with the world, I asked him if he thought that perhaps his Fold-Ins, which took images and then subverted them to evoke their opposite once the page was folded, were somehow symbolic of living between the two worlds of the Yiddish, religious shtetl in Lithuania and New York City. He nod-ded and said, "Yes, I think that is right."

As I hugged him and his vibrant wife, Joyce, goodbye, I felt profound gratitude to this artist who had brought those worlds together and delivered them to mainstream America and by so doing taught all of us to have a deeper awareness of the complex, multilayered reality of postwar American life.

(2016)

MADness in anatolia

Michael Benson

NKARA IN the early '70s. The city operates according to a mysteriously cyclical logic. Five times a day, the call to prayer reverberates from megaphone loudspeakers bolted to pencil-shaped minarets in the city below. Every morning just before eight, a marching band in full dress uniform issues forth from a gate up the street, turns clockwise, and proceeds to the flagpole in front of the presidential guard HQ, directly across the street from our house. Two of them high-step forward, stiffly unfold the Turkish flag, and affix it to the cable. At eight sharp, the bugler honks out the national anthem. Clustered notes ricochet off guardhouse cement as the crescent moon and star rises.

I watch, aged fourteen. A diplomatic brat with little experience of America, I'm a stranger in a strange land. Like many a "third-culture kid"—the coinage is by sociologist Ruth Useem—I spend my time gleaning shards of meaning about this and that. Mostly a Turkish *this*, and an American *that*. The latter's ostensibly home, despite being two continents and seven time zones away. The former's where I actually live. Apart from my parents, who are from New York City, I'm assisted in my incipient Americanness by Ankara Air Station, a US Air Force facility adjacent to Balgat, a ramshackle town of red-tiled roofs at the city's edge. Effectively a bubble of the home country, pinched off and transported to Asia Minor, the station contains a reasonable simula-crum of the USA. It has milkshakes, bowling, burgers and fries, touch-downs, and my school, where we recite the pledge of allegiance every morning. Outside, the American flag flies over a commissary, PX, swimming pool—and the Stars and Stripes, a well-stocked newsstand full of US periodicals. It's where I grab new issues of *MAD* magazine the minute they appear.

Like most other US nationals my age, all but a handful of us military kids, I vacuum up whatever's at hand to provide grounds for a cul-tural identity. Those of us who live off the base are assisted in this by a steady stream of buses in Air Force blue, which link the city with the air station and also the movie theater, run by AAFES, the Army and Air Force Exchange Service. We're in much the same position as the rest of the world, dazzled by the stories pumped steadily out of South-ern California. They're a major source of American "soft power"—not that we'd ever put it that way—and even if we occasionally return stateside on home leave, they quickly supplant those fading memo-ries. Because what are we citizens of, exactly? The real place, or the one we can see with our own eyes? And one appeal of *MAD*—not the only one, but a biggie—lay in its sardonic extended riffs on the Hol-lywood blockbusters that appeared regularly in Ankara. Exactingly drawn by Mort Drucker with a kind of High Renaissance genius for isolating and accentuating the facial features that define how we see individuals, particularly famous ones, *MAD*'s spoofs skewered the movies of the day. They turned them until done.

It's the '70s: we're talking disaster movies. *The Poseidon Adventure*, about passengers struggling to survive inside a capsized ocean liner, became "The Poopsidedown Adventure" (#161). *The Towering Inferno* was "The Towering Sterno" (#177). And so on. Drucker and his collab-orators, writers like Dick DeBartolo, Larry Siegel, and Arnie Kogen, tackled more serious fare as well, as readers of "The Oddfather" (a high point in the genre, #155) and "A Crockwork Lemon" (#159) can attest. A confirmed fan of another Kubrick production, I practically inhaled "201 Min. of a Space Idiocy" (#125), in which the man-apes of *2001: A Space Odyssey*'s "Dawn of Man" sequence are confused by their location—could it be the set of *Planet of the Apes*?—as they caper around "the **mysterious big black thing** that's supposed to **excite us** and make us want to do **intelligent things!**" as one of them puts it, causing another to comment, "Y'know, you're right! I feel like doing an intelligent thing . . . ! I **FEEL** like **QUITTING** this stupid movie—**RIGHT NOW!!**"—this inside a classic Drucker frame depicting a flung bone bouncing off Kubrick's monolith. (All phrases in **bold** are **exactly** as in the **original**.)

Despite my solemn fascination with *2001*, I found this hilarious, as was DeBartolo's channeling of the film's supercomputer, HAL, here named SID: "Don't be silly, Poof! A **machine** can't have feelings! And besides—would you mind not **talking** about me? It's very embarrassing!"

Actually it'd be accurate to say that this aspect of my nascent American identity formation was a kind of alloy, compounding the satirists at 485 MADison—as the masthead put it—and their targets. Sure, the country and its films colluded. And sure, like the rest of a world besotted by both, we eagerly lapped it up (albeit in our case with a self-conscious sense of association). But on top of that another conspiracy was underway, in which Hollywood's visions pinged further off *MAD*'s funhouse mirror, a re-projection paradoxically adding signal to the noise, not the other way around. And *that* was the ouroboros, the serpent eating its tail forever, arriving reliably from the good old USA, and provided in fact by a US military touchingly intent on making sure its troops were entertained.

That's not to say that one took precedence over the other—far from it. If anything, *MAD*'s satires of American film and TV productions delivered truths that the big-budget commercial filmmaking and mainstream television of the early '70s couldn't or wouldn't, simply because they upended the suspension of disbelief that fiction requires. *MAD* took its readers behind the camera, to where producers and directors bickered, actors traded sarcastic quips about the vacuity of the films they were starring in, and everybody knew the fix was in and the audience was the fall guy.

Because it's one thing to wring humor from the SS *Poopsidedown*'s upended state ("Doctor . . . where are you **going?**" "We're all going back to the **front** . . . !" "But that's **wrong!** you have to go **forward** to the **back!**" "**Oh no!** It's **up** to the **bottom**, and then **back** to the **front!**" "No! It's up to the **bottom**, and then **forward** to the **back!**"), but then DeBartolo and Drucker sprinkled on some of *MAD*'s patented metaphysical pixie dust. The debate between the leader of one group of passengers and another cuts to a frame in which Drucker's Gene Hackman (as Reverend Shout, pastor of "Our Lady of Perpetual Motion") dismisses his flock's concerns with a jerk of his thumb at the other group. "Reverend Shout, is it possible **they're** going the **right** way, and **we're** going the **wrong** way?" "**It's possible!** If you want to follow an **Extra** leading a bunch of **Walk-ons** who don't even have **speaking parts**—go ahead! The rest, stay here and look for **supplies!** I'm going to try to find the route to the **Engine Room!** While I'm gone, each of you will have your **very own big scene** to do so the movie audience will get to **know** you so much better!"

Apart from producing a "What, me worry?" grin, this was heady stuff for a fourteen-year-old. Because along with *MAD*'s other readers, I'd been invited into a knowing little community, one where a disbelief already barely held at bay by the acting, direction, and cinematography of these productions was decisively inverted, not unlike the SS *Poopsidedown* itself, producing a wider, longer view—a cynical one, sure, but larger and arguably more honest. A bigger story, booby-trapped by the cathartic sense of recognition that well-executed humor can trigger.

And a community in the know about everybody getting their **very own big scene**, so the audience could get to **know them better**.

The day pans by and shadows lengthen. At 6:00 P.M. the marching band returns, lowers the flag, folds it into a triangular red lozenge, and thumps back home. Drums fade into ambient city noise, the presidential gates clang shut, and our night watchman arrives. He smiles a benevolent greeting and heads to the subbasement door, where a small table and a few square meters of cold cement floor constitute the indoor parts of his nightly rounds. Hanging from a strap under his arm is a Detex watch-clock—a disk-shaped, vaguely maritime chronometer with a brass keyhole.

I've been exiled to the farthest subterranean bedroom for fighting with my former roomie, a.k.a. my kid brother. My new room has windows onto the woodpile in back, staffed by a rotating cast of feral cats. In practice this means the watchman and I live in direct proximity, at least after the sun goes down. I kick back on my bunk with the latest *MAD*, vaguely aware of his activities. His rough-hewn English is good enough to let me know, in a kindly way, that ideally I would refrain from banging across his floorspace when he spreads his rug on the floor, points it toward Mecca, and kneels in prayer. Not least because I find the whole thing fascinating, I quickly amend my ways, and we constitute a peaceable community in exile. He does his thing and I do mine. His time is divided between obeying the muezzin's call, which echoes eerily up from the city below, and following the mechanical dictates of the Detex, which propels him out the back door to a chain of metal boxes mounted along our property's perimeter, keys dangling inside. Twin imperatives governing his nights and ensuring he stays awake.

By now I've switched on the light and moved from *MAD*'s movie parodies to the reliably brilliant, perpetually wordless "Spy vs Spy." Conceived and drawn by exiled Cuban cartoonist Antonio Prohías, it features two identical pointy-snouted spooks, each equally determined to off the other by whatever means necessary. Dynamite. Knives. Guns. It's all good. The only discernible difference between them is one's dressed in black, the other in white, each under broad-brimmed hats indistinguishable apart from their color.

In "Spy vs Spy," elegance of execution (each one-page strip is a miracle of compression) invariably reveals Prohías's genius for kinetic, fine-lined physical comedy, a kind of latter-day graphic iteration of a lineage originating in Commedia dell'arte and the silent films of Charlie Chaplin and Buster Keaton. Despite their beaky features, our homicidal spies have been imbued by their maker with an extraordinary range of expressions. In one strip Black Hat, in a captain's uniform and peering through a periscope, sees White Hat on a life raft in a wetsuit, reading a book titled *How to Disarm a Torpedo*. Black Hat immediately pulls a lever, launching a torpedo at White Hat, who jumps off the raft and directly onto it, then proceeds to disassemble it with a screwdriver from the back, leaving a frothy trail of nuts and bolts in his wake. Arriving at the torpedo's nose cone, he pries it off—and an angry shark explodes from the front. In the last frame, the shark can be seen looming with serrated teeth over White Hat, as Black Hat grins from his sub, hands raised in twin "V for Victory" gestures.

All this in only eight frames. Actually Prohías could do as well with fewer. One classic "Spy vs Spy" featured a single frame containing two

'60s-vintage space capsules, a white one rocketing up to a black one. Off to the side, his pointy glass space visor sheathing his beak, Black Hat can be seen spacewalking, his long umbilical cord trailing behind, attached to his capsule. White Hat leans out of his white capsule, one hand still on his controls, and padlocks shut the black capsule's door with the other—cutting off both Black Hat's oxygen and means of escape. Directly below, a horizontal chain of dots and dashes spells out Prohías's signature, the author's name in Morse code.

Apart from encapsulating the Cold War space race (no pun *intended* or to be *inferred*), "Spy vs Spy" helps me understand aspects of our existential situation, not only in the broader context of great power competition, but here in Ankara. A NATO member, Turkey's a frontline state, the only one actually bordering on the USSR. There's no runway at the air station, or it'd be called a base. It doesn't need one because most US Air Force personnel in the capital are engaged in intelligence gathering, not flight activities. In short, they're spooks. East of us, forests of antennae and radar installations are scattered across the country. They extend intermittently to Mount Ararat, which looms over Yerevan, the capital of Armenia, from the Turkish side of the border. Armenia being a Soviet republic, as is Georgia, which flanks Turkey directly to the north, on the Black Sea.

So it would be no exaggeration to say I saw spies every day, and went to school with their kids. Years later I learned that Prohías had been widely recognized as Cuba's foremost cartoonist, and was honored personally by Fidel Castro after the revolution, in part for his anti-Batista political strips. After turning his pen against the new regime for its press censorship, he was accused of working for the CIA. He immediately quit his position at *El Mundo*, the country's leading paper, resigned as president of the Cuban Cartoonists Association, and escaped to New York. After spending the spring of 1960 building up a portfolio, Prohías appeared unannounced in *MAD's* offices, accompanied by his daughter, who translated. A few hours later he left bearing a check for $800—more than $8,000 today—for the first three of the more than two hundred "Spy vs Spy" strips published in the magazine between 1960 and 1986.

One stock character he had to retire on leaving Cuba, El Hombre Siniestro, always wore a hat, had a long, pointy nose, and left a reliable trail of mayhem wherever he went. Although operating solo, El Hombre was clearly the immediate ancestor of our thrashing, stabbing, ever-more-inventive spies. In 1983, Prohías commented, "The sweetest revenge has been to turn Fidel's accusation of me as a spy into a money-making venture."

Trapped in its rugged bowl of hills, Ankara has some of the worst air pollution in the world in the 1970s. Every winter, as temperatures drop, chimneys across the city start pumping out smoke from high-sulfur lignite, a low-grade, locally produced brown coal. Billowing past the mosques, coiling around the square columns of Ataturk's Tomb, it fills the air above the wind-shielded capital, staining the sky darker and darker as winter unfolds. Trucks piled high with shattered chunks of the stuff come and go, inexorably adding more toxicity to the air. By February the elderly and infirm start to die, of "respiratory complications."

But we're Americans. We have all the latest tech. Every room in our house has an electrostatic air purifier. Like bug zappers, they periodically buzz, with each fizzy discharge marking the electroshocked termination of a particle that otherwise might have embedded itself in our lungs. I subconsciously process these irregular zaps through a sonic filter grounded in the work of *MAD* man Don Martin. *Thwizzik . . . ZAK! PFFT-FRACK! Shtoink. PAF.* Sounds ostensibly made on or around, nearby or by, Martin's clownish potbellied geeks with their projecting doorknob noses, rotund mincing figures bumbling about in supermarkets, morgues, operating rooms, Philadelphia, and the great outdoors.

For his loopy silent soundscapes alone the cartoonist, who died in 2000, deserved an Oscar for Best Comic Textual Sound. Martin's *bloops* and *poings* still go *klakka dakka* in my memory of his strips, most of them too politically incorrect to detail in our woke times—though I find myself wondering what he and Dave Berg, *MAD's* in-house reactionary Republican, would've made of the contemporary American landscape, with its priggish censorious lefty scolds and dummkopf Foxzombie Trumpist white nationalists. They may well have concluded that both sides, the woke and the dud, are equally deserving of the resounding *SPLADAP* of a wet fish smacked in their faces.

This is not to suggest that my worldview, even when reduced to just those few years, was mostly formed by the Usual Gang of Idiots at 485 MADison. That would be too simple. Still and all, the magazine provided a passport to, and formed a synergistic whole with, a distant country—*my* country, teeming, febrile, and fucked-up, a place of corrupt hypocritical pols, cynical film producers, arrogant self-righteous wingnut conservatives, bellbottomed dim-bulb hippies, bombshell bikini babes, ridiculous overlarge cars, kneejerk overconsumers, nitwitted football coaches, dumber TV sitcoms, and more.

In short, nothing like Ankara, Turkey. And a glorious place to spend time.

brueghel of the bronx

Daniel Bronstein

ENSCONCED IN American popular culture, *MAD*'s mascot, Alfred E. Neuman, became as recognizable an icon as Mickey Mouse and Superman. As *Time* magazine's Richard Corliss writes, to say that the *MAD* approach to humor influenced American comedy is "to understate the case. Almost all American satire today follows a formula" generated by the creative father of *MAD*, Harvey Kurtzman. As Paul Buhle and Denis Kitchen write, "Without Harvey Kurtzman, there would have been no *Saturday Night Live*. . . . [He] taught two, maybe three generations of postwar American kids, mainly boys, what to laugh at: politics, popular culture, authority figures."

MAD was spawned from several parents, including EC Comics and *MAD* publisher William M. Gaines. Founding editor Harvey Kurtzman was the overall architect of *MAD*, while his friend and colleague Will Elder played a key role in translating Kurtzman for the masses. Shorn of the artistic contribution of his friend Will Elder, Kurtzman's *MAD* work would not have packed the same punch. If Kurtzman and his *MAD* artists "can be compared to another bunch of early '50s comic smarty-pantses the Sid Caesar writing staff," writes Corliss, then "Elder was Mel Brooks." As Kurtzman made clear, Elder could "carry my stuff forward and enrich it by a multiple of five." Even within an institution teeming with professional humorists, William M. Gaines declared Elder to be *MAD*'s "funniest artist" and "unquestionably the nuttiest guy that ever walked in the doors here.... [He] probably became the most popular artist in *MAD*," a position he maintained over the course of many years.

Born Wolf Eisenberg in 1921 and raised in the Bronx, he was always a joker and was called "Meshugganah Villy" by his family. Although twice rejected, first at age seventeen and later at nineteen, for a cartooning job at Walt Disney Studios, Elder, along with several other *MAD* artists, was among the first graduates of New York's High School of Music and Art. He was also a veteran of World War II who helped draw maps for the Normandy D-Day invasion, as well as posters warning GIs about venereal disease. It was only after the war that he legally changed his name from Wolf William Eisenberg to Will Elder, in homage to the sixteenth-century Dutch artist Pieter Brueghel the Elder.

Together with his work on other EC Comics, Elder contributed to *MAD* from its first incarnation as a comic book through its transition into a magazine, spanning the years 1952–56. Known for his remarkable mimicry of almost any cartoon style, Elder meticulously aped other artists while still humorously eviscerating cultural luminaries, such as Donald Duck, Archie, Popeye, and Superman. Elder possessed a remarkable gift for replicating the design of other cartoonists.

Elder's artwork for "Mickey Rodent!" (#19, January 1955), Kurtzman's Disney parody, is a flawless impersonation of classic Disney's distinct style. "Darnold Duck" is shamed by Goony (Goofy) for walking around in public without pants. Here Elder offers a vision of what Donald Duck might look like experiencing an anxiety attack. The *Archie* comics parody, "Starchie" (#12, June 1954), portrays Mr. Weatherby—here Mr. Weathernot—as sexually harassing the Betty and Veronica counterparts, Biddy and Salonica. That spin on *Archie* would have been plenty, but Elder added other details. The two female students are pockmarked, with Biddy packing a hypodermic needle in her purse along with unlabeled pills, hand-rolled joints, and a deck of cards. As Elder noted, all the "things that are wrong with people in society registered on those pages" of "Starchie."

Elder's drawing skills coupled with his talent for parody set a high bar for all of *MAD*'s artists. As Jack Davis, another founding artist of *MAD*, later recounted, Elder "started the trend of putting in funny little things in the background." Elder, he said, was "kind of the original *MAD* artist. He'd put in crazy things that had never been done before." Elder called these tasty additions "chicken fat," schmaltz in Yiddish. Elder's acolytes dubbed him the "Marx Brother in cartooning." Like the Marx Brothers' work, Elder's was composed of layers upon layers of gags—the schmaltz to the main storylines, adding globs of extra Jewish flavor.

Monty Python's Terry Gilliam, among the many humorists who learned their craft via Elder and Kurtzman, described the chicken-fat format as the layering of "jokes on jokes on jokes." Cartoonist Daniel Clowes also takes a crack at defining "chicken fat," writing that "Elder articulates his Milt Gross/Marx Brothers–Yiddish–vaudevillianism," which was in some manner a "descendent of Bosch and Brueghel . . . The backgrounds are literally cluttered with information about the artist himself and the very specific urban culture from which he has risen. . . . The interplay of chaos and control is orchestrated . . . [and provides] his crystal-clear vision of a world gone mad."

Kurtzman, a talented artist with a truly original style and a legion of disciples, wrote most of the scripts and laid out storyboards for every panel of *MAD*, before he and Elder left the magazine in 1957 (Kurtzman and Elder then went on to collaborate on three magazines, none of which lasted long: *Trump*, *Humbug*, and *Help!*). As Gaines recounted, he was "like a conductor of an orchestra, made a pencil sketch, pretty tight pencil sketch, of every single panel of every single story and God help the artist who tried to change it!" But Elder's comic appendages festooned and even transcended Kurtzman's visual scripts for the *MAD* stories.

Kurtzman would "roughly set it down on paper in these little panels and written dialogue and sound effects," Elder recounted,

> and I would work with that as a base. Basically I would use that to start throwing things in. And he never said a word; because he figured whatever I did would only enhance the humor of what he did. And it was a good combination. It worked well. Before you know it, I was throwing in the kitchen sink and the dumbwaiter. Every blessed thing that came into my mind, which ended up in a hilarious clutter, as he put it.

Elder later recalled that

> if it was a crowded scene, I have everybody doing the wrong thing. Instead of having just the concentration on the hero or heroine, it would be simultaneous action elsewhere, and something to do with the story—it was unrelated—it had something to do with the story. . . . I consider myself like the Marx Brothers. It was chaos, but it was kind of organized.

This is significant because Elder's flourishes created a new tier of humor for Kurtzman's already funny work. "Harvey would say, 'Everybody will be reading Will's sight gags and not even my stories.'" Kurtzman affirmed, "Willy was much funnier than me."

In Elder's art, like Brueghel's *Fight between Carnival and Lent* (1559), or *The Triumph of Death* (1562), there is a multiplicity of individuals, each requiring particular attention. Like Bosch's *Garden of Earthly Delights* (1490–1500), there are a host of stories within stories, each requiring particular focus. Elder's scene of mass fright on the splash page of "Woman Wonder!" (#10, April 1954) includes an aside of skeletal legs jutting out from a coffin running along with a fleeing mob. Similarly, "Ping Pong!" (#6, August–September 1953) contains several scenes of crowds fleeing in terror. Elder's recurring trope of mass chaos might suggest the painting *Colossus* (ca. 1812, also known as *The Giant* or *Panic*) attributed to Francisco de Goya, depicting a mass of tiny figures fearfully scattering in every direction from a lumbering giant. Throw in a bit of the untidiness and shock value of Paul Cadmus but with perhaps less cynicism—and lots of Jewish comedy— and you have a Will Elder crowd scene.

Elder's comedy also included wordplay. Elder enjoyed affixing superfluous text onto background visuals. Following the precedents of cartoonist Bill Holman's *Smokey Stover* (syndicated 1935–73) and Roy Crane's *Wash Tubbs* (syndicated 1924–88) he deployed hosts of puns and other language-based humor, and used panels breaking down the fourth wall separating the art from the reader.

The parody "Shadow!" (#4, May 1953) offers some juicy examples of Elder's word games. In one panel Elder throws in a sign saying, "Try the new breakfast cereal 'Hush'! Doesn't snap, pop or crackle!" Using a saloon scene from the same story Elder inserts a sign on a wall saying "No Drinks to Miners," illustrated, of course, with a picture of a miner. Elsewhere in "Shadow!" he uses the backdrop of a gas station to display a sign reading, "Eat and get gas." "Ping Pong!" includes a glimpse of a man reading a magazine with the same cover format as *Life* magazine but titled "Death." Elder also adds an image of stereotypical natives boiling a man alive in a large pot. A closer look shows an inscription on the pot: "Advice for thin people. Don't eat fast!!! Advice for fat people. Don't eat—fast!!"

Larding Kurtzman's scripts with comic ephemera, Elder's generous dollops of "chicken fat" often employed the humor particular to the New York Jewish milieu of Elder's upbringing, explicated in Lenny Bruce's now-famous riff on what it meant to be a New Yorker: "If you're from New York and you're Catholic, you're still Jewish." Although Elder and Kurtzman departed from *MAD* in 1957 under less-than-happy circumstances, Elder's chicken-fat style was nevertheless preserved by his artistic successors and endured in the pages of *MAD* for half a century. Still, as his son-in-law and chief biographer, Gary Vandenberg, writes, "Will and Kurtzman were hitting [the readers] over the head with Jewish humor. . . . American humor had been set down a path where Yiddish sensibilities were never very far from the surface."

Elder's Jewish comedy was rarely hidden. Take his first *MAD* collaboration with Kurtzman, the story "Ganefs!" (Yiddish for "thieves") from the very first number of *MAD* in November 1952. Unlike most of their other collaborations, "Ganefs!" was mostly an Elder creation. "Ganef" was just the first of the story's many Jewish signposts. Elder and Kurtzman used a peculiar Jewish New York dialect and referenced New York culture. Relying on words like "furshlugginer," also spelled "fershlugginer" (a favorite invented Yiddishism), they had their own satirical self-referencing system—the Bronx answer to the *New Yorker*'s sophistication.

Some New York Jewish–specific material was foreign to some fans: "What in the world is 'borscht'?" demanded a reader. "Please tell me what in the world 'Furshlugginer' means," pleaded another. "Ganef" was coupled with words like "farshimmelt," and even references to "halavah," as Martha Reidelbach has pointed out, seemed "strange and exotic" to readers of the early *MAD*.

Issue #7 (October–November 1953) included the Sherlock Holmes parody "Shermlock Shomes," with a recurring gag of the sleuth mistakenly kissing a hand that he believes to belong to a beautiful woman but really is that of Mrs. Gowanus, an unkempt and unsightly cleaning lady who always seems to enter the scene shortly after cleaning cesspools. As many New Yorkers knew, the Gowanus Canal was infamous for its pollution, filth, and malodorous condition. For *MAD* readers in the rest of the country, this offered a glimpse into the distant and even exotic, multicultural city of New York.

Elder's Jewish points of reference were frequently gastronomic. For example, issue #3 (February–March 1953) included a parody of the police *Dragnet*, "Dragged Net!" Searching through a cave for the bad guy, "Glotz," the two detectives are shown walking by what appear to be hanging hams, stamped both with "Swifts"—one of America's venerable meatpacking companies—and the word "kosher" in Hebrew as well as English. Another ongoing gag in the story revolved around borscht. The detectives interrogate Glotz in a restaurant while the latter gorges himself on an octopus, frog, what appear to be a human arm and hand bones together with prehistoric creatures, modern worms, and a chick coming out of an Easter egg. In the midst of this gluttony and over the course of several panels, Elder shows a series of signs behind the characters proclaiming, "WE GOT BORSCHT," "BORSCHT WE GOT," "BORSCHT YOU BET!" "WE'RE RUNNING LOW ON BORSCHT," "SORRY! NO MORE BORSCHT."

Kurtzman and Elder's *Popeye* parody, "Poopeye!" (#21, March 1955), includes a showdown with "Superduperman." In Elder's version of the Man of Steel, the letter "S" on his chest is replaced in one instance with the label for Fleischmann's Yeast and in another with the very words "Chicken Fat." Early in his tenure at *MAD*, Elder began putting visual representations of chicken fat in various stories. In the fifth issue, for example, a container labeled "Jar of Chicken Fat" is inserted in the story "Outer Sanctum!" (#5, June–July 1953). The *Mandrake the Magician* parody, "Manduck the Magician" (#14, August 1954), includes a photo of bodybuilder Charles Atlas, another cultural icon, wearing trunks with the words, "I was raised on chicken fat." Elsewhere in the story, a woman is shown eating various foods from a box labeled "Manischewitz." Another example of Elder's gastronomically based humor is found in a 1954 *MAD* story (#16), really a cultural study, titled "Restaurant!" showing the ups and downs of having a family meal at a Chinese restaurant. (The splash page itself offers enough material to occupy one's attention for many years.) In yet another aside, Elder adds a sign to a restaurant booth saying "Today's Special: Egg Foo Yong with Gefilte Fish."

Perhaps Elder's most notorious display of Yiddishkeit was his take on Clement Moore's poem "A Visit from St. Nicholas," popularly known as "The Night Before Christmas," from the very first issue of *MAD*'s sister publication at EC, *Panic* (February–March 1954). Never as successful as its predecessor, *Panic* drew from the same stable of artists but was edited—far less strictly—by Al Feldstein, later editor of *MAD* magazine after Harvey Kurtzman's departure. Although "The Night Before Christmas" parody was not a result of collaboration with Kurtzman, its content would still have fit well in *MAD*.

Responding to the line "A bundle of toys he had flung on his back / And he looked like a peddler just opening his pack," Elder drew Santa Claus as what appeared to be an archetypal Lower East Side fish peddler. As refracted through the mind of Will Elder, another stanza about Santa being "dressed all in fur, from his head to his foot, / And his clothes were all tarnished with ashes and soot," finds visual

form in a blackface Al Jolson singing "Mammy." But what most ran-
kled was Elder's portrayal of Santa's sled as a car bearing the sign "Just
Divorced!" along with a YMCA bumper sticker. The sign and bumper
stickers were secondary jokes; Elder's visual interpretation of the
stanza actually centered on literal portrayals of the names of Santa's
reindeer.

Elder's "The Night Before Christmas" caused *Panic* to be banned
in Massachusetts. As Gaines recalled, "The trouble we had with the
Santa Claus story was Bill Elder. . . . Now how do a bunch of iconoclastic, atheist bastards like us know that Santa Claus is a saint and that he
can't be divorced and that this is going to offend Boston?"

In a faux biographical sketch of Elder from *MAD*'s "Special Art
Issue" (#22, April 1955), the toddler Elder is described as "shmear-
ing" chicken fat on towels, bald heads, visitors' dresses, and conve-
nient walls. "Today those shmears . . . are hung in various museums
and signed with Elder's various pen names such as 'Braque,' 'Matisse,'
'Picasso.' etc." The difference between Elder and Brueghel, Bosch, or
Goya is not simply that Elder's work unfolded in cheaply sold comic
books rather than as paintings on display in the Prado. Elder, unlike
the classical artists with their fierce satires, was focused on making
people laugh.

Elder's "layered, free-for-all approach," as Daniel Clowes describes
it, "influenced the cartoons of R. Crumb and films like *Airplane!* and
the *Naked Gun* series." David Hajdu observed that while "earlier comic
book artists like Joe Shuster and Bob Kane may have invented the
superhero . . . Will Elder made possible [later comedies like] *Super-
bad.*" Ultimately, as noted in *The New York Times* obituary for Elder,
the chicken-fat "approach to humor seeped into the rest of the magazine and the DNA of the contributors. . . . It set the tone for the entire
magazine and created a look that endures to this day."

Elder-era *MAD* occupied the same world as those comedians designated at the time as "sick": Mort Sahl, Jules Feiffer, and, of course, the aforementioned Lenny Bruce. Kurtzman and Elder's work also laid the foundation for the 1960s counterculture comics of Crumb and Gilbert Shelton. Alongside comedians like Monty Python members John Cleese and Terry Gilliam, San Francisco hippies like musician Jerry Garcia pointed to Elder as an important creative influence. Still others have linked Elder's chicken-fat style to Louis Malle's film *Zazie dans le métro* (1960) and to the Firesign Theatre.

Thanks to Will Elder, the schmaltz of Jewish humor was distilled into the chicken fat of American comedy. By instilling a distinctly Jewish comedic sensibility into *MAD*'s parodies of mainline American culture, Elder's work also exemplifies how the melting pot of American popular culture was laced with Jewish humor, and when digested became an essential ingredient of the humor consumed by Americans of every faith, creed, and stripe.

(2016)

MAD's Jewish America

Nathan Abrams

HE JEWISH influence of *MAD* magazine has been profound but strangely overlooked. *MAD* functioned as a secular Talmud for a generation of Jews and non-Jews alike in America and beyond. Like its religious forerunner, *MAD* was intertextual, self-referential, and arguably even formatted similarly. And like the Talmud, its influence extended outward—from the comic book world, it inspired graphic novels, television, movies, and more. Only recently, graphic novelist Art Spiegelman pronounced it his "Talmud." Without *MAD*, arguably there would have been no *Maus*. He was not the only one. Nor perhaps would there have been Stanley Kubrick's *Dr. Strangelove* or the other countercultural satires of the 1960s, such as *Catch-22* and *M*A*S*H*.

Although it debuted in 1952, it was not until 1955 that *MAD* magazine, as we know it, burst onto the scene. A high proportion of its staff was Jewish. This "Usual Gang of Idiots," as the magazine referred to them, included its founder Harvey Kurtzman, editor Al Feldstein, artists Mort Drucker, Al Jaffee, Will Elder, and Dave Berg, and writers Larry Siegel and Lou Silverstone. In many ways, *MAD* stood for a group of alternative New York Jewish intellectuals.

Born in the 1950s, *MAD* lived contemporaneously with that generation of writers, poets, essayists, and literary critics who came to be

known as the New York Intellectuals, as well as such iconoclasts as
Bob Dylan, the Beats, comedians Mort Sahl and Lenny Bruce, movie
director Stanley Kubrick, cartoonist Jules Feiffer, novelist Joseph
Heller, and those who would form the New Left and counterculture. This group of Jews, centered in New York, had come to political awareness during the Great Depression. Their religious and ethnic
heritage had a direct and important influence on their work.

Marinated in the same urban Jewish culture, *MAD*'s commitments
mirrored theirs and arguably were part of the same debates, particularly in the post-Holocaust world. A detailed examination of *MAD*'s
pages in the 1950s and the 1960s shows that it engaged with the same
dilemmas and paradoxes as these intellectual New Yorkers, producing
an alternative New York critique, which skewered the key intellectual
concerns of those decades: suburbia, psychoanalysis, existentialism,
Freudianism, intellectual airs, bohemianism, technology, disarma-
ment, and containment.

MAD's Jewish background had a direct and important influence.
MAD was very much humor in a Jewish vein (*MAD*'s first numbers, as
a book, had been called *Tales Calculated to Drive You MAD—Humor
in a Jugular Vein*). Elder, for example, pioneered the "chicken-fat"
method. That is, he laid the schmaltz on thick, piling joke upon joke
upon joke, filling the frame with details and wasting no space.

Because *MAD* refused to include advertisements from 1957 to 2001,
it had the freedom that other publications lacked. Having neither
advertising nor strict regulation, *MAD* could target almost anything it
wished, and indeed the major icons and iconography of America came
into its sights. Ironically, the magazine's offices were located in the
heart of American corporate advertising, MADison Avenue. Instead
of adverts, it produced spoofs for such bogus products as "Ded Ryder
Cowboy Carbine" rifles and "Shmeer's Rubber Bubble Gum."

It even sent up other comics. In "Starchie" the innocent teenagers Archie and Jughead became chain-smoking juvenile delinquents. "The Lone Stranger" was transformed from a western hero into a schlemiel. And "Superduperman" was not the triumphant superhero but a schlimazel. The magazine also asked "What If Batman Were Jewish?" (#516, August 2012) and "What If Superman Were Raised by Jewish Parents?" (#325, March 1994).

It loved to target Disney, whose founder had a reputation for antisemitism. His central wholesome icon, Mickey Mouse, became the gray, rat-faced, vermin thug Mickey Rodent, whose fingers and tail were caught in mouse traps.

It supplied a phrasebook of "handy phrases" for American tourists traveling to Russia during the Cold War. "Waiter, there's a dictaphone in my borscht!" was transliterated from a purported Russian translation as "Tsam, hyu med tsee pahntz tu lung!"

MAD was not afraid of directing its satirical talents at any target, including movie stars, pop singers, presidents, politicians, and the British royal family. Even World War II and the Holocaust were not safe. One of its earliest allusions to the Nazis came in its parody "Frank N. Stein!" (#8, December 1953–January 1954), in which Dr. Frankenstein succeeds in creating his monster. On the final page, the monster's face is revealed, to the horror of the soldiers sent to detain him: "There it is!" "Look at its face!" "What a horrible face!" and "I can't stand it!" In the next panel, we see that it looks precisely like Hitler. (In the end, the Hitler-like monster flies away because, as it turns out, Bumble stole a "fershlugginer" bird brain!) The following December, *MAD* parodied the play and movie *Stalag 17* (directed by Billy Wilder in 1953) as "Stalag 18!" (#18). Here the overweight and aging Kommandant, named Johann Sebastian Shmaltz, complains: "Oh for der good old days ven dey made us Nazis in der movies, tough, good-lookin' guys mit der blonde crew-haircut . . . mit der shnappy uniforms mit der daggers in der belts." In January 1967, under the heading of the "Mein 'Kamp' Humor Dept.," "Hokum's Heroes" (#108) parodied the television show *Hogan's Heroes*, which ran from 1965 to 1971.

MAD also helped change the nature of comedy by redrawing the boundaries of orthodoxies of taste. Earlier Jewish humor had been dominated by the Borscht Belt comedians, those Jews who played the kosher resort hotels in the Catskills like Grossinger's and Concord and gently poked fun at Jewish life for Jewish audiences. Black or sick humor became fashionable, paving the way for Sahl and Bruce, as well as the absurdism of Ernie Kovacs and Stan Freberg, who couldn't be further disconnected from the tameness of the Borscht Belters.

MAD used parody to criticize a predominantly Protestant culture from the perspective of the Jewish outsider. As Stephen E. Kercher has pointed out, "Kurtzman's *MAD* comics mercilessly lampooned a host of square-jawed, goyishe American tough guys, from the upright, virtuous marshal played by Gary Cooper in *High Noon* to Marlon Brando's motorcycle bad boy in *The Wild One*." In February 1955's "Cowboy!" (#20), Kurtzman juxtaposed the "movie and television version" of a cowboy—a handsome, clean-shaven man named, significantly, Lance Sterling ("Could you ever picture a cowboy hero called Melvin Poznowski?")—with John Smurd, a "100% genuine cowboy" who wore, like all his fellow cowboys, a "nauseating mustache." Unlike Lance Sterling, "old John Smurd worked like a horse," and since "there was no cowboy union then," he had little time or energy for "shooting it out with bad guys."

MAD also foregrounded issues of racism, intolerance, and prejudice. In so doing, it exploded the myths that America was truly democratic and tolerant. As Al Jaffee recalled:

I think that for Jews of my generation especially, social consciousness came naturally for those of us who suffered from a lack of civil rights and were discriminated against. Social consciousness really is in a way self-serving. Because by being in favor of civil rights for example, in a like way you're really saying, "Jews have suffered without civil rights for so many centuries that we know what not having civil rights is, so we cannot possibly impose this on someone else, not to have civil rights." I think it's a gut reaction: I don't think either Harvey Kurtzman or I or anybody who works in the entertainment business—comedians, writers—sit down and say, "I owe something to society." Basically, we're trying to be funny, and a good source of humor is the stupidities in society, and certainly bigotry is one of the biggest stupidities. And Jews have experienced it firsthand and they know how stupid it is, so we go after it.

MAD's Jewish creators also managed to poke fun at their own co-religionists so that, in effect, no one was safe from satire. In this way, the magazine bore more than a passing resemblance to the films of Mel Brooks. As Brooks said,

The roots of my humor are in very old-fashioned Yiddish comedy . . . which is based on some failure—making fun of the inept, which is cruel. . . . So, Jews taking off on unfortunates, it's always compelling. Because you're saying in a strange way, "Oh thank God, it's not me." You enjoy the humor because you are not the butt of the joke. It's cruel but effective.

Like *MAD*, Brooks has been accused of being childish, scatological, and vulgar; his detractors claim he makes films in bad taste. Consider the farting-around-the-campfire scene in Brooks's *Blazing Saddles* (1974). Perhaps *MAD* even supplied the blueprint for Brooks, who was a writer for Sid Caesar. In 1959 and 1960, Caesar contributed four stories to *MAD*.

MAD's humor was grounded in Yiddishisms, sarcasm, and self-mockery—all defining features of Jewish humor. It employed a whole lexicon of Yiddish phrases, both real and imaginary—making, for the unqualified, Leo Rosten's *The Joys of Yiddish* (1968) a required companion text. Elder and Kurtzman, observe Denis Kitchen and Paul Buhle, "added a peculiar Jewish New York dialect, from 'Mrs. Gowanus' (a reference to the Gowanus Canal in Brooklyn) to . . . 'fershlugginer' (a made-up Yiddish word)." This was announced from the very first issue, when a strip titled "Ganefs!"—Yiddish for thieves or crooks—appeared. *MAD*'s Yiddish-inflected terminology included the more familiar terms such as "schmuck," as when it ran the strip, written by Al Jaffee, "Don't You Feel Like a Schmuck?!" in March 1973 (#157). But this also included words less known in middle America: "schmaltz," "shmear," "oy," "feh," "borscht," "ganef," "veebleftzer" (made up), "farshimmelt," "kibitzer," "schlepp," "schnook," and "halavah." In one column (the two-part story "Murder the Husband!/Murder the Story!", #11, May 1954), it printed Yiddish in Hebrew letters meaning "a Danish king [has] come to a memorial service in Copenhagen." Readers often wrote in to complain of the strange and exotic-sounding words that saturated the magazine.

Similarly, in a reversal of the name-changing process so beloved of Jewish Hollywood stars during the heyday of the studio system, *MAD* Yiddishized names, turning Batman and Robin into "Bat Boy and Rubin," GI Joe into "GI Shmoe," and Sherlock Holmes into "Shermlock

Shomes." The name "Shadowskeedeeboomboom," used for various heroes and foes, was a name inspired by the Yiddish comic singer Aaron Lebedeff. In this way, *MAD* reacted to the de-Semitization of the Hollywood studio system, which was often at pains to sideline or ignore Jewishness and Jewish characters, in what Henry Popkin has called "the great retreat." During Hollywood's heyday, Jews were hidden on-screen both literally and figuratively as the Jewish moguls, often prompted by pressure from Jewish organizations and the Hays Office, which exercised tight control over the portrayal of religion and ethnicity, promoted a strategy of assimilatory Americanization. Jewish actors changed their names, as their Jewish bosses, for commercial reasons, as well as fear of inciting antisemitism even further, calculated that their predominantly white working-class audiences did not want to watch Jews on-screen.

By contrast, *MAD* foregrounded Jewishness. "Dragged Net!" (#11, May 1954), its second spoof of the TV show *Dragnet*, was punctuated with a heavyset middle-aged Jewish woman intermittently shouting, "VIL-LEE." In the final panel, she catches up with little "Villie Elder!" who, naturally, can be found in the bathroom. "Strangely Believe It!" (#42, November 1958), written by guest contributor Ernie Kovacs, featured a "Dr. Sidney Klutz." A "Prof. Rumblemacher" appeared in "Shrunk World," written by Sid Caesar (#49, September 1959). In its parody of the 1968 film *Rosemary's Baby*, renamed as "Rosemia's Boo-boo," Dr. Abraham Sapirstein (Ralph Bellamy) was renamed the more obvious "Schlepperstein."

In *MAD*'s "Credits for the Common Man" (#42, November 1958), a whole galaxy of Jewish characters appeared. Sam "Red" Schlepp ran "a luncheonette so bold and different that only a schnook like Schlepp would dare attempt it!" There was also Irving Siegel, Seymour Cohen, Herman Katz, Phil Spieler, Stanley Klatch, and Bernie Levine. Even the very idea of the spread, giving credits to the "common man" as stars and crew received credits for movies, could be argued to have derived from Jewish memories of the "dos kleine menshele" ("the little man") so fundamental to *Yiddishkeit* and Yiddish literature.

MAD also took on Judaism. Its view of the religion and especially what had happened to it in the United States curiously resembled that of an ultra-Orthodox rabbi who took a dim view of the reforms made by the more liberal branches of Judaism. This is most clearly articulated in "The *MAD* 'Religion in America' Primer" (#153, September 1972). Clearly, with its tongue placed firmly in its cheek, *MAD* introduced Judaism as a whole thus:

> The Jews do not believe Christ is their Savior.
> Who *do* they believe He is?
> They believe He is a nice Jewish boy
> Who went into his Father's business.
> So much for our first lesson in religion.
> Now you know why religion has been running for over
> 2000 years.
> You also know why the Jews have been running for over
> 2000 years!

It then went on to break Judaism down into its constituent parts of Orthodoxy, Conservatism, and Reform. It described the latter group as hardly observing any religion at all, concluding "To the other two groups / Reform Jews have another name. / They are known as 'Christians'!" Their Temple was easily locatable because it was "the one with the Christmas tree in front." Thus, when a Catholic and Protestant decide to get married and compromise, in Dave Berg's "The Lighter Side of . . . Weddings" (#152, July 1972), they choose a synagogue. *MAD* lampooned the rabbinic leadership as being more concerned with food than spirituality: a morose-looking rabbi postpones a bar mitz-vah "because the caterer didn't show up," before adding, "How much suffering can the Jews stand?" On the subject of Jewish food, it carica-tured the stereotypical overbearing Jewish mother, depicting her as an overweight matriarch who stuffed her family with oversized bowls of soup while imploring them to "eat! Eat!"

But *MAD* was "Jewish" in another way. Underneath its rowdy sur-face was thoughtful social commentary, as it sought both to entertain and to educate. *MAD* also often railed against alcohol, drugs, tobacco, licentiousness, deceit, and hypocrisy. One theologian, Vernard Eller, detected in 1967 a biblical morality lying beneath the magazine's surface: "*MAD* is every bit as preachy as that old codifier Moses. Beneath the pile of garbage that is *MAD*, there beats, I suspect, the heart of a rabbi."

MAD's alternative Jewish sensibility permeated the entire maga-zine. It was subversive, held no golden calves or even tablets of stone. Its humor was very much that of New York City, mirroring that of Joseph Heller, Jules Feiffer, Lenny Bruce, and Mort Sahl. It showcased the best Jewish comedy talents of the 1950s and 1960s while predicting what was to come from those of the later '60s, '70s, and '80s, including Woody Allen, Mel Brooks, and the team of Zucker-Abrahams-Zucker. It was surely no coincidence that *MAD* artist Jack Davis went on to design one-sheet posters for Woody Allen's *Bananas*, among many other films.

MAD of the 1950s and '60s very much articulated the position of the Jew in genteel (read: Gentile) society: one who does not quite belong. Through aggressive, Yiddish-punctuated, and often foul-mouthed satire, it expressed a brash urban Jewishness and a deliberate outsider status, while challenging the status quo, highlighting its hypocrisy, and reveling in the absurdities of everyday life.

(2013–14)

with a little bit of ecch: MAD and the movie musical

David Hajdu

IT HAD everything *MAD* was against. *My Fair Lady*, the musical repurposing of Shaw's *Pygmalion* as a last defense of English magnificence for a world in the midst of disproving it, was a project of corporate culture, a triumph of marketing, and a testament to the persistence of outdated, old-fashioned ideas. The Broadway production, which opened on March 15, 1956, had been set up through a savvy cross-merchandising plan devised by Goddard Lieberson, the head of Columbia Records, who arranged to fund the stage show in exchange for a high 40 percent royalty on sales of the cast recording in the emerging delivery medium of long-playing albums. The vinyl discs the company manufactured went on to dominate the record charts for years and, in time, sold more than thirteen million copies. Record sales, in turn, fueled sales of tickets for road-show productions across the globe. By the beginning of the 1960s, when *MAD* was settling into the mode of formatted adolescent insolence that would define it forever, *My Fair Lady* was everywhere: on the record players in every paneled rec room in America and under the lights in theaters in countless cities where the sun was finally setting on the British Empire.

My Fair Lady, a hoary paean to submission and conformity with songs by Alan Jay Lerner and Frederick Loewe, neatly embodied all that *MAD* objected to in its satirical cartoon features about the advertising industry, the government, the military, and parents. Henry Higgins, the patrician phonetician determined to turn the peasant Eliza Doolittle into the veddy image of a proper lady, personified all the bloated, entrenched forces *MAD* saw as threatening to exploit the powerless—that is to say, the young people reading *MAD*—and strip them of their treasured individuality and status as outliers. If Higgins could transform a surly flower girl into a model of upper-crust propriety by training her to follow given codes of speech and comportment, the ad agencies on Madison Avenue could turn TV viewers into zombies of consumption, the army could make draftees into khaki-uniformed killers, and parents could condition their children to become something kids saw as inconceivably terrible: more adults.

MAD had been carrying parodies of movies in a mix with spoofs of comic strips and comic books since the first year of its anarchic original incarnation under the editorship of Harvey Kurtzman. From its sixth issue, in 1953, to its thirty-sixth, in 1957, *MAD* published nineteen satires of films, nearly all recent releases of the time geared to adults, such as *From Here to Eternity* (twisted into "From Eternity Back to Here!"), *The Barefoot Contessa* ("The Barefoot Nocountessa!"), and *The Seven-Year Itch* ("The Seven Itchy Years"), with deliriously silly text by Kurtzman himself in nearly every case; a variety of early *MAD* artists, including the impishly creative Will Elder, handled the drawing. It was not until the 1960s that the spoofs in *MAD* took a turn under the magazine's second editor, Al Feldstein, who had taken over *MAD* after Kurtzman left. Feldstein opened up *MAD* to more topical (and often less funny) social critique, along with its established fare of wacky goofball humor.

In April 1960, the fifty-fourth issue of *MAD* included a seven-page assault on its favorite target, Madison Avenue, in the form of a fictive musical entitled "My Fair Ad-Man." It was not precisely a spoof of *My Fair Lady* but a twist on the plot (the Pygmalion story) and a takeoff on the songs Lerner and Loewe wrote for the musical. The script was by Nick Meglin, a twenty-four-year-old *MAD* writer who would eventually become coeditor and ended up working at the magazine for a total of forty-eight years. (Meglin once carried business cards identifying him as *MAD*'s Tennis Editor.) The art was by the supremely gifted caricaturist Mort Drucker, who had a rare capacity to convey impeccable likenesses with elegant line work and precisely lacerating exaggeration. The feature Meglin and Drucker concocted was a loopy nightmare pastiche comprising elements of *My Fair Lady*, pointed commentary on the cynical opportunism of the ad business, and random pop culture allusions.

It began as a splash panel conjuring the manic glitz of a big, brassy Broadway opening number. Characters from midcentury advertising iconography—Mr. Clean, Tony the Tiger, Speedy the Alka-Seltzer boy, the Mobil winged horse, and more—parade down Madison Avenue as a traffic cop with the face of Dean Martin belts a parody song with words set to the music of "On the Street Where You Live":

> People stop and stare
> At the colored signs
> Telling them to buy their beer from Schlitz
> and beans from Heinz

A couple of passing ad execs with the faces of Cary Grant and Charles Laughton launch into a debate over the quality of advertising copy: Is it or is it not so insipid that someone with no training or experience could write it? As a test case, in the manner of Eliza Doo-little, they stop a wandering beatnik—a handy symbol of indolence and ineptitude, complete with baggy turtleneck sweater, beret, and a goatee—and proceed to indoctrinate him in the banality of advertising and the mindless art of back-slapping one's way to success in the corporate culture. The beatnik, shaved and groomed in gray flannel, now looks fully like the Frank Sinatra of the Kennedy era. Why Sinatra—and Dean Martin, Cary Grant, and Charles Laughton—as visual references? To young readers in 1960, they would be unlikely to mean very much specifically; they would read mainly as famous middle-aged white men whom adults seem to think are important for some reason: symbols of commercial success who show up from time to time on the same TV screens as Mr. Clean and Tony the Tiger.

In a sophisticated mirroring of the musical's integration of story and songs, "My Fair Ad-Man" relays much of its critical content in the parody lyrics by Meglin. He wrote full sets of words to eight of the show's songs: "On the Street Where You Live," "Wouldn't It Be Loverly?," "Get Me to the Church on Time," "With a Little Bit of Luck," "I Could Have Danced All Night," "I've Grown Accustomed to Her Face," "Why Can't the English," and "The Rain in Spain," which Meglin used to make a clever meta joke. "Repeat after me," the Cary Grant exec tells the transformed Sinatra: "An ad that's bad will end up spoofed in *MAD!*"

Meglin was crafty and wrote words that not only scanned nicely over Lerner's melodies but frequently matched—or exceeded—Loewe's lyrics in cleverness. In his variation on "Get Me to the Church on Time," for instance, Meglin has the beatnik Sinatra sing cheekily about adapting to business hours:

> I've got to be there in the morning
> Can't let the boys in Westport down

No more expresso
My new address-o
Is somewhere with the squares uptown

Anyone alive in 1960 would be able to sing all the tunes in the satire from unavoidable exposure to the playing of those millions of original-cast albums that Columbia Records had sold, as well as performances of the songs on TV variety shows every week. It was not necessary to learn the tunes or even like them; everyone was cultivated by pop culture to know them.

After "My Fair Ad-Man," *MAD* published one musical parody every year or two, almost (but not always) pegged to the movie version of the show. There's a full list of all the *MAD* film parodies on Wikipedia, and to scour it for musicals is to be startled by how few there were: only six for the entire decade of the '60s, compared with forty-four satires of non-musical films—and even more spoofs of TV series in the same period. ("My Fair Ad-Man" is not on the Wiki list, because it was based on the stage musical, rather than the movie to follow in 1964.) The dozen or so musical satires from the magazine's peak as a popular phenomenon in the '60s and '70s seem to retain an out-size place in *MAD* readers' collective memory. This, I think, is partly a function of their rarity among the *MAD* spoofs; they stood out, and they stuck with us because they were done so well, with artfulness and an arch sense of play—qualities most *MAD* features shared—and something additional: admiration veering to the brink of envy.

While the musical satires used the musical form in a variety of ways, they rarely did much to mock the form itself, and when they did, the ribbing was gentle, as if the writers and the artists (or artist, since Drucker drew the majority of the musical satires) were reluctant to get rough on something they cared about. The first two *MAD* musicals to follow "My Fair Ad-Man" both carried on its approach and adopted the story outlines and song structures of the shows (and films) to critique something other than the shows. "The Producer and I," with text and lyrics by Meglin, took off on Rodgers and Hammerstein's *The King and I* to look at the ways power-drunk Hollywood moguls exploit vulnerable starlets; and "East Side Story," with text and lyrics by Frank Jacobs, applied the rival-gang scheme of Leonard Bernstein and Stephen Sondheim's *West Side Story* to satirize the East and West in Cold War geopolitical rivalry. A few years later, when Lerner and Loewe's *Camelot* was adapted for the screen, Jacobs turned it into "Can a Lot," a fierce (and more serious than funny) critique of corporate America in which management and labor compete for power like medieval fiefdoms.

The opening number, a play on "I Wonder What the King Is Doing Tonight," has Arthur King, head of the Excalibur Wax Fruit Company, in a duet with the chairman of the board, Merlyn M. Merlyn. Wondering what the larger firms are doing that day, Merlyn sings:

> And oh, the trepidation
> As they're forced in arbitration
> And they find that Labor's heart
> is made of stone!

Frank Jacobs, who had started writing for *MAD* in 1957, not long after Feldstein had taken over, wrote more of the musical parodies than any other *MAD* writer. In fact, he wrote more features of all kinds than any other *MAD* writer, with nearly six hundred bylines to his name over his fifty-seven-year association with the magazine. When he died, in April 2021, *The New York Times* emphasized his work on the musical parodies, praising his "pitch-perfect verse and lyrics."

In the first years of the twenty-first century, I interviewed Jacobs (and other *MAD* artists and editors) for a book I was writing on comics and teen culture in the postwar era, and he brought up the pride he and his colleagues took in the musical spoofs. "I think they were the best thing we ever did," Jacobs said. "I would spend hours working on a single line, making sure it was just right. I'd put a lot of time into every rhyme."

I pointed out that he had just come up with a rhyme pretty easily, and Jacobs recoiled. "Yeah—too easily," he said. "I wouldn't use that. Our rule was that the parody lyrics had to be as clever as the original lyrics. If you're trying to poke fun at something and what you do isn't as good as the original, the joke is on you."

With the features based on Broadway shows, Jacobs, Meglin, a few other writers, and Drucker were not just making fun of musicals; they were *making* musicals. This was both homage and preservation, an effort to honor an art form that had been drifting further and further from the center of pop culture since *My Fair Lady* opened in 1956. By the 1960s, most of the early masters of show music—Jerome Kern, the Gershwins, Irving Berlin, Cole Porter, Harold Arlen, E. Y. "Yip" Harburg, Richard Rodgers, and their peers—were gone, no longer active, or well past their creative prime. The musical was essentially a historical art.

MAD kept it going in the quirky form of cartoon magazine satires for young readers who, as the years passed, grew ever less likely to have any idea how to sing "I've Grown Accustomed to Her Face." From the mid-1960s to 1974, when *MAD* hit its all-time highest circulation of more than 2.1 million readers, *MAD* published a string of musical features spoofing subjects other than musicals themselves: "007: The James Bomb Musical," in which Jacobs used the structures of songs from *Oklahoma!* to mock the Sean Connery Bond films; "West Coast

Story," in which Jacobs again reset the songs from *West Side Story*, this time in a tale of battling hippies and right-wingers in California, with art by *MAD*'s prolific big-foot specialist, Jack Davis; "Antenna on the Roof," a cutting take on suburban living, with Jacobs adapting the songs by Jerry Bock and Sheldon Harnick from *Fiddler on the Roof*; and "My Fair Laddie," with Jacobs now using the Pygmalion story and Lerner and Loewe songs to skewer the '70s singles-bar scene.

Nick Meglin, who wrote the first *My Fair Lady* takeoff in *MAD*, would eventually try his hand at writing musicals for the stage, collaborating with the composer Neil Berg on a song-and-dance sequel to *A Christmas Carol* and a musical version of the movie *Grumpy Old Men*. But Jacobs and Drucker needed no such outlet. They were creating successful musical comedies in the pages of *MAD*. With winks in the direction of Broadway, they were content to make a cartoon art of discontent on the creative territory they owned, and they stayed on the street where they lived.

MAD
and the insurrectionists

Clifford Thompson

You'd better give up
On Christmas this year
You haven't a chance
With relatives here—
Sam and Roz are coming to town!

They're bringing their kids
To add to your fun
They're staying ten days
You thought it was one—
Sam and Roz are coming to town!

They'll monopolize your bathroom
Destroy your solitude
They'll eat you out of house and home
Then complain about the food

The only way
To save your Noël
Is give 'em the house
And take a hotel—
Sam and Roz are coming to town!

HE LINES above were set to the tune of "Santa Claus Is Coming to Town." I read them in *MAD* sometime in the 1970s, when I was growing up, and I have quoted them from memory. The lyrics, and my ability to recall them more than forty years later, suggest several things to me. One is that I have a strange memory, which is a subject for a different essay. What I do not have is total recall, which means that, at one point in my life, I had both the time and the desire to read these lyrics repeatedly; and that, in turn, suggests both a particular stage of my development and the animating spirit of *MAD*: adolescence. That is a time of questioning things once thought to be beyond reproach, of which there is no better example than Christmas. And that makes the demise of *MAD*, and its particular spirit of questioning, very sad indeed—because we could use more of that spirit.

Oh, there is still questioning going on. On January 6, 2021, a group of citizens questioned the results of the previous year's presidential election to the point of violent, deadly conflict at the US Capitol. It would be easy to draw a line stretching backward from the insurrectionists' arrested adolescence to the spirit of eternal childishness supposedly fostered by cultural entities such as *MAD*, but there is a crucial difference between the two, which can be illuminated by a look at *MAD*'s mascot.

My impulse is to go to the Internet, like a responsible writer, and find a reputable-looking source to tell me about Alfred E. Neuman's history and the idea behind his creation. I am going to resist that impulse. Really, what does it matter? As with anything presented to the public, what is important is not the idea but what millions of readers saw. Here is what this reader saw:

A grinning, dorky-looking boy of indeterminate age. Was he nine?

Fourteen? Whatever his age, he always seemed to me a little old for that missing tooth, which suggested someone also a little slow in his development. His grin made it seem that he was okay with that, that he was okay, really, with everything—the bliss of ignorance. His motto, the only thing he was ever known to say, was "What, me worry?" *MAD* put that happy acceptance in its gunsights: *Wake up, kid! The things you like are stupid!* Of course, Alfred liked what we liked—all the stuff *MAD* made fun of—suggesting that Alfred was us. But hold on: that stupid-looking kid was also on all the magazine's covers. It seemed that he stood for the magazine too, meaning that *MAD*—and here is that crucial difference I mentioned—did not place itself above what it questioned. The magazine was its own first target, because if Alfred was us, *MAD* was us, too, part of a goofy trinity doing a collective facepalm: *Look at what we hold dear! How dumb can we get?* Don't forget that *MAD*'s creators always called themselves "The Usual Gang of Idiots." The title of one of the parodies was partly a dig at *MAD*'s (our) own ignorance: *Who's Afraid of Virginia Woolf?* became "Who in the Heck Is Virginia Woolf?"

The questioning and ridicule then turned outward, gleefully. What were the things we held dear, those balloons begging for *MAD*'s needle? TV shows were a big one. One of the panels in a feature called "Where Else But on TV . . . ?" was a drawing of the character Richie Cunningham from the sitcom *Happy Days*, shown breezing through the front door of his parents' house wearing a light sweater and a big, carefree grin; the caption was something like . . . *is there never any rain or inclement weather of any kind (except on Christmas Eve, when it suddenly starts snowing everywhere)?* (I'm pretty sure I have the parenthetical exactly right.) Then there was "Bawde," a parody of *Maude*. *MAD* was not deterred by the fact that the show was already, to an extent, a spoof of upper-class liberal cluelessness. In one panel, Bawde asks a man, "Do you prefer to be called a *Chicano* or a *Mexican-American*?" The man responded, "Well, like most *Bolivians*, I don't particularly care for *either one!*"

Where I have placed italics, *MAD* used bold letters. The stresses the writers placed on certain words reflected their keen ear for speech. Then there were the drawings: those renderings of Richie and Bawde/Maude were not just vague likenesses—they were dead ringers. If *MAD* and its creators were us, they were us at our sharpest. They were also us at our humblest. They questioned their own tastes, and by extension—unlike the insurrectionists—they questioned themselves.

One day in the mid-1970s a friend asked me which was better: *MAD* or *Cracked*? He was not asking my opinion, because this was not a matter of opinion; he knew the right answer and wanted to know if I did. "*MAD*," I said, and he nodded his approval. About the best you could say for *Cracked* was that it didn't try to hide what it was up to. *Cracked* was a straight-up copy of *MAD*, or an attempt at one, right down to the idiot-boy mascot and the short "a" in its one-syllable title, published with the brazenness of a hostile takeover—or an attempt at one. Beyond that, *Cracked* might have been created solely to show how good *MAD* was. The drawings were okay, but the writing was lousy—those guys didn't even know how to punctuate. Maybe worst of all, *Cracked* seemed to forget half the time that its job was parody; its feature on Fonzie from *Happy Days* read like a fanzine. If *MAD* represented our better instincts, *Cracked* stood for one of our worst, which is to take the wrong things at face value. To fail to understand that *MAD* was better than *Cracked*, surely, was to fail to understand much of anything.

My conversation with my friend was a testament to *MAD*'s reach (and *Cracked*'s, too, I suppose). Our exchange took place in an all-

Black section of then mostly Black Washington, DC, in the middle of the low-income housing project where this friend and most of my other friends lived; I lived in a small, semi-detached private house across the alley. I've never read anywhere who *MAD*'s imagined readers or target audience were, or if they had any, but if they did, I don't imagine they were my friends and me. It's not that the humor was at all racist; it wasn't, at least in my memory. Rather, it is that if *MAD* and I were considering the same objects of ridicule and laughing at them for the same reasons, *MAD* was seeing them from a slightly different angle.

One issue of the magazine demonstrates what I mean and also exemplifies other core characteristics of *MAD*. One recurring feature, "The Lighter Side of . . . ," had three- and four-panel strips poking fun at some aspect of the given subject. Several "Lighter Side" entries were variations on the theme of summer, like "The Lighter Side of Swimming Pools" (#121, September 1968). The only thing I remember is that in Dave Berg's strip, the characters sat by their pool. If *MAD* was—in some respects—me, here was, nevertheless, the difference between us. I knew exactly one family who had their own pool—cousins way off in the suburbs—and the only other pool I knew about, period, was the one at the high school down the street, where my mother, very much against my wishes, signed me up for swimming lessons in the summer of '76, when I was thirteen, lessons that were emphatically unsuccessful. What I'm saying is this: if I had to guess at *MAD*'s target readers, they would be the suburban adolescents of summer with the comfort and time for the boredom that would turn their mocking attention to the world around them. That attitude was the heart of *MAD* itself. (Of course, if being Black does one thing for a person, it is to make that person skeptical. So maybe *MAD* and I took different routes to the same place.)

Why summer? The magazine was not published only during the summer, of course; I'm pretty sure "Sam and Roz Are Coming to Town" appeared as Christmas approached. But the summers of adolescence were the perfect time to find a comfortable spot and lazily turn the pages of *MAD*. The magazine itself seemed, on some level, to know this.

That was summer for us geezers, anyway, even the non-suburbanites among us. Children of subsequent generations—as I know, having helped raise two of them—have lives so packed year-round with activity, aimed at impressing the right high schools so they can impress the right colleges, that those hot, empty, aimless, endless summer days seem relegated to the past. We cannot turn back the clock, and it is useless to want to. Still, something has been lost. Those days could be boring, but they were also great for dreaming of what might come— maybe while walking slowly up the alley on your way to nowhere with a couple of friends, the sun high in the sky, maybe while staring at your bedroom ceiling in the middle of the afternoon. That dreaming involved, maybe inevitably, disdain for parts of the present. When *I* grow up, I'll write a TV show that's better than *this* crap, of which I've seen all the episodes, some of them three and four times. Those adults sitting around the pool in "The Lighter Side of Swimming Pools"—I know adults like them, my parents are kind of like them, but that's never going to be *me*, I'll tell you *that* much. You can rest easy, world. I'm here now.

Then we get older. We may move on from large swaths of pop culture, the subjects of *MAD*, or they may move on from us, after which the magazine, for that and other reasons, begins to hold less appeal. Mostly, our tastes have changed. Our summers fill up with work. If we're lucky, or hardheaded, or both, we never lose the impulse to dream, but those dreams tend to range less far from Earth. And if we have accrued any wisdom along the way, we come to some realizations about our relationship to the world. If we are lucky, and good, we may leave the world a little better than we found it—but leave it we will. Somehow, it will go on, just as it did before we came. We are not the world, nor are we above it; we are merely of it, until we aren't.

MAD knew that all along. It was, after all, created by adults. It put the evidence in front of us when we were kids; the memory of it winks at us now that we, too, are grown, now that we understand. *You made it*, this wink says.

Well, some have made it. Others never saw the email about how they are not the world, or its center, how the objects of one's skepticism and questioning should always include oneself. A number of things motivated the 2021 insurrectionists, and those things do not need enumerating here, but what underlies all of them is the deep-down realization that the world they had been promised, along with their place in it, was built on shifting sand. It is easier for them to rage at the truth than to question the lie. Their fury momentarily spent, they headed home to pay further tribute to their odious leader, no doubt looking for inspiration to old issues of *Cracked*.

"spy vs spy" vs. PROhÍas

Bonnie Altucher

N 1960, Antonio Prohías, a Cuban satirist living in political exile with his wife and children in one room in a
cruddy Queens fleabag, began putting together a portfolio
to show the editors of *MAD* magazine (which he already loved for its
"sublime, crazy" name but would never be able to read in English). The
thirty-nine-year-old cartoonist had just fled from Havana. His award-
winning career with *El Mundo* and other prominent media outlets
had ignominiously collapsed. Prohías left *El Mundo* in February 1959.
Later that year, Castro, having only recently presented Prohías with
the Juan Gualberto Gómez Cartoon of the Year Award (comparable to
a Pulitzer—Prohías had won it five times before), began sharply limit-
ing freedom of the press. The defiantly liberal Prohías, once known for
his cartoons mocking American-backed dictator Batista, had become
disenchanted with his revolutionary successor, now cozying up to the
Soviets. A kangaroo court of Prohías's newspaper colleagues, anxious
for political cover, called for his execution by firing squad.

In New York City, the fugitive cartoonist can only find employ-
ment as a presser in a garment factory, barely covering rent on the rat-
infested hotel room he shares with his wife and two children. On the
day of her fourteenth birthday, daughter Marta, an unconfident inter-
preter, accompanies her father to the appealingly shambolic offices of

MAD, whose creatives make do without support staff and are liable to spontaneously burst into opera. Despite the linguistic obstacles, Prohías's accomplished sketches seal the deal, and he exits with a hefty check. "Spy vs Spy" debuts its six-decade run.

This is the opening scene for a biopic I've been writing in my head for years about the persecuted political cartoonist who went on to create an enduring pop culture legacy. (And, yes, I realize I'm about to be scooped by a Ron Howard property featuring Ryan Gosling and, according to the *Daily Mail*, "physical and highly visual action . . . with two spies going mano a mano in ruthless fashion"). My own movie, light on physical action, would flash back to the urban Atlantis of prerevolutionary Havana, not the lurid playground for Mafia king-pins and Hollywood celebrities we know from the usual representations. Not to trivialize the social ills of sex work, the drug trade, and gambling, or to overlook the eco/human tragedy of the surrounding rural provinces despoiled by the extractive American sugar industry. But who could resist a time-travel hit of the sophisticated, progressive tropical city thriving in spite of Batista's kleptocratic rule, still flush with American corporate investment, boasting arcaded baroque palaces and futuristic art schools, a syncretic musical culture that launched a cascade of dance crazes worldwide and an energized creative class responsible for making Havana the media capital of Latin America?

Prohías grew up as the handsome, vaguely bohemian child of a respectable middle-class family, defying his father's practical ambitions to establish himself as a political cartoonist, winning the highest professional honors while still in his mid-twenties. Despite his reputation as a supportive, affectionate father, and friend, Prohías's Cuban work displayed a cruel, Buñuelian streak. One cartoon shows a woman whose trip to the "Venus de Milo Beauty Shop" results in her emerging sans arms. Castro, in last-resort negotiation with the Soviets, could not have been thrilled with the panel depicting a hungry skeleton struggling to eat his dinner with a hammer and sickle.

I first learned of the Prohías saga from my late friend Robert Morales, pop culture savant (and author of *Truth: Red, White and Black*, the secret history of Black Captain America). Our long friendship was partly cemented by our common experience as two shrimpy, alienated '60s kids eager to widen the scope of our immigrant upbringing by reading anything irreverent we could get our hands on, beginning with *MAD*. I still remember the pre-readerly focus demanded by the Rube Goldberg plotlines of "Spy vs Spy," the enveloping spell of a narrative sequence that didn't make sense to me yet. As Peter Kuper, the artist most associated with the strip after Prohías retired in 1990, observes, "Spy vs Spy" was a gateway to *MAD* for the preliterate. Prohías compensated for his lack of English fluency with an elaborate Esperanto of rigged alarm clocks, falling bowling balls, deceptive wind-up toys, exploding chicken eggs. And then there was the stylized ambiguity of the spies themselves, long-beaked humanoids with gleaming, psychopathic eyes, their neotenous bodies cloaked in monkish spy-wear. The cartoonist's knack for humanizing specificity—a quizzically hunched shoulder, string-bean arms, perversely dainty boots, the naked-looking hands and feet—conjures a semi-relatable pair of unkillable predators. (The same insinuating mix of intimacy and derision elevates Prohías's caricature of Castro as a Rabelaisian military blowhard, beard metastasizing everywhere like curly pubic hair.) Though the strip's Cold War context may have been obscure to younger readers, its situation—an inseparable dyad married to their nihilistic tit-for-tat—must have felt depressingly familiar to certain children. My mother and father spent nearly a decade in a vicious court battle over my custody, only to hand off the raising of me to my grandparents. Marta Prohías recalls her father's encouraging correspondence with one child from an unhappy family who had enclosed his own artwork in fan mail. Kids growing up with that kind of contentiousness had a head start in grokking the absurdist hellscape of "Spy"-world.

Every "Spy" installment is predictable. Despite the farcical complexity, we always know how it will end. Repetition and symmetry are encoded in "Spy vs Spy," both in the antagonists' indistinguishability and in the formal diptych structure of each episode, beginning with a self-contained splash panel in which one spy's victory forecasts his defeat at the end of the main sequence and vice versa, each methodical reversal as formally elegant as a playing card, and as pointedly stilted as *Last Year at Marienbad*. (The diptych format persisted for nine years, until it was simplified in 1969.) At the core of this frenzy lies stasis, a vacuum where nothing can live. Like the roughly contemporaneous *Dr. Strangelove*, "Spy vs Spy" specifically dramatizes the way in which Thanatos manifests itself in geopolitics, showing the arms race more as masculine psychosis—a phallic acceleration toward mass oblivion—than rational statecraft.

Prohías triangulates this dynamic with a voluptuous Eros, the Lady in Grey, appearing from 1962 to 1965. Her plump-shouldered, blond sensuality, harlequin glasses, and blistering grin evoke an eerie hybrid: Cheshire Cat plus Doris Day. One glimpse of this picture-hatted femme fatale relaxing in a hammock with her naked toes piquantly curling discombobulates the spies like a hit of military-grade LSD, plopping them into the traps she (via Prohías) devises for them. In his words, "The lady spy represents neutrality." I think she serves as a feminine proxy for the author himself, whose refusal to propagandize for any party eventually made him non grata, along with his family. "The sweetest revenge has been to turn Fidel's accusation of me as a spy into a money-making venture," he told the *Miami Herald*. At *MAD*, he pivoted to a more abstract indictment of Cold War brinksmanship.

Act Two of my movie takes place in 1961, right after our humiliating debacle in Cuba's Bay of Pigs. My fictionalized cartoonist, finally feeling like he may have landed on his feet, is approached by two identically suited agents, maybe over *picadillo* in a bustling Cuban café. Why wouldn't there be a dossier on Prohías on file somewhere at Langley? Especially in light of the FBI's well-documented paranoia regarding not-very-radical *MAD*. A chat along the lines of "It would be a shame if those nice kids of yours had a problem with their visas," concludes with "We need you to do us a favor, though." Cue one of the agency's many ludicrous plots to assassinate Castro: botulism-tainted cigars, an exploding seashell (Fidel was an avid scuba diver), or the old room-service/depilatory trick, in which a hotel "chambermaid" powders *El Jefe*'s army boots with a systemic toxin guaranteed to make his beard fall out. There are more where those came from. No scheme is implausible.

With animated spies jabbering at each ear—Black and White, unreliable strategists—my Prohías manages to give his handlers the slip and survives the insane operation. Which is really a MacGuffin to allow for a rich slew of zeitgeisty set pieces, from the gemütlich to the ridiculous. On any random stroll through New York City in that era you might have encountered the Women's Strike for Peace or seen high and low art making Ben Day–dot babies in Bonwit Teller's Fifth Avenue windows, courtesy of Andy Warhol. People still gazed at each other while striding incredibly swiftly and young children played in the street unsupervised. There were too many epoch-making performances to choose from—Bob Dylan opening for John Lee Hooker, Miriam Makeba onstage with Nina Simone. A thousand used bookstores. And everywhere, immigrants, buying newspapers in so many languages, flooding out of the sweatshops and restaurant kitchens and onto the subways. And how many thinking, *It's not home and we're broke, but at least we'll survive here. It isn't the firing squad.*

mind the gap

Sarah Boxer

I'M GONNA be honest with all you *MAD* lovers. I never got past Alfred E. Neuman's face on the cover and I don't care. I don't think I was meant to get past it anyway. That big-eared, glassy-eyed, gap-toothed snot was *MAD*'s bouncer. Alfred E. Neuman stopped me by being so unappealing that I had no wish to see what was beyond him. His mug was a giant "No Girls Allowed!" sign on the clubhouse.

By the time I was in college, I came to associate *MAD* magazine with the mean, male humor that reigned at the *Harvard Lampoon* in the 1970s and '80s. Although I loved comedy and comics and had some vague idea that I might like to try stand-up, I steered clear of the *Lampoon*. I was afraid of the hazing involved, and besides, I didn't like the snorting, snucking vibe. Somewhere lurking in the background was my recollection of Alfred E. Neuman's smug smile.

Repelled though I was, I was fascinated, sucked in, by one detail—the gap in the grin. I couldn't look away. That gap—which has a name (diastema, from the Greek word for "space"), a reputation (it has been used to signal female lust ever since Geoffrey Chaucer wrote of the "gap-toothed Wife of Bath" in *The Canterbury Tales*), a movie (*Gap-Toothed Women* by Les Blank, 1987), a diagnosis (Williams Syndrome), and a history (as you'll see)—was, for me, a portal to the mysterious realm beyond it. It was my way into *MAD*. So here goes: let's dive into the teeth of that placid, self-satisfied, "What, me worry?" face.

Before drawing the gap-toothed boy, Norman Mingo was known primarily for his pictures of Vargas-style pinup girls, his movie posters, and his ads. He began drawing the kid who would become Alfred E. Neuman in 1956, when he was sixty years old. But he did not invent that glazed doughnut of a face. It was borrowed, copied, stolen. Even Alfred E. Neuman's motto, "What, me worry?", wasn't original, as Harvey Kurtzman, one of *MAD*'s founders, freely admitted. In fact, it was Kurtzman himself who dug up some of the original sources, in the hopes of skirting a copyright infringement lawsuit.

In 1965, *MAD* magazine was sued by the widow of a cartoonist named Harry Spencer Stuff, who had, some fifty years earlier, drawn a smiley, big-eared, freckle-faced, gap-toothed boy for a dentist. Copyrighted in 1914, the image was dubbed "The Original Optimist," or the "Me-Worry?" Boy. But that was not its first appearance. Not by a long shot. As Sam Sweet observed in a 2016 article for the *Paris Review*, the Me-Worry Boy had a long history both before and after its 1914 copyright. "He was there on a 1942 matchbook for an auto-parts store in Longhorn, Texas; on the label of Happy Jack, a soda produced in 1939; on the menu for a coffee shop in Ashland, Nebraska; in a 1908 calendar for antikamnia, a cure-all painkiller spiked with heroin; in a 1905 ad for 'painless dentistry' . . . and in a 1902 playbill for Maloney's Wedding Day, a small-market musical comedy."

In *Completely MAD: A History of the Comic Book and Magazine*, Maria Reidelbach took the Me-Worry Boy back further—to an 1895 advertisement for Atmore's Mince Meat and Genuine English Plum Pudding: "The kid's features are fully developed and unmistakable," she noted, "and the image was very likely taken from an older archetype that has yet to be found." Then a patent attorney, Peter Reitan, found an earlier rendition—an 1894 ad for *The New Boy*, a London farce. Under his face are the words "What's the Good of Anything?—Nothing!"

In every precedent, as Sweet noted, the boy has "mussed red hair, saucer ears, and a shit-eating grin, minus a tooth." And in most cases, he also comes with a who-cares motto. Once the court saw those ancestors of Alfred E. Neuman, they ruled in favor of *MAD*: "Neuman was a fatherless mutant of the public domain." He was there for the taking. *MAD* ran with it, made it its own, used it on hundreds of covers until the Me-Worry Boy was inextricably linked to *MAD*.

This seems to have been a big part of *MAD*'s strategy—borrowing and, in some cases, burying the debt. I guess this is pretty obvious. *MAD was* after all a magazine of parody and satire. Without the originals, *MAD* probably would not have existed. So, it's no shock that *MAD* was always anxious about its sources. On its masthead, listed just after "Creative Consultant" and just before "Logistics," was a position simply called "Lawsuits." Apparently, this job was not mostly for obscenity or libel cases, as one might guess, but for copyright infringement.

In many instances, in its parodies of ads, poems, songs, television shows, and movies, *MAD* proudly laid bare its borrowings. But there is a thin line between making fun of others' work and making off with it. In *Completely MAD*, Reidelbach notes that in the early 1960s, after producing "Sing Along with *MAD*," a booklet of songs that included such parodies as "I Swat You Hard on the Skin" (to be sung to the tune of "I've Got You Under My Skin") and "When They Bring in the Machine" (sung to "Begin the Beguine"), *MAD* was sued by the Music Publishers Protective Association on behalf of Irving Berlin, Richard Rodgers, and Cole Porter.

The 1963 ruling was mixed. Twenty-three of the parodies were ruled fair game, but two of them—"Always," a song about endless psychotherapy, and "There's No Business Like No Business"—were ruled too similar to the originals. The music association, unhappy with the verdict, pressed their case and their luck, but ended up in even worse shape. Irving R. Kaufman, the new judge (who was best known for sentencing the Rosenbergs to death), defended the rights of *MAD*, saying "we believe that parody and satire are deserving of substantial freedom—both as entertainment and as a form of social and literary criticism."

I agree. I support a right to parody, especially when it is social criticism, and even more when it's funny. Some of *MAD*'s parodies were one or the other or both. The spoofing ad for Carry-on cigarettes (*MAD*'s twist on Tareytons), drawn by Al Feldstein, proclaiming "Us Cigarette-Makers will fight rather than quit," certainly qualified as social criticism. And *MAD*'s print parody titled "Hochman's Heroes," conceived by Al Siegel and set in the fun bunks of the Buchenwald concentration camp, did a fine job pointing out what was offensive about *Hogan's Heroes*. In a bit of biting dialogue, one of the pinstriped inmates yucks it up: "Yes, sir—this is American Television Humor at its best!"

But what about something like "Superduperman!" dreamed up by Kurtzman and drawn by Wally Wood in 1953? Is it social criticism? Is it funny? What does it add to the original? The drawings are energetic, funny, and expressive—I actually prefer them to Joe Shuster's originals—and there are some priceless moments in them. I particularly admire the phone booth scene, where Clark Bent, nebbish supreme, sheds his clothes to become Superduperman while an angry line forms for the phone. But the underlying message stinks. The Clark Kent character, a sniveling "man assistant to the copy boy," lusts after Lois Pain, a shallow, bored snob. What's the social commentary? This: working women are nothing more than steel-hearted bitches and the men who work with them do not view them as potential allies or competition but only as possible pieces of ass.

I have no idea what the owners of *Superman*, National Periodicals, thought of the blatant misogyny (and misanthropy) of "Superduperman!" but they clearly thought that *MAD*'s satire endangered *Superman*. As Maria Reidelbach notes in *Completely MAD*, National Periodicals "threatened *MAD* with a lawsuit for infringement." Ultimately *MAD* was advised to avoid parodies of *Superman*, but the magazine, recognizing that its whole future depended on such borrowings, totally ignored the recommendation and went on its merry way, as if to say, "What, me worry?"

But *MAD*'s devil-may-care facade has, I think, always pointed to a bedeviling worry—to the fear of being seen not only as a thief but as an incompetent and unfunny thief. As NPR's Stephen Thompson, speaking of "Weird Al" Yankovic's parodic gifts, recently observed, "One of the central rules of satire, of parody—you have to be able to do the thing you're parodying or satirizing as well or better than the source material. And if you don't, people can see the strings." That is, "Eat It" must be roughly as good as (and a helluva lot funnier than) "Beat It." Otherwise, what's the point?

I hear an objection out there. *MAD*, you protest, was a lot more than parody. And that's true. There were, for instance, original cartoons by Mort Drucker, Don Martin, Sergio Aragonés, and others. But if you look into some of the things the magazine is best known for—not just Alfred E. Neuman's face, but Al Jaffee's "Snappy Answers to Silly Questions," and Antonio Prohías's comic "Spy vs Spy"—you will see that even these features have progenitors. And some of those ancestors are pretty well buried.

Take Jaffee's "Snappy Answers." In an interview that ran in *Vulture*, Jaffee, who invented "Inferior Man," a comic featuring a superhero who changes into civilian clothes when the going gets tough, and the magazine's trademark Fold-In, a clever reversal of *Playboy*'s foldouts, recalls how he came up with "Snappy Answers" in October 1965, while fixing an antenna on his roof: "Suddenly, I heard my son climbing up this ladder. He asked me a question that he asked every time he came home from school: 'Where's Mom?' And I answered, 'I killed her and I'm stuffing her down this chimney.' He knew I was kidding, obviously."

Never mind the casual misogyny. There's a notable absence, a gap, in this origin story: in 1908, decades before "Snappy Answers," Rube Goldberg began drawing "Foolish Questions," one-panel comics offering snide answers to stupid questions for the *New York Evening Mail*. For example, "Foolish Question No. 4" shows a man coming into his house soaking wet with an umbrella. His wife asks: "Why, dearie, did you get wet?" He responds: "Of course not—the rain is dry today." (Once again, a woman is the butt of the humor.) "Foolish Questions" was invented almost sixty years before "Snappy Answers," a fact that the obituaries for Jaffee in *The New York Times* and *Rolling Stone* both neglected to mention.

What about "Spy vs Spy"? I'd always assumed this was a wholly original *MAD* feature. But it's not precisely so. "Spy vs Spy," drawn by Prohías, a Cuban artist, beginning in January 1961, stars two beaked creatures, one black, one white, bent on mutual annihilation. The crazy contraptions that these two spies set up to destroy each other harken back to Rube Goldberg's inventions, which date to 1914. The creatures themselves seem to owe a lot to Paul Terry's Heckle and Jeckle, two identical wisecracking magpies, who had their first flight in 1946. And their endless war has at least two precedents, the forever battles between the Roadrunner and Wile E. Coyote, which began in 1949, and those in George Herriman's *Krazy Kat* comic, starting in 1913.

I do like "Spy vs Spy." And I think Prohías was clever to have repurposed these old original sources into a new Cold War–era cartoon. Besides, the history of cartooning, like the history of jazz or art, is filled with quotes and borrowings. Still, I have to say that a lot of *MAD*'s knock-offs make me long for the originals. I'd rather look at the work of George Herriman or Rube Goldberg or Paul Terry any day of the week. And I don't like it when forebears are forgotten. To put it in modern terms, imagine if "Weird Al" Yankovic were to blot out Michael Jackson.

This brings me back to the gap-toothed boy. I believe that the "What, me worry?" face actually camouflages and betrays a real worry, which happens to be closely tied to both *MAD*'s genius and its animus. In *The Anxiety of Influence*, Harold Bloom pinpointed the greatest anxiety of great artists and poets: "what strong maker desires the realization that he has failed to create himself?" *MAD* was not merely in the business of parody and satire, but also in the business of cover-up, of hiding its debts to its progenitors. Why? Could it be because *MAD* worried that its knock-offs would be viewed as inferior?

Parody is a form of domination. It thrives on biting (and in some cases devouring) the hand that feeds it. This is painfully clear in Will Elder's *Wonder Woman* knock-off "Woman Wonder!" (#10, April 1954). The original *Wonder Woman* comic, created by William Moulton Marston, a feminist who dreamed of women ruling the world, featured a race of superwomen who need no men. In the parody, a guy in a bat costume, who uses the name Nivlem (Melvin spelled backwards), takes away Woman Wonder's bullet-repelling bracelets and overpowers her. She ends up on a pile of glass shards as Nivlem stands over her proclaiming: "Woman Wonder! Now that your face is lifted to me, so tenderly in tearful supplication, I can do only one thing . . .

Smash it in with me hob-nailed boot! . . . I've been planning for years to beat you to a bloody pulp!"

Geez. Violence much? The last frame shows the former Woman Wonder married to Nivlem. She is beaten down, slaving over a hot stove, while her horrible children scream and run wild. Yes, I suppose you could read it as a hilarious spoof of male supremacist fantasies, but to my eye, the unbridled joy taken in this drawing of a female superhero trampled, humiliated, and defeated expresses pure misogyny. And my guess is that behind this hatred of women there is envy. Envy? Of what?

As I've said before, my sole way into *MAD* was the gap in the "What, me worry?" face. The gap in the grin, as I see it, betokens the dark, mysterious, feminine place where men and boys—always the primary audience for *MAD*—fear to tread. I believe this gap points straight to a profound angst—to the fear that all of one's best ideas have come from others, that one is, at heart, uncreative and unfruitful. In short, it's a close cousin to womb envy (a concept theorized by the neo-Freudian Karen Horney), which is marked by a compulsion to compensate for one's procreative deficiencies by creating male-only worlds and by denigrating women. Now I think I know why Alfred E. Neuman, the very heart and soul and face of *MAD*, blocked my passage. Behind that insipid grin, *MAD*'s bouncer was betraying a most primitive male fear. To those who dare enter the *MAD* world, I have a little advice: mind the gap.

**G**ROWING UP IN SWEDEN, I WAS FIRST INTRODUCED TO MAD MAGAZINE IN THE SHAPE OF ITS SWEDISH EDITION WHICH INCLUDED LOCALLY PRODUCED CONTENT MOCKING SWEDISH TV SHOWS, MOVIES AND CULTURE IN GENERAL. IT WAS EDITED BY LEGENDARY WRITER AND COMEDIAN LASSE O'MÅNSSON, WHOSE EDITORIALS PROVIDED AN INIMITABLE TOUCH IN LINE WITH THE HONORABLE SWEDISH TRADITION OF DESPERATE AND ABSURD HUMOR. ALREADY PAST ITS PEAK BY 1973 WHEN I DISCOVERED IT, TOGETHER WITH THE POCKETBOOK REPRINTS OF THE COMICS BY KURTZMAN, JACK DAVIS, WILL ELDER AND JOHN SEVERIN, IT WAS STILL ENOUGH TO TURN MY ELEVEN-YEAR-OLD WORLD UPSIDE DOWN. MAD IS NOW CANCELLED BUT THE WORLD REMAINS IN THE SAME POSITION.

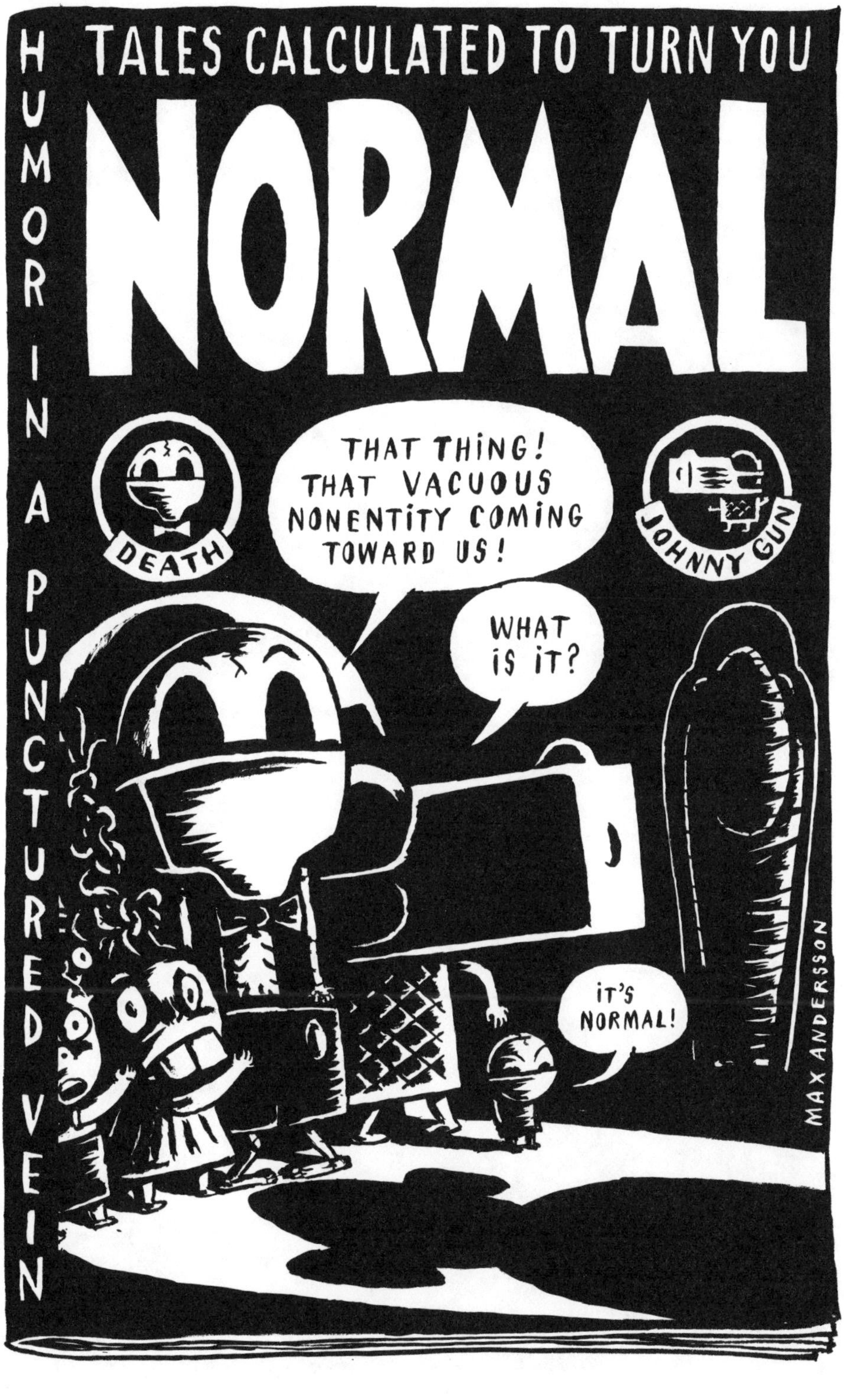
TALES CALCULATED TO TURN YOU
NORMAL
HUMOR IN A PUNCTURED VEIN
DEATH
JOHNNY GUN
THAT THING! THAT VACUOUS NONENTITY COMING TOWARD US!
WHAT IS IT?
IT'S NORMAL!
MAX ANDERSSON

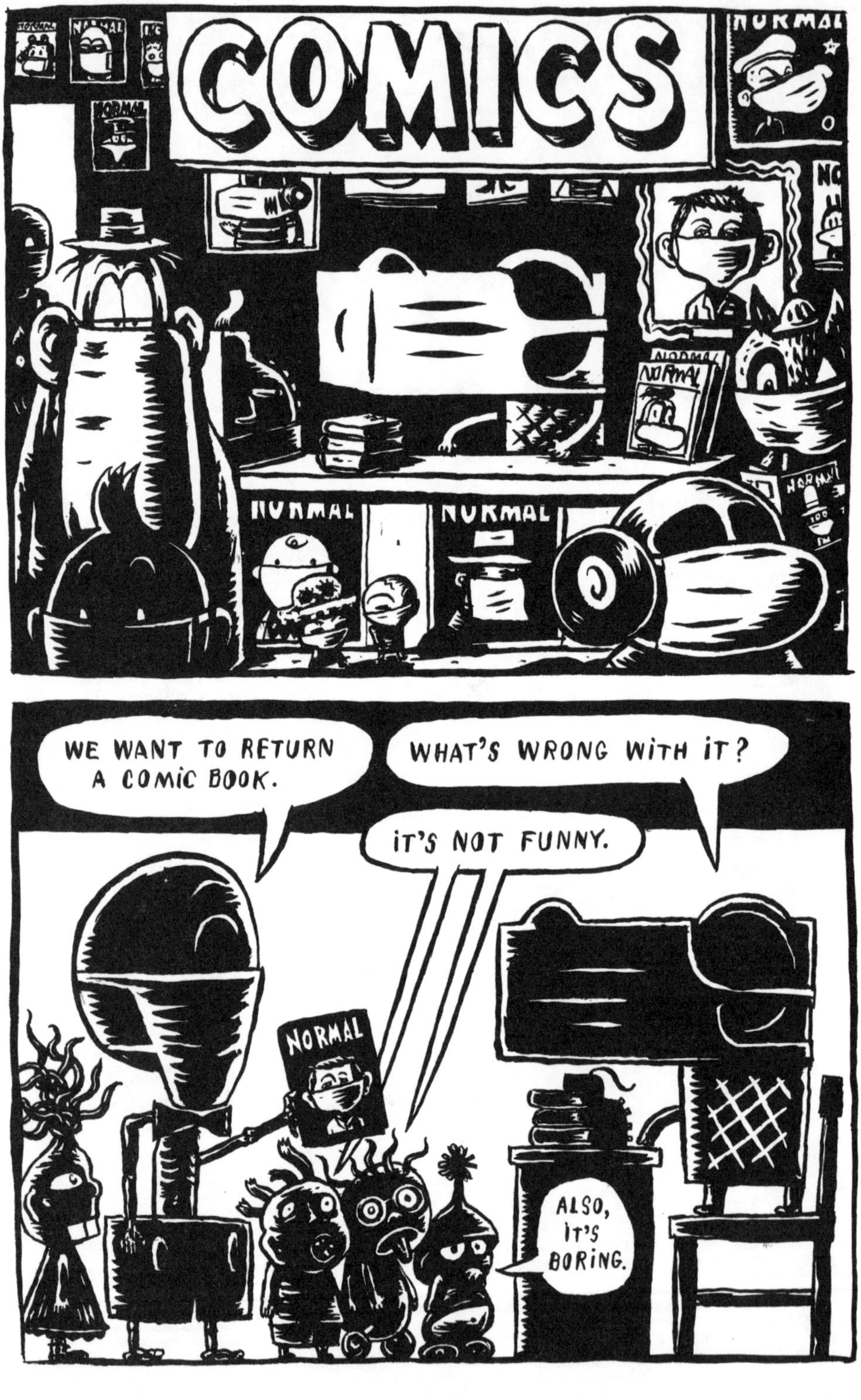
NORMAL
NORMAL
NORMAL
COMICS
NORMAL
NORMAL
NORMAL
NORMAL
NORMAL
NORMAL
WE WANT TO RETURN A COMIC BOOK.
WHAT'S WRONG WITH IT?
IT'S NOT FUNNY.
NORMAL
ALSO, IT'S BORING.

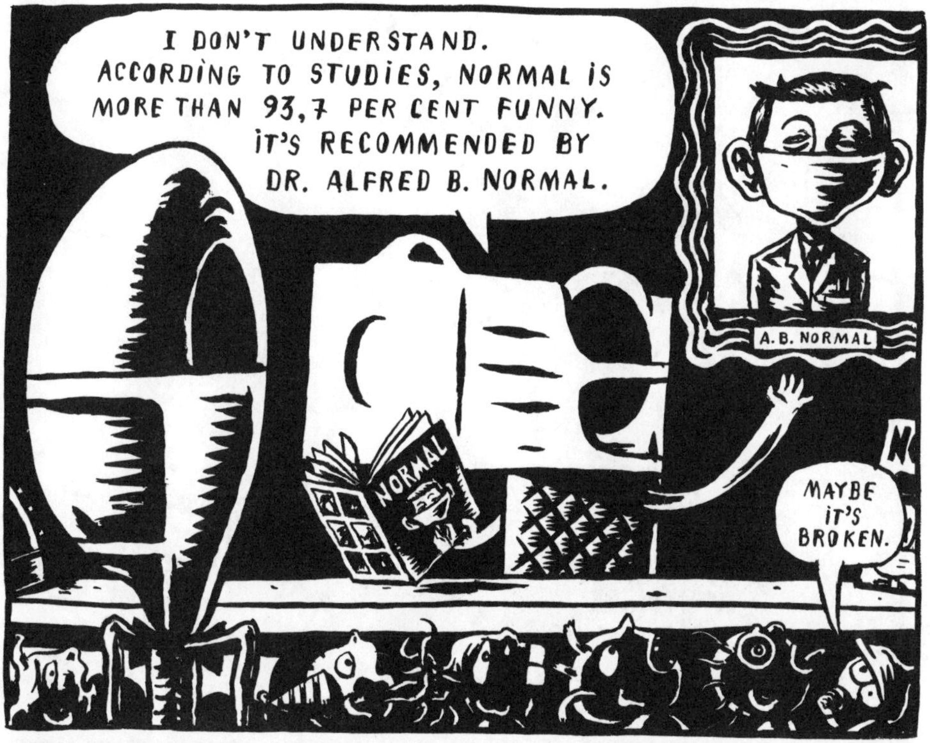
I DON'T UNDERSTAND. ACCORDING TO STUDIES, NORMAL IS MORE THAN 93,7 PER CENT FUNNY. IT'S RECOMMENDED BY DR. ALFRED B. NORMAL.
A.B. NORMAL
NORMAL
MAYBE IT'S BROKEN.

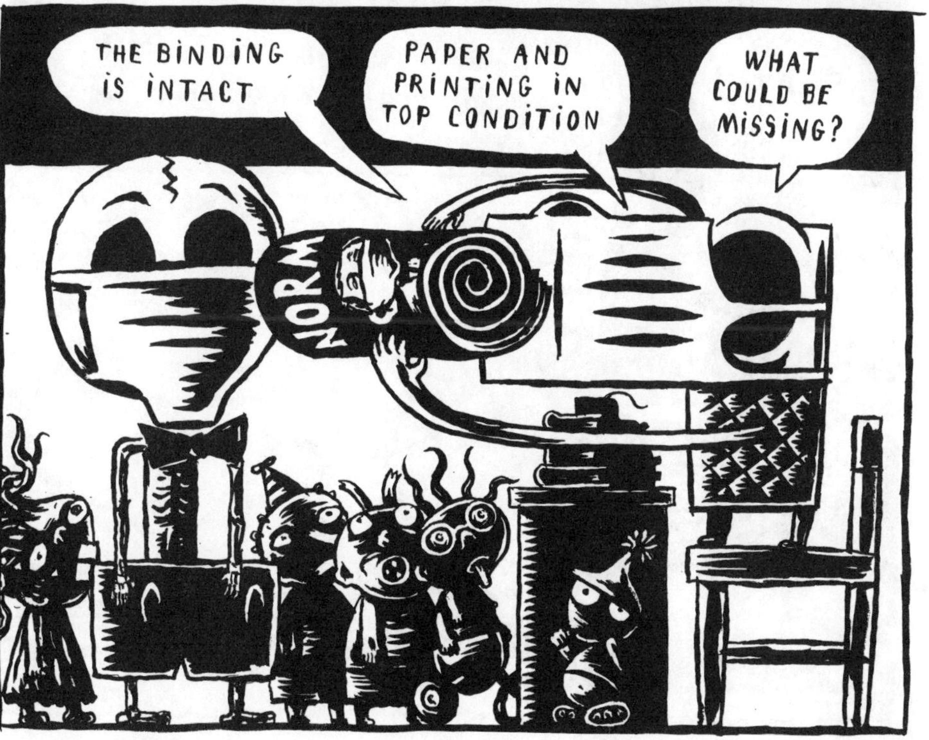
THE BINDING IS INTACT
PAPER AND PRINTING IN TOP CONDITION
WHAT COULD BE MISSING?
NORM

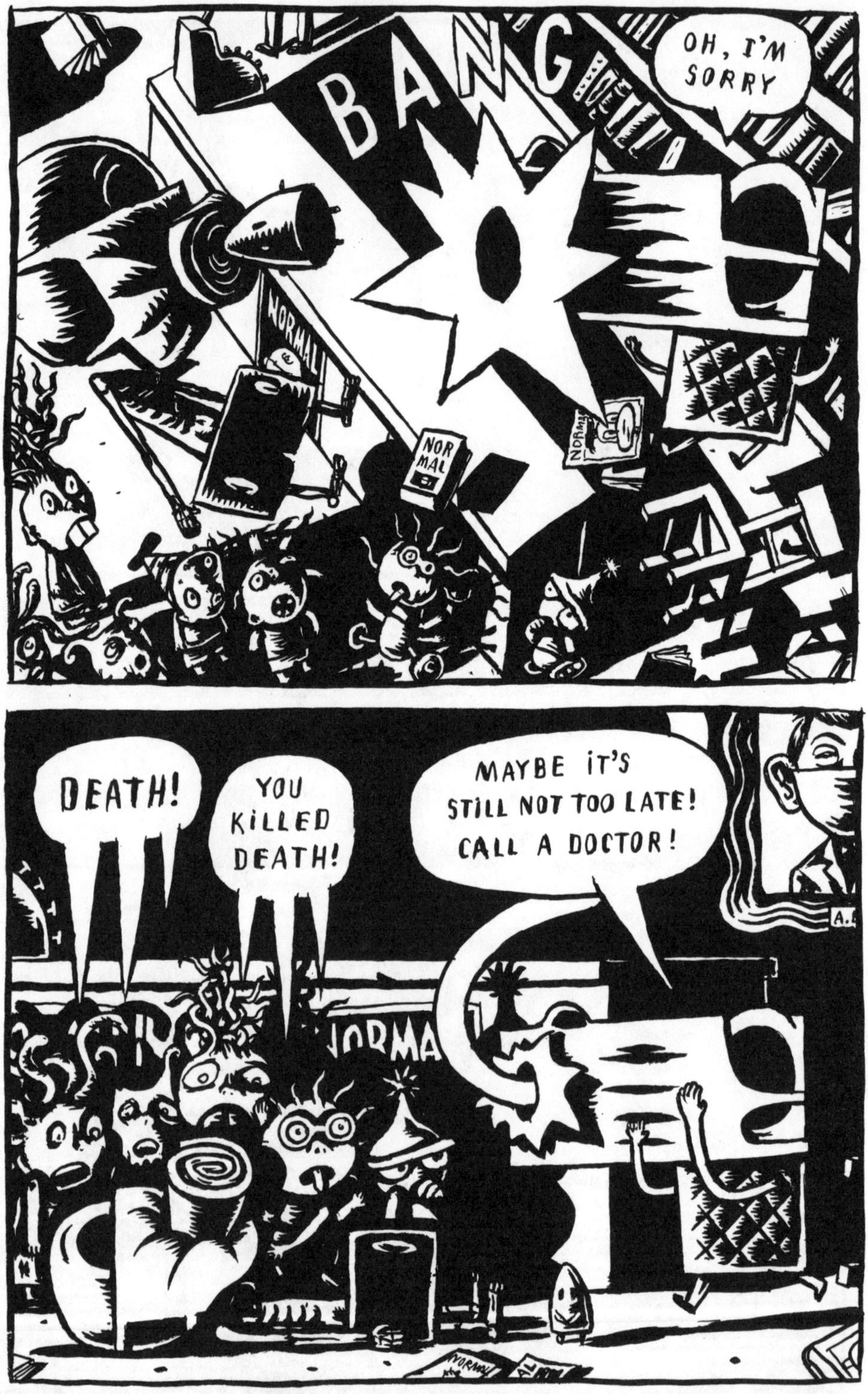
BANG
OH, I'M SORRY
NORMAL
NOR MAL
DEATH!
YOU KILLED DEATH!
MAYBE IT'S STILL NOT TOO LATE! CALL A DOCTOR!
NORMA

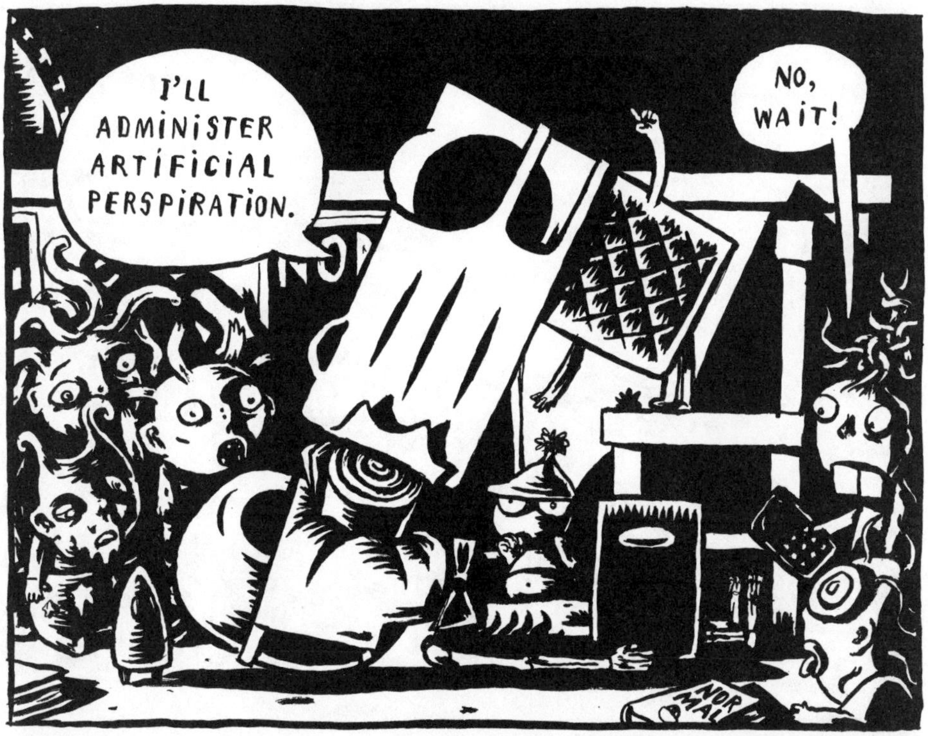
I'LL ADMINISTER ARTIFICIAL PERSPIRATION.
NO, WAIT!
NORMAL

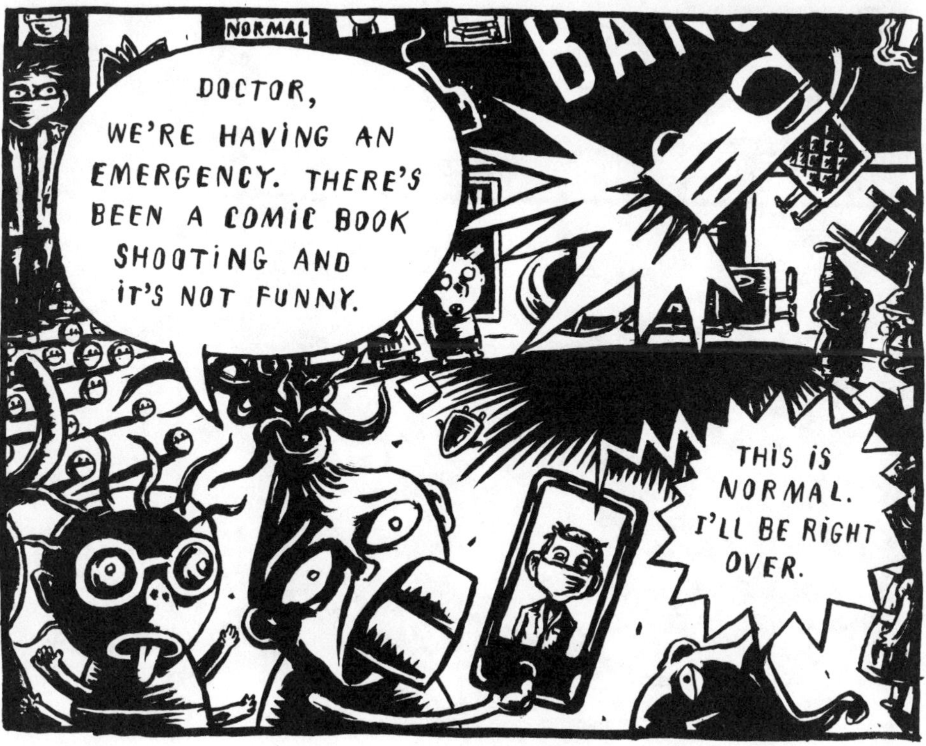
NORMAL
BANG
DOCTOR, WE'RE HAVING AN EMERGENCY. THERE'S BEEN A COMIC BOOK SHOOTING AND IT'S NOT FUNNY.
THIS IS NORMAL. I'LL BE RIGHT OVER.

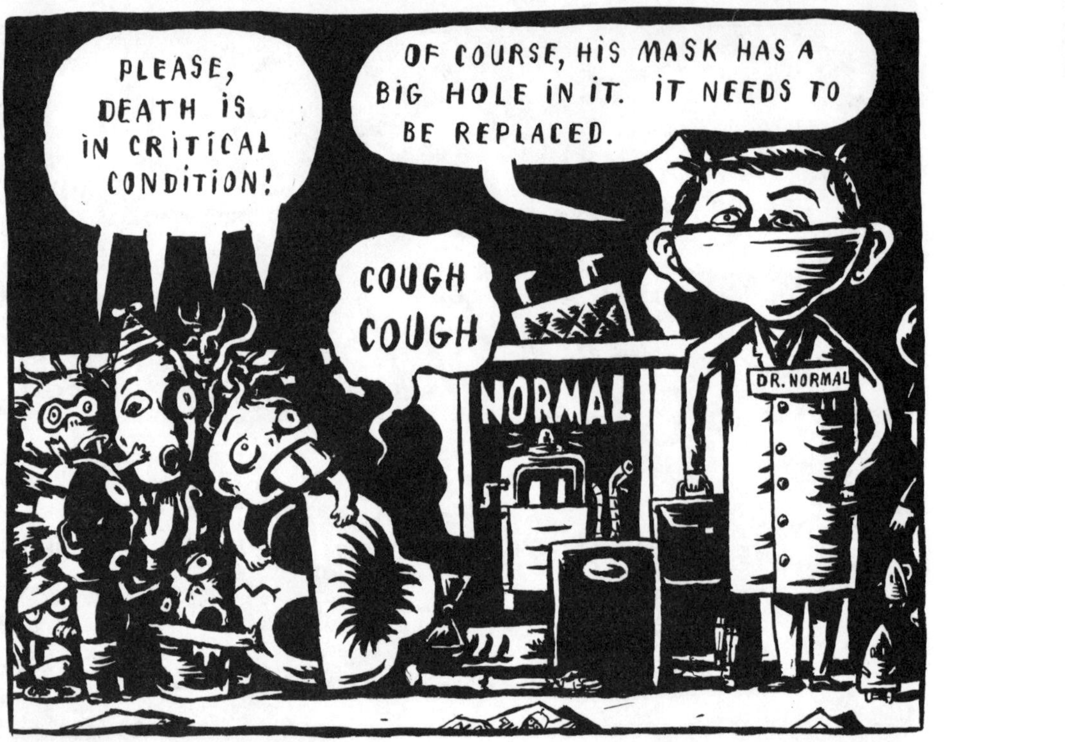
PLEASE, DEATH IS IN CRITICAL CONDITION!
OF COURSE, HIS MASK HAS A BIG HOLE IN IT. IT NEEDS TO BE REPLACED.
COUGH COUGH
NORMAL
DR. NORMAL

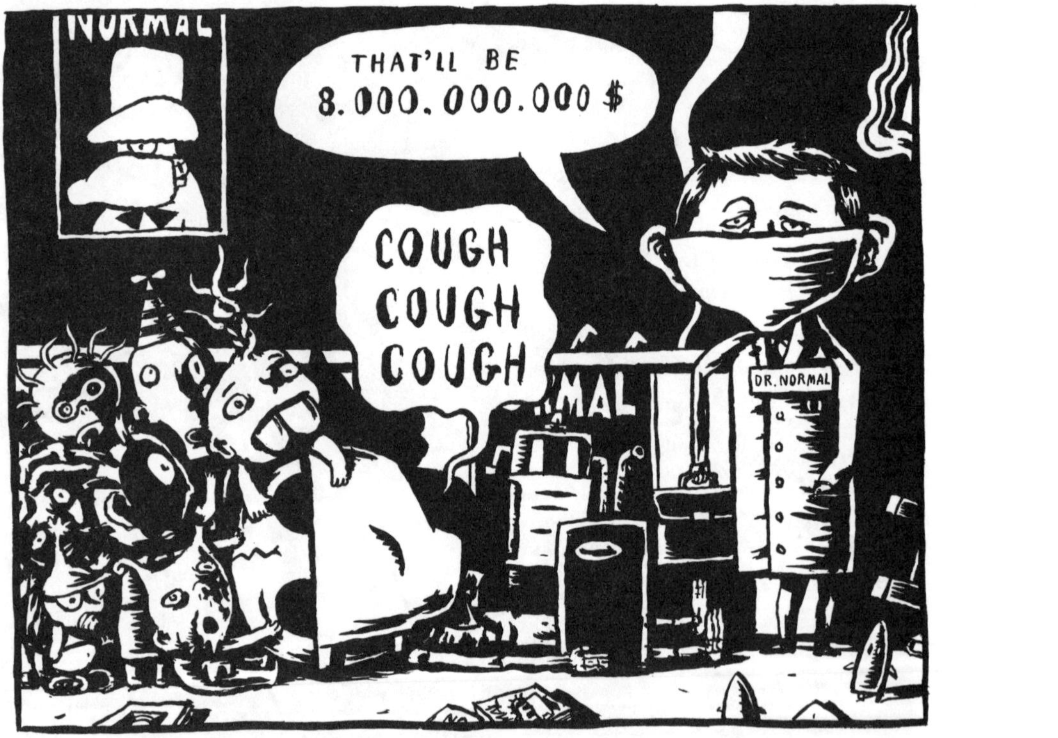
NORMAL
THAT'LL BE 8.000.000.000 $
COUGH COUGH COUGH
DR. NORMAL

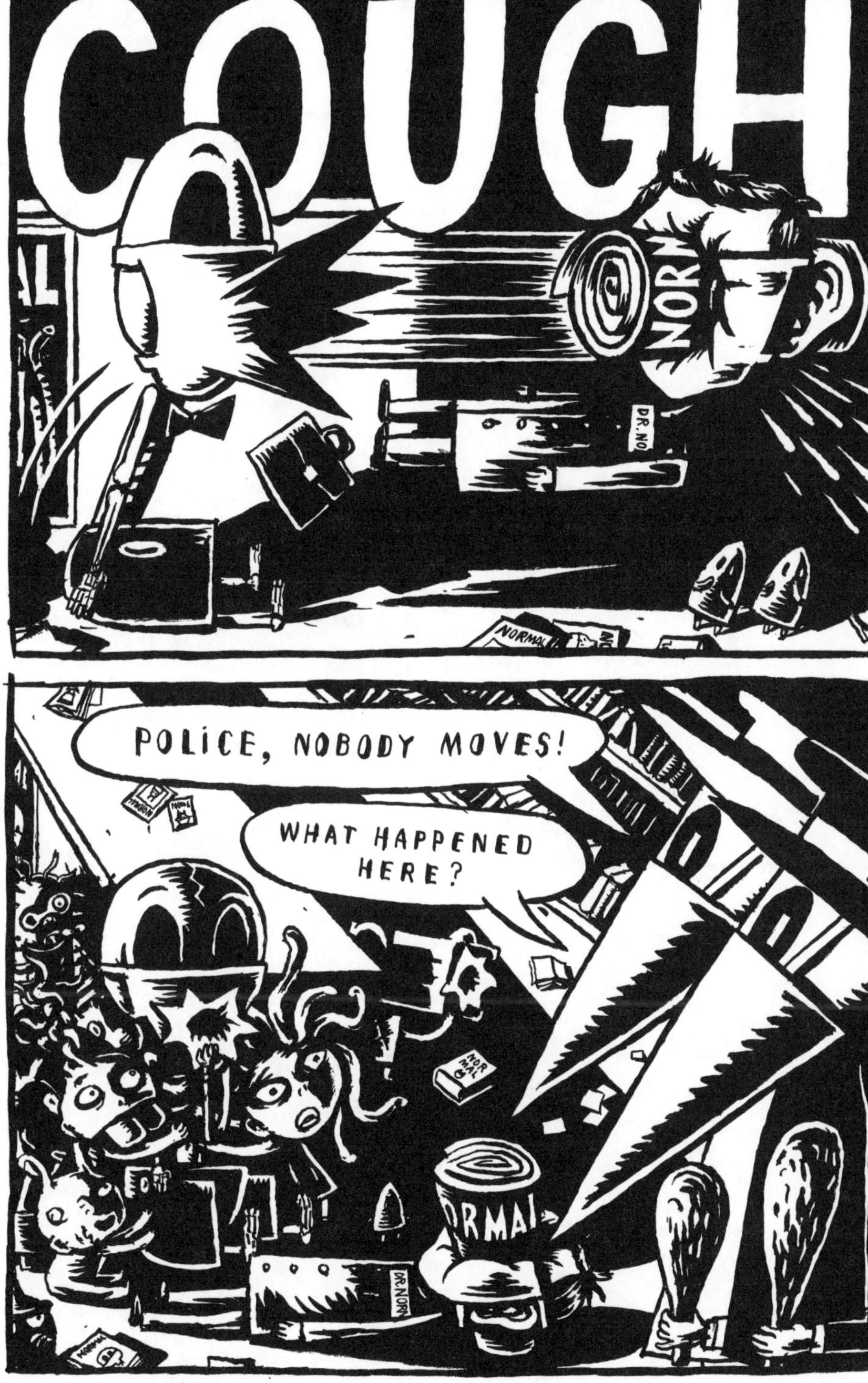
COUGH
NORMAL
POLICE, NOBODY MOVES!
WHAT HAPPENED HERE?

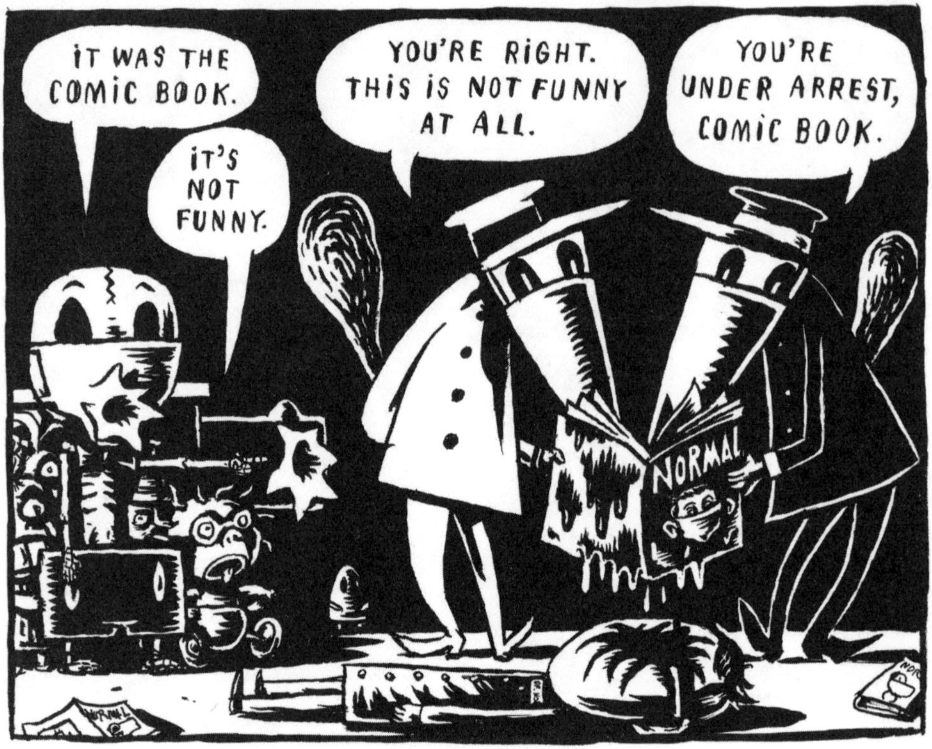
IT WAS THE COMIC BOOK.
IT'S NOT FUNNY.
YOU'RE RIGHT. THIS IS NOT FUNNY AT ALL.
YOU'RE UNDER ARREST, COMIC BOOK.
NORMAL

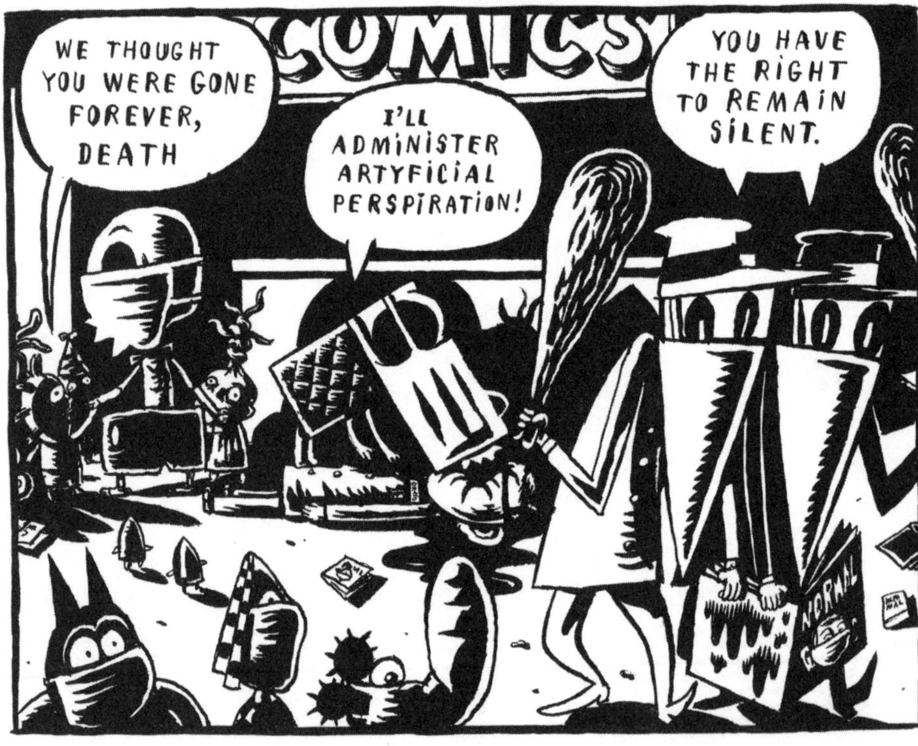
COMICS
WE THOUGHT YOU WERE GONE FOREVER, DEATH
I'LL ADMINISTER ARTYFICIAL PERSPIRATION!
YOU HAVE THE RIGHT TO REMAIN SILENT.
NORMAL

MAD, the '50s, and the '60s: a (slightly) dissident view

Adam Gopnik

"THE BIBLE "of twelve-year-olds"—that was the critic Paul Goodman's somewhat but not entirely dismissive summing up of the role of *MAD* magazine in '50s culture, in his once famous 1960 book *Growing Up Absurd.* *MAD* belonged, then, it seemed, to the literature of juvenile delinquency, for good or ill. Goodman's subject—and, it seemed, the satiric magazine's—was the internal revolt of teenagers and younger people, identified clearly as a class, an interest group, a subdivision of the population, for perhaps the first time in history. They had a music (Elvis and Chuck Berry), a set of movie stars (Brando and Dean), and, in the form of Alfred E. Neuman, the mascot of *MAD*, at last a court jester.

This sense of what *MAD* might have been, and of what the '50s were, is by now so deep-set as to be close to an American legend, or even a kind of myth. By now, the insistence that *MAD* was the one place that was *not* mad is commonplace; it's seen as a kind of isolated, underground beacon of under-crust lust and underclass revolt—with the underclass in this case not being the oppressed or *Misérables* of the street but the eighth-grade outcasts, forced into shop class. *MAD*, like the companion invader of rock 'n' roll, was a kind of bacillus resisted by the bulwark-like immunities of American conservative culture—or, perhaps better, a series of pimply sappers, undermining it. The battle for the underground man—or, in this case, underground adolescent—was eventually won, but is always being refought, with the twin demons of commercial co-option on the one hand and censorship on the other always threatening.

This hero epic of subversion and resistance is so central to the way we tell stories about ourselves that it seems essential to retell them again and again. It's very important for the makers of American pop culture to insist on their own history of persecution—even when it was, in retrospect, nonexistent or minimal. We hear a lot about what rock 'n' rollers weren't allowed to do—about Elvis's hips or Mick Jagger's lyrics—even though we know that, in the fight between repression and rock 'n' roll, there's no question which side won, and won by a rout. The truer story is harder to tell—the story of a "mainstream" far more inclusive (and commercially avaricious for novelty) than our heroic legends may capture, and of a dissent far more varied and handmade than the stories of persecution suggest.

The facts of *MAD*'s origins are often and briefly told. Harvey Kurtzman, a typical lower-middle-class Jewish kid from Brooklyn, had gone to work for the most notorious of all the New York comic book publishers, EC Comics, whose line of existing grisly horror comics—*The Vault of Horror, The Crypt of Terror*—occasioned Frederic Wertham's once famous polemic *The Seduction of the Innocent* and eventually led to the self-censoring comics code. Kurtzman, though working for a living, disliked the horror comics and sought to humanize them by making "war comics" into a recognizably realistic form, conscientiously, even obsessively, researched to reflect the truths of combat. In 1952, he urged William Gaines, the owner of EC, to issue a satiric publication, and the result in the autumn of 1952 was *MAD*. Kurtzman turned his attention to the whole exploding world of the American media, as it was blossoming in the first fully televised age. He and his colleagues mocked Howdy Doody and the western and the new youth movies and even classic comic books.

Kurtzman's *MAD* was the first satiric enterprise that got its effects almost exclusively from parodying other forms of popular entertainment. Like Lenny Bruce, whom he influenced, Kurtzman saw that the conventions of pop culture ran so deep in his audience—and already stood at so great a remove from real experience—that you could create a new kind of satire just by inventorying them. As I wrote thirty years ago, almost all American satire today, from *The Onion* to the ongoing *Saturday Night Live*, follows a formula that Harvey Kurtzman invented for *MAD*.

Like all entrenched histories, this origin story of *MAD* has as much truth in it as not, and yet, like all entrenched histories, it also contains elements of myth. First, because the '50s, far from being a cultural desert of frightened sensibilities diving underground to mutter their truths, was a high period—arguably the highest—of "aboveground" American satire. From Phyllis McGinley to Nichols and May and beyond, as Philip Roth once pointed out, it was an era that valued literary-minded satire—and *MAD* was literary-minded, in the root sense of feeding on other writing—more than any other in American history. It is the mainstream nature of *MAD*—and its mainstream acceptance—that is far more striking in retrospect than any place it held outside it.

When *MAD* emerged in the 1950s, it was easy to insist that it was in some way an underground magazine. But in truth it belonged very much to that mainstream of American satire then very much in bloom. Far from being part of some subterranean samizdat, it was very much part of mainstream '50s culture—which was already broadly dependent on mockery and satire of other forms of pop culture. *MAD* was much closer to Sid Caesar's legendary mockery of foreign film on his two television series, or to Mel Brooks's already much practiced two-thousand-year-old man, than it was to, say, Bruno Schulz, or any genuinely oppressed or subversive Eastern European writer.

What is most impressive about *MAD* in its time was that it was so successful and so widely adopted. Writing that Harvey Kurtzman was responsible for the shape of American satire to the present day, though meant on this writer's part as eulogistic praise, was not meant strictly and exclusively as praise. There were already kinds of satire in America that were more intricate and eloquent in their way than the burlesques of pop culture that Kurtzman helped make the unique style of American satire. Any novel by Peter de Vries—or for that matter any mordant panel by Jules Feiffer—held more restrained poetic power in its scrutiny of American manners.

But, whether on *Saturday Night Live* or even the superior *SCTV*, Kurtzman's instinct is now what satire means—some bit of pop culture impersonated, more or less perfectly, and then juxtaposed surprisingly with some other bit, with TV commercials most often the heart of it, and TV news, or situation comedies, or, more rarely, foreign films and musical theater placed within the mockery. ("Imitations, with a funny hat and a leer" was Pauline Kael's frustrated name for this style.) Looking back on memories of fifty years of *Saturday Night Live*, it is very hard to recall truly funny sketches that were not in some way less about life and manners and more about other things on television. (*Seinfeld*, to be sure, is an exception to this rule, and for all that it bashfully insisted that it was a show about nothing, it remains startlingly perennial exactly because it is a show about the biggest of somethings—social and erotic manners and their ironies and complications.)

Far from being "subversive," satire was so fertile in the '50s because satire is, as countless professors and historians have shown over time, a conservative genre in the first instance. It was at home in a more self-possessed era than our own. Satire posits a realm of sanity and obvious order from which some current craziness has diverged, and its purpose is to redivert the current to the flow of normal sanity. Its purpose is to make us aware of the absurdities of what has come to seem normal.

That's why Jonathan Swift mocks the absurdities of reflexive religious politics in England by imagining the Big-Endians and Little-Endians, whose arbitrary choice of where to break the morning egg is as trivial, and as passionately held, as sectarian difference. Swift's point was not, so to speak, that the Lilliputians were foolish to eat eggs. It was that it didn't really matter where you broke them. In the same spirit, the legendary early satirical pieces in *MAD*—"Mickey Rodent!" "Superduperman!"—weren't really subversive appeals to some other better set of values that commercial comics culture concealed. They didn't call for an end to bad comics. They were, instead, the eternal call of satire to the reality of things—that a mouse is a rodent, that Clark Kent was more likely to be snubbed and exploited than chummily befriended by a real Lois Lane, and that, when someone cries out, "It's a bird! It's a plane! It's . . . ," well, likely, actually, to be a bird. The truth that, in the simple elegant formulation of the greatest of '50s satirists, Lenny Bruce—in certain ways the most conservative: "There is no 'what should be,' there is only what is."

This instinctive desire to show not "what's wrong" but "what is" was, one suspects, the real force in what *MAD* did. And the subsequent irony is not that *MAD* helped unlock a current of subversive emotion that eventually led to the revolts of the '60s, but that the revolts of the '60s were so utterly unlike the practices of *MAD*. In place of knowing realism, the cultural keynote of the '60s was mystical longing—a desire to move back *past* twelve, to the condition of childhood. It was all about what might yet be, never about what is. "Ah, I was so much older then. I'm younger than that now," Bob Dylan's legendary renunciation of political activism and the message song, is not a satiric moment. It's a wholly romantic one. In a cultural irony greater than is perhaps often meditated upon.

The cultural space that Kurtzman and *MAD* opened blossomed in the succeeding decade into the underground comix, particularly in the work of R. Crumb and his lesser fellows. But their theme was not at all brightly satiric like *MAD*'s, but heartbreakingly nostalgic, looking back on a lost America of blues musicians and telegraph poles and humpbacked cars and all-night diners. Crumb filled the space opened by Kurtzman with a completely different emotional valence. What began as satire turned into psychedelia.

If this meant that, over the years, *MAD* itself ran down into a kind of strange enclosed and repetitive corral, that is, in a sense, the fate of all magazines. Like *Playboy*, its companion in the art of the seemingly scandalous magazine, *MAD*'s special virtue, in retrospect, was the optimism of its style. Just as *Playboy*, never read by any playboy, imagined a nonexistent world of indoor masculine pleasures, *MAD* presupposed a kind of boys' club of Jewish kids who were "on to it." That emotion of being clued in, knowledgeable, not fooled, involves a kind of joy in mutual recognition.

Those moments of mutual recognition, mediated by a magazine, are part of the American heritage of possibility. The exaggerated claims for *MAD*, and for Kurtzman, miss the more appealing truth: that, now and then, from improbable sources, works of intelligence and charm rise and join in the free movement of images and ideas that are a positive part of any open society. George Santayana, in his book

Character and Opinion in the United States (1920)—and in an insight wiser perhaps than his more famous one about repeating the past— insisted that all our cultural life is posited on an American boomer- ang that tends to produce, in one decade's wisdom, the next decade's absolute opposite, with all of us sharing amnesia about where we were immediately before. Satiric realism blossoms—but turns not toward political activism, but, in the hands of a Dylan or Crumb, into roman- tic imagining of an imaginary American past. "What is" becomes "what's gone." Kurtzman threw a boomerang, and like all such, it turned around and hit him, and us, in the head. Is that not the very best thing American boomerangs can do?

THE "OBSCURE AND AWESOME" WOMEN CARTOONISTS of MAD

Rachel Shteir

ON MARTIN from *MAD* magazine did that for me a lot when I was a kid," said Lynda Barry in a 2008 interview. "That" being the thing comic artists do best, which is make readers happy.

Barry was talking about the wacky, bulbous drawings of Martin, one of *MAD*'s longtime, legendary cartoonists whose zany riffs on and outlandish parodies of TV shows, poems, plays, anything, helped make the magazine iconic. Barry is not the only revered female cartoonist of the twenty-first century to cite *MAD* as an influence. Roz Chast (who appears in this volume) was drawn to the magazine too. As she told Adam Gopnik, she "liked the fake ads and, of course, Al Jaffee. I even liked Dave Berg, and I know it's not cool to like Dave Berg." Alison Bechdel, a child subscriber who recalls the brown wrapper the magazine came in, described herself as a "*MAD* magazine addict." And yet famously, for most of the magazine's sixty-year history, *MAD* counted few women among "the Usual Gang of Idiots."

But women appear in the pages of *MAD*. Like burlesque shows, drive-in, *Playboy*, the Borscht Belt, Lenny Bruce, television, and other cultural creations of the 1950s, *MAD* did not ignore women.

Don Martin himself drew them—or crackpot versions of them, anyway. Depending on the artist, *MAD* showed realistic-looking dames, curvy babes, and nonhumanoids. However, into the 1990s, few women contributed to the magazine as writers or artists. Amy Gillett, *MAD*'s first woman intern (in 1989), could not remember any. "They [*MAD*] weren't making an effort," she said. But she loved the magazine regardless. *MAD*'s social and critical skewering, driven by a desire to tear down slick exclusive Madison Avenue, tickled her. As it did many women from the first years. Women all over the country were reading *MAD*, reveling in its naughtiness, wanting to be a part of it, and rejecting it, using it to drive them to other styles.

As I asked cartoonists, curators, and comics aficionados about the subject of women at *MAD*, the name that kept coming up was Leslie Sternbergh, who died tragically in 2019 at age fifty-eight, a few months before the magazine stopped publishing new content. Sternbergh was one of the "obscure and awesome women cartoonists of the last two decades of the twentieth century," as the cartoonist Ned Sonnenberg put it. She had waist-long red hair and was a well-known figure in the underground comics scene, contributing to *Wimmin's Commix*, *Cherry Pop Tart*, R. Crumb's *Weirdo*, and *Dori Stories*, a festschrift for her friend the artist Dori Seda, who herself had died young in 1988.

Sternbergh, like other woman comic artists of her generation, became interested in comics by reading *MAD* paperback reprints (Gaines kept ninety-three *MAD* paperbacks in print between 1954 and 1993) and *Playboy*'s Little Annie Fannie as a child. Although her style seemed too savage, pornographic, and autobiographical for *MAD*, she would contribute around ten comics to the magazine, and her freehand, phantasmagoric panache helped make it possible for more women to draw there in the aughts.

Published in 1994 when she was thirty-four (her birthday was in June and this appeared in May), Sternbergh's first piece in *MAD*, "College Roommates from Hell," pairs hellish dorm cohabitants on each page. One is a hoarder: the door can barely open because of the mountain of stuff behind him, threatening to spill out. Another is a born-again Christian wearing a "Jesus Loves You" T-shirt. In the front of this panel sits a copy of Charles Darwin's *Origin of Species*, taunting the viewer. Sternbergh has positioned you as the freshman, standing at the door looking at these unnerving figures. The pictures give you the panic attack you would have if you were meeting them on the first day of college.

"They opened up their style. They were more varied," said the cartoonist and comics historian Trina Robbins, explaining how by the time Sternbergh began drawing for *MAD* in the '90s the magazine's format had loosened, allowing a range of aesthetic approaches. But Ned Sonnenberg, who knew Sternbergh in those years, said: "The few projects there were quite demanding, and she felt frustration that there was no guarantee of steady assignments." While Sternbergh was drawing for *MAD*, she moonlighted for underground feminist comics magazines. Yet the pieces of hers that *MAD* published burned. In 1995, a year after "College Roommates," she drew "Another MTV Generation" and "A Parental Guide to MTV." Both socially conscious strips expose a grotesque world in which the TV blazes as the watchers wither, like twentieth-century Dorian Grays. In Sternbergh's take on MTV, it doesn't matter if you are Black, white, young, old, poor, or rich, the device has you in its maw. In one panel, a group of watchers seem to be gravely discussing Michael Jackson. One page shows five different TVs, each sucking an ever more depraved audience into its screens, while another shows a kid affixed to MTV and imagining a succubus standing on a dump of skeletons and skulls reaching toward him. The "Parental Guide" is even more sinister. "Bored, Ignored

90210" is one caption. Another displays a corpse of a rock-n-roll animal with the caption "serve chilled" tied onto his toe.

By the time Sternbergh appeared in *MAD*, female cartoonists already had their own scene; some were bursting into the mainstream. A few got syndicated, wrote their own books, or flourished in the many alternative periodicals and zines. But Sternbergh kept delivering pieces to *MAD*. In 1996, at the height of Madonna's fame, she drew "Maternity Girl," a parody of "Material Girl." Longtime *MAD* contributor Frank Jacobs did the lyrics to the song. Sternbergh's full-frontal pregnant Madonna waves a cigar above her head like some army general. Her baby bump bursts out of her trademark Gautier corset and her porcine face stares unblinkingly at the reader. A teddy bear in an S&M harness and a baby in stilettos float around the margins. Two years later, "Approaches to Avoid When Your Child's Pet Dies" parades macabre families, each more indifferent than the rest. Each panel advises parents how not to handle the death of their little darling's furry friend, including weeping profusely, turning away from the event, serving the pet for dinner, or pouring its ashes over your child's hands. In most of the panels, the parents are spectacularly indifferent to their children's suffering.

Sternbergh's last contributions to the magazine appeared in our century. In 2000, her lighthearted "Products for Your Aging Hippie Parents" includes images of a bong, a copy of Abbie Hoffman's *Steal This Book*, and a walker for the octogenarian Harley rider headed to Sturgis, North Dakota. The following year, a few months after *MAD*, desperate for revenue, began accepting advertisements, Sternbergh's "Job Opportunities for the New Millennium" moves to an even darker mode. In large, loosely drawn panels crowded with ugly imagery, she depicts the despair of her generation—dead-end, even violent jobs, fearful faces, bullying, and cruelty. That would be Sternbergh's last piece for *MAD*. She spent the remaining two decades of her life focusing on stories she felt she could only tell in alternative comics. But there's no doubt that she used what she learned at *MAD*.

Sternbergh was not the only female contributor to *MAD* in the '90s. Shary Flenniken, the creator of the feminist, Seattle-lampooning strip *Trots and Bonnie*, drew five pieces for the magazine—some sharply addressing sexism at work, others the overreach of the women's movement or the absurdities of sex.

Despite *MAD*'s reputation as a magazine for snot-nosed, wise-assed boys, women were part of it from the beginning. Marvel's colorist, Marie Severin, colored for *MAD* in the magazine's first years, before it went black and white. In 1955, after William M. Gaines became publisher and Albert B. Feldstein became editor, a handful of women contributed. But of these, in the first three decades of the magazine's history, few sent in more than one or two ideas or pieces. Despite the wealth of *MAD* information available on the Internet and an archive of Al Jaffee material at Columbia University, I found little information about the early "obscure and awesome women cartoonists." Were their names pseudonyms? Some seemed Jewish, like many *MAD* male contributors of that era. Here is a short list of the women who were what John Ficarra, editor-in-chief of the magazine from 1985 until 2018, called "one-hit wonders" in the '60s and '70s: Connie del Vento, Isabelle Di Caprio, Rochelle Davis, Darlene Rutherford, Mary Sarazin Timmons, Marcelle Goodman. Carol Lay worked for the magazine in the '90s.

All the one-hit wonders made inventive contributions. One surprised me. The March 1966 cover "Alfred Hides Shakespeare in *MAD*" is bylined Betty Rollin, then a magazine writer and editor for *Look*, girlfriend of Arthur Herzog and, shortly afterwards, supporter of the women's movement. Illustrated by the prolific Spanish cartoonist Sergio Aragonés, this cover comically reverses kids' habit of hiding *MAD* inside a respectable book.

A majority of the "one-hits," as well as the two- and three-hits, satirized feminism and domestic subjects. Spoofs of *Ladies' Home Journal* and the "feminine mystique" popped up before Betty Friedan wrote her opus in 1963. In 1961, there appeared the first of Pearl Belkin's three pieces targeting children, "A Realistic Children's Book . . . for Realistic Children," written with Gary Belkin, an early *MAD* writer who moved into television. "A brother is to blame things on," a caption for one panel read. Pearl Belkin's subsequent two pieces, "Kids' Letters to Other World Leaders" and "How to Succeed at Childhood," ridicule conventional child-rearing practices. But after that, Belkin disappeared. In May 1969, the New Theatre Workshop on East Fifty-Fourth Street produced two plays by a Pearl Belkin—*Who* and *Hard Labor*. Then the woman disappeared again.

After women's lib exploded in the late 1960s, a new pool of illustrators gravitated to *MAD*. These bold satirists took aim at the women's movement, the Me Decade, and one usual suspect—CULTCHA. In the early 1970s, Marcelle Pesek and Gloria L. Rich each wrote ideas that Al Jaffee worked on. "Snappy Answers to Stupid TV Commercials" railed against the squawk box. "You Know It's Really Over When . . ." by Gloria L. Rich ridiculed the humiliations of dating in the supposedly brave new world. But the battle between the sexes was not the only subject women attacked: they contributed other hilarious panels that fit successfully into the *MAD* brand. In 1976, Marilyn D'Amico wrote three pieces. In "A Collection of Paired *MAD* Thick and Thin Books" in which, bookended by Alfred E. Neuman, we get "A Life in Pictures" by Jacqueline Kennedy and Howard Hughes and "Friends I

Have Made Through My Work" by Xaviera Hollander and Rona Barrett. D'Amico produced two other pieces, "Old Math v. New Math" and "A Guide to the American Class System."

The one-, two-, and three-hit wonders appear and disappear, like the rabbit in the magic shows that were popular in the mid-1950s, or like burlesque performers who never became Gypsy Rose Lee. Like... centerfolds. *MAD* staff artist Sam Viviano remembered one more prolific early woman writer for the magazine—May Sakami. She was born in 1921 in Philadelphia to Japanese parents and studied at Temple University's Tyler School of Fine Arts. She married in 1943 and had three children, but lost her husband in 1963 when he died at the age of fifty. According to a 1974 feature about her in a Pennsylvania newspaper, she somehow met *MAD*'s Paul Coker and in December 1966 (#107) the magazine published "The Astrodome (With apologies to 'Kubla Khan' by Samuel Taylor Coleridge)." The three-page spread featured Tom Koch cowriting and Don Martin doing the illustration. It begins:

> On Houston's soil did millionaires
> A garish Astrodome foresee:
> A palace where the baseball fan,
> 'Mid climate hideous to man,
> > Might loll more pleasantly.

The magazine likely paid Sakami around $100 (around $842 today) for this anti-Astrodome piece. Her next effort, published in July 1967 (#112), was "What Is a Final Exam?", also cowritten with Tom Koch. Sergio Aragonés illustrated with sight gags in the margins: people throwing up in front of final exam announcements, or falling into manholes while thinking of theorems, clouds coming out of their heads. "What Is a Final Exam?" is on the literary side for *MAD*. "Along the perilous road that runs from Matriculation to Graduation . . ." it begins. It uses a lot of text—two whole pages—though much conjures pratfall images of physical suffering endured by exam-takers. "It [the final exam] finds his Breaking Point by forcing him to sit jammed between a rhythmic sniffler and a pathological knuckle-cracker."

In September 1967, Sakami began contributing to *MAD*'s "Horrifying Clichés" series, which had debuted the previous year. Paul Coker illustrated. In one piece Sakami supplied "embracing A BELIEF," in which the belief is the monster; he reappears as the resolution in "introducing A RESOLUTION" and as the confrontation in "avoiding A CONFRONTATION." But in 1974, after six of these features, Sakami, like Pearl Belkin, disappeared from *MAD*. She had other interests and a successful career—under her married name May Schlosberg, she painted on marble, creating labor-intensive pieces depicting royal figures such as the king of Sweden as well as athletes, among others.

Ronnie Nathan, who wrote doggerel for *MAD* in the same era as Sakami, specialized in satiric ditties. Published in the fall of 1968, her "A CBS-TV Summer Memo to the Smothered Brothers," illustrated by Jack Rickard, scolded TV suits for their lame politics. John Ficarra met Nathan years later in the office when she came in with her grandson. "She reminded me of my aunt," he said. But Nathan, who had directed a few musical skits for local organizations in Great Neck, New York (where she lived with her family), before turning to *MAD*, churned out one hilarious taunt after the other, including "A *MAD* Look at Hugh vs. Helen" (#126, April 1969), a spoof of the well-known editors of *Playboy* and *Cosmopolitan*; "Ordure of the Day" (#143, June 1971); the deliciously apocalyptic "The Facts of Life (& Death)" (#133, March 1970); and "An Offer They Could Refuse!" (#161, September 1973). Then she stopped contributing. From "The Facts of Life (& Death)":

The cars that we drive
Are lethal, they say,
And so is the air
We breathe every day.

I turned thirteen in 1979. I did not read *MAD*. I was the oldest child, daughter in a suburban home of repressed, middlebrow, assimilated Jewish parents. Much popular culture was banned from our household. The only TV we watched was *Electric Company*. Years later, I started reading graphic novels and alternative comix, where female cartoonists were doing highly autobiographical work or grappling with more intimate and feminine topics than *MAD* editors seemed interested in. I wanted feminist comix, a raw, grotesque edge barely leavened by wit. Less the jovial bro-ish *MAD* style. More the comic artist Aline Kominsky Crumb, R. Crumb's wife, and her magazine, *Twisted Sisters*, than Dave Berg and his "The Lighter Side of . . ." But looking at it now, I could see how the writers and artists I like might not have existed without *MAD* to bump up against.

John Ficarra thought there might be other reasons why *MAD* attracted so few female cartoonists. "*MAD* bought all the rights and some women balked at that," he said. And "Nick (coeditor Nick Meglin until 2004) and I made concerted efforts, but it was very difficult. . . . We reached out to things like *Bustle*. We had women in for dinner in the offices. Twenty women in the office!" Indeed, in its last years, *MAD* did publish more women. Some just stopped by, like the TV writer Megan Ganz, who read *MAD* as a teenager, interned there while she was still in college, and sold them a joke.

A more substantial contributor to the form was Teresa Burns Parkhurst, who in the aughts wrote and drew maybe forty pieces for the magazine—more than any other woman. But what's as notable as the volume is her versatility. She seems able to squeeze something funny from almost any subject—dogs, *Fifty Shades of Grey*, phones.

MAD stopped publishing new material in 2019, two years after the #MeToo movement gained wide recognition. Maybe that is one of the things that pushed *MAD* into obsolescence, just as stripping made burlesque obsolete and internet pornography killed *Playboy*. Last weekend, trying to finish this piece, I went to see *Chicago Comics: 1960s to Now* at the Museum of Contemporary Art in Chicago. As I walked through the rooms (packed in mid-2021, with COVID-19 rates still high), absorbing the rich history of the artists the show promoted—many of whom did not mention *MAD* in their biographies—I realized something is missing in our landscape: an irreverent mainstream magazine that inspires (and infuriates) female comic artists. Something to strike back at. Maybe a new venue will arise, with more female contributors and new forms of storytelling. If that happens, I hope it lives as long and does as well as *MAD*.

TO ANTARCTICA AND back

Chris Ware

IN OUR sixth grade, I'm pretty sure that my copies of *MAD* were the only ones that'd been to the South Pole. I'd inherited them from my mother's second husband, a meteorologist who'd traveled to Antarctica in 1957 as part of a now seemingly prescient climatological expedition (a glacier still bears his name, at least as long as it lasts). He was a strange fellow, favoring leisure suits, survival rations, the John Birch Society newsletter, and bundling himself up in a blanket in the basement to watch television in the dark. My mom told me years later that it took her only about six weeks to realize she'd made a terrible mistake by marrying him—apparently influenced by my innocent request for "a dad" when she'd asked me what I wanted for Christmas at age seven—a marriage that she then took a terrible seven years to extricate herself from. But it was the 1970s: misaligned marriages, like macramé, were common, along with inflation and *The Love Boat* (one of the shows he'd watch, bundled up in that basement).

Thing is, (1) I hadn't had a dad before, so he provided, for a time, a convincing takeoff of one, plus (2) he came with that stack of old *MAD* magazines. Some of these *MAD*s had parachuted to the Antarctic ice with other mail, rations, and heavy equipment when it was too snowy and dangerous for supply planes to land. Dating from the late

1950s, the yellowed paper and vaguely sinister glowing Frank Kelly Freas covers fascinated me in my preadolescence, and when there was nothing else going on I'd spend weekend afternoons in my room poring over their redolent, acidic pages, the references to television shows and presidents I'd never heard of puzzling me while my mother and less newish dad progressively got along less well with each other downstairs.

A digression for readers born during or after the Clinton administration: in those days, acquiring information—such as how to carve a Cub Scout neckerchief slide into the shape of a guitar amplifier, the functional population of the USS *Enterprise*, and/or key details of female anatomy—was a gauntlet of frustrated dead ends, guesses, and bad information, sometimes entailing visits to the public library but most often newsstands, comic book racks, and your and other parents' dressers, closets, and sock drawers. "Finding things out" was pretty much entirely the domain of paper, secrets locked behind bindings, inside stapled spines, and within folded papers under stacks beneath other folded papers. There were no search words, other than perhaps "I sure wish . . ." or "How am I gonna . . . ?" This deep ocean of print through which *MAD* drifted included, but was not limited to, comic books, real books, newspapers, office photocopies, catalogs, gas station gag brochures, respectable newsmagazines, unrespectable magazines, private newsletters, and public funeral pamphlets, among unimaginably vast quantities of other ephemera, very little of which was actually accessible. In fact, during the single 100-watt-ceiling-bulbed and cigarette-smelling shag-carpeted '70s, if one was friendless enough, a whole hour could be passed simply turning the pages of the local phone book. My friends and I all fed on this publishing slurry in our own personal ways, whatever conclusions drawn from which were later to be shaped by the opinions of older siblings or at the school lunch table, where various hypotheses were tried out until something sounded sorta right or you just got punched.[1]

I'd grown up reading comic books and collecting comic books and copying comic books, and so by the time of fifth or sixth grade I had somehow cemented myself into recognition as the kid Most Likely to Grow Up to Be a Douchebag. Incapable as I was of any sport, drawing was the only way I could find any respect or attention among my peers, and I sought, not so secretly, to become an artist, or even, if I could, a cartoonist. One of my closest friends at the time was, like all the other boys, naturally athletic, but he also had a collection of *MAD* magazines, so an occasional Saturday afternoon might be predicated on that common point alone. Bought at local 7-Elevens and grocery

---

1. Also: television. Those born into a world with all answered by that phone in one's pocket must understand the near-imperceptible high-pitched pull of perpetual on-ness that the cathode-ray tube had on one's central nervous system in the 1970s and 1980s; there's probably a reason CBS chose a single, open eye for its logo. I myself had a black-and-white Zenith in my room, on basically 24/7, regularly monitored with half of one of my own eyes for any sign of activity and directly in front of which I'd pass out every night, my fingers oranged with Dorito dust, an emptied two-liter of Sunkist nearby.

And sometimes, it'd happen. I remember when the film *Logan's Run* (1976) was televised: the censors had apparently not been savvy to a scene in which the female lead, compelled by the chilly air of an ice-cave, is compelled (of course) to completely disrobe, offering 1.75 seconds of full-frontality before donning sexy fur pelts—which yes I myself witnessed on national broadcast television, a nacho chip suspended in disbelief. But there was no rewind, no review, except in my mind. Did I really just see it? I think I did.

Or did I? Those lucky few whose imminently divorcing parents had splurged on the randy new technology of videotape were, at that time, the select elite who were first able to go back, check, rewind, see again—a preview of our contemporary consciousness, now entirely taken for granted. The poorer of us back then had to sift our even poorer memories, make do with the fan magazines and comic books, or, in some cases, read *MAD*.

store newsstands, his were not from the Antarctic 1950s, but contemporary to our 1970s, and thus won hands-down as the way cooler
stash. They were also seemingly dirtier, with the occasional "damn"
or "hell" or even alluding to worse ("A Crock O' BLIP! Now," etc.). We
both liked Sergio Aragonés's "marginals," the tiny drawings set in the
magazine's peripheries analogous to where we'd doodle in our school
textbooks, and Antonio Prohías's "Spy vs Spy"—albeit completely
pruned from its Cuban political grounding—and of course Al Jaffee's
Fold-Ins and especially the weird, Matta-esque floppy-footed drawings of Don Martin with their sleepy eyes and spongy noses. But if
the afternoon's activities devolved into some outdoor sport with the
surprise visit of other tribal males, it was not unusual for the two of us
to excuse ourselves from each other's company in an implicit hand-
shake agreement of divergent interests and skills, and I might spend
some time perusing his *MAD*s while he went outside to throw balls
around with the normal kids. (Since his own [real] dad also had some
hardcover collections of *Esquire* and *Playboy* cartoons shelved in his
library, I was always ready to pursue a cause of self-betterment.) Over
time, and despite my mother's initial objections, I managed to con-
vince her at the grocery store to start buying me new issues of *MAD*
and so supplemented my inherited collection with up-to-the-minute
pop culture knowledge, thrilled that the magazine covered TV shows
I recognized and R-rated films I had no chance of seeing—and, even
more importantly, reported back on valuable events that were inac-
cessibly fleeting: when *Star Wars* was released, I unironically studied
the *MAD* parody several hundred times to try to recapture the feeling
of the film until I was able to get my mom to drive me to the movie
theater to see it again.

Thing is, I'd never really thought of *MAD* as comics, or even, really,
as all that funny. This is not to say that it wasn't funny—just that I was

too dumb to notice it. The "Usual Gang of Idiots" produced it from an office on "MADison Avenue," which, I genuinely believed was so named because the street was an honorific for the periodical. *MAD* seemed like a sort of port into an adult world that was otherwise closed off to my twelve year-old self. While I of course knew that real artists actually drew its pages, beyond the potent distillations of Hollywood actors Mort Drucker somehow seemingly effortlessly condensed out of those wiggly ink-commas, I didn't really try to copy them; at that age I was still studying the world of superhero comics,[2] pasting drawings of my own face onto masked muscular bodies in capes. There was something distant and clinical in *MAD*'s typeset speech balloons which made both the text and even the drawings semi-visible and not-quite-comics. Besides, why would I want to draw like Dave Berg? His "Lighter Side of . . ." pen-and-ink drawings creeped me out, capturing a peculiarly antiseptic leisure-suit ad-supplement quality I couldn't put my finger on. (I should add that as an adult, however—and not that it matters—I greatly admire his work exactly for this reason. His earliest ink-wash illustrations are also just plain terrifying, bathed in deep shadows: a dark 1950s feature about how future shopaholic Americans would eventually stop walking entirely and ride motor scooters everywhere, evolving into round-bottomed polyps, has proved frighteningly oracular.)

So, when I first discovered that the thick-spined "*MAD* Specials" would occasionally bind in a newsprint comic book reissuing material from the earliest days of the magazine under the title "The Nostalgic *MAD*," I was suspicious. I thought the magazine was lying, that

---

2. I will remind the younger reader, this was at the time the lowest of the low in terms of culture—risible and worthy of derision, not the subject of major motion pictures or billion-dollar franchises. Sexually eligible males didn't traffic in it, nor even speak of it.

it wasn't actually a "10¢-Type Comic Book of *MAD* Collector's Items from the '50s," but a parody of one (what was "Humor in a Weathered Vein," anyway?). I simply wasn't smart enough to arrive at the epiphany Art Spiegelman did when he was a kid—namely, that *MAD* had clued him into the fact America was a put-on. *MAD* had only clued me into the fact that *MAD* was a put-on.

Which, originally, it was. Created in 1952 as a quicker and easier comic book for cartoonist/writer/editor Harvey Kurtzman to produce along with the two heavily researched, planned, and horrifyingly serious war comics (really, antiwar comics) he was already delivering to EC Comics managing editor William Gaines, the original *MAD* comic book allowed the loud-voiced, snappy rhythm and liquid layouts Kurtzman first composed into his "Hey, Look!" filler gag pages[3] for Stan Lee's (yes, Stan Lee) Timely/Marvel (yes, superhero) comics line in the 1940s to expand into its own comic, a parody of comics itself. Writing the scripts and laying out the compositions, Kurtzman deployed many of the artists who already drew the crime, science fiction, western, and horror comics of EC's other titles to make fun of the crime, science fiction, western, and horror comics which were paying their rents and mortgages. They seemed to relish the opportunity, as did the readers; the comic book was an immediate success. I arrived way late, however, first seeing *The Nostalgic MAD* #6 in 1977, two decades after its original publication. Nevertheless, I was riveted. Somehow, the hand-lettering (permit a young cartoonist his psychological limitations) made the whole thing feel more familiar, and somehow, I could "see" it better. Plus the work was great: the

---

3. Cartoonist Dan Clowes once told me that reading the 1991 book collection of "Hey, Look!" strips after a long night of work would make him want to get up and immediately start drawing all over again.

Melvin Mole story, originally from *MAD* #22 (April 1955), chronicles a parodic biography of major *MAD* artist Will Elder, jokingly proffering the strip as his ultimate comics "masterpiece," and deploys a repeating, almost musical structure through which the main character, an incarcerated criminal, repeatedly escapes jail by digging his way out of increasingly cave-like confinement with increasingly lesser tools (shovel, spoon, toothpick, and finally a single nose hair). Along with being a useful storytelling lesson for budding cartoonists, it's one of the funniest (I actually laughed at this one) and weirdly horrifying stories *MAD* ever published, turning on fears of confinement, live burial, and, of course, death.

"Gasoline Valley" (#15, September 1954) is another masterpiece, parodying *Gasoline Alley* creator Frank King's sui-generis-genius idea of a newspaper comic strip where the characters age at the same rate as the reader, capturing the tragic ineffable passage of life and allowing, at least in King's original case, for the first seriously emotional graphic fiction. In *MAD*'s parody, the repeated panel of Skizziks's ("Skeezix" in King's original) brother Caulky ("Corky") remains a baby throughout, increasingly surrounded by medical monitors, with an exclaimed "Caulky's still the same!" chiming like a clock while Skizziks gets rapidly, nightmarishly older, speeding toward death, though not without a first daring gag of him "erecting" into a teenager when he first sees a buxom Nin(a) O'Clock. Even cleverer, Will Elder signs every page with a large, intrusive, double-punning "Elder" in imitation of King's signature, time-stamping each with a relentless sense of a final Sunday-strip gag panel, even though there isn't always something funny to laugh at.

As those original *MAD* comics progressed, they became less traditional parodies and more adventurous, original, and *Tristram Shandy–*esque, with disorienting near-blank pages, fake ads, typeset blocks of text, and repeated fourth-wall breaks, the strangeness of the material eventually extending into the complete comic book object itself, offering up some of the greatest magazine covers ever, nearly postmodern in their "challenging"—as my later college art teachers seemed fond of saying—of "the reader's relationship" to the printed object, from the all-orange cover to the composition-notebook cover to my favorite, the parody of the Johnson Smith back-cover ads or cheap novelty gag items—all ending with a last big typeset THINK. Taken in total, all twenty-three of the original *MAD* comics are the richest example of the aesthetic and expressive potential of the comic-book-as-art presented in the least prissy of ways[4] before the underground comics of the 1960s—which I'm pretty sure most every one of those underground cartoonists would credit as a primary inspiration.

Harvey Kurtzman was practically born a cartoonist, raised in New York picking "through his neighbors' trash searching for the Sunday papers his own family didn't get, so that he wouldn't miss even one comic strip." Reportedly, the inspiration for *MAD* was also found in the same art gallery: "I picked up in the garbage, or somewhere, some college magazines. They impressed me as being a new kind of humor. . . . Of course what they were, were youth magazines."[5] The Jewish origins of *MAD* were completely opaque to me as a kid; on the spectrum of cartoonist ethnicity, I'm probably farther to the goy than Charles Schulz, growing up a sheltered midwestern WASP. But the directness and implicit sentiments ("don't take yourself seriously" and "all human effort is essentially trash") sure stuck.[6] And while the

4. Unlike this pretentious essay.

5. All quotes from Harvey Kurtzman are taken from Maria Reidelbach, *Completely MAD: A History of the Comic Book and Magazine* (Boston: Little, Brown, 1991).

6. Sadly, the words "furshlugginer" and "potrzebie" didn't resonate as they should have, however.

magazine *MAD* was cool, those early comic book *MAD*s spoke more directly. There's something innately low-class and always accessible about the comic strip's garbage-y mashup of words and pictures, and *MAD* tied itself not only to comics but also drew a direct kinship to earlier gangs of idiots: the *Harvard Lampoon, Ballyhoo, Puck, Judge,* and *Punch*. Even George Cruikshank's *Comic Almanack* (1835–53) and Albert Smith and Angus Reach's 1847–49 *The Man in the Moon* contain Aragonés-esque "marginal" drawings, the latter sporting a Jaffee-worthy foldout comic strip pasted into each issue.[7] Less isn't more, more is more—and in this vein, *MAD* was crammed to the edges. It seemed to suggest that you should enjoy life now, since things could all change suddenly, without warning, tomorrow. Which things, in fact, did. One Monday morning I arrived at school to discover my friend with several pages of his own in-progress *MAD*-esque magazine, a stapled-pencil-on-notebook-paper confection that to my horror had attracted the attention of all the other boys in our homeroom. It was good. And funny. And about all the things that make adolescent boys laugh (titled, appropriately, "GROSS"). I was absolutely crushed, my identity as cartoonist dashed, even though I hadn't even really attempted anything myself yet at all. Crestfallen, after some time—maybe a couple of days?—I stapled together my own paper and started my own imitation, not of *MAD* but of my friend's *MAD* imitation. Crucially, mine was not funny; it was just bad. And it had an even worse title: "HUMOR."[8] All I wanted in my feral state was,

7. The always excellent David Kunzle's most recent book, *Rebirth of the English Comic Strip: A Kaleidoscope, 1847–1870* (Jackson: University of Mississippi Press, 2021), offers a fascinating, funny, and unpretentiously readable survey of completely forgotten and nearly completely forgotten early British comic strip material.
8. It's probably unnecessary to mention, but various publishers had done the same—for decades—with lame-ass watered-down imitations all calculated, well, to make

pathetically, attention. My paper stack went with me everywhere, and I kept adding to its pages, going for quantity over quality, scratching and erasing during countless study halls, a pastiche of drawings lifted from the comic-book era *MAD* adjusted to my own ends filling its pages. My friend, initially rightfully annoyed, eventually encouraged me, perhaps sympathetically intuiting as the sibling of three brothers—I was an only child—my misplaced inclination to primate-compete. (Besides, he was on to something better.⁹) In retrospect, I was almost sort of like Hugh Hefner, who was himself an imitative cartoonist before going on to his career of parasitic life-ruining—talk about secrets in folded paper!—also funding Kurtzman's various post-*MAD* projects, strips, and magazines (weirdly, one named *Trump*), all to be eventually smothered by Hefner's stifling editorial surveillance. The Baby Boomer boyness of *MAD*—not many girls read *MAD*¹⁰— also gradually lost its interest for me, which probably relieved my mom, since I'd imagine the magazine also reminded her of a time in her life she'd very much rather forget.

---

money: *Cracked, Sick, Crazy, Zany, Nuts, Loco, Frenzy,* and on and on and on. The *MAD* editors, not one to waste an opportunity, created their own imitation, *Panic,* which lasted several creditable issues. (Mine lasted only one.)

9. Electric guitar.

10. Though apparently Roz Chast—a contributor to this volume—did. And so did my wife, who told me once that growing up with the magazine (along with its disreputable cousin *National Lampoon*) around the house in her experimental three-parent household—her dad upstairs, mom's boyfriend in the basement—made her feel "sort of cool and in-the-know," even though the neighborhood's awareness of her unusual family arrangement embarrassed her deeply. She also said Alfred E. Neuman gave her the creeps.

Inexplicably, as the universe apparently likes jokes, she also lived for a year in the Playboy Mansion after Hefner sold it to the Art Institute of Chicago for use as a student dormitory. She discovered bunny ears in the basement and a large, dark, empty indoor swimming pool.

My mom eventually remarried (a nice guy) and we moved far away; I lost touch with my *MAD* friend, put my *Star Wars* toys in storage, finished high school, went to art school, drew comics for the student newspaper, did terrible paintings, ran my hand through a table saw, moved to Chicago for more art school, broke both my legs jumping off a building, started publishing my own comic books, got married and had a daughter, now heading off to college. Somehow, through it all, I still held on to my second father's *MAD*s. How, or why, I'm not sure. Now even more yellowed and acidic and strange, the things I look for in them aren't laughs or secrets of the adult world or tricks of ink wash—okay, sometimes I'll look for tricks of ink wash—but some sense of briefly recapturing a feeling, moment, or sensation that I can't even begin to name or identify.[11]

11. Recently, I returned to my hometown and was dining at a restaurant with my wife and daughter across from—I suddenly realized in a shocked moment—the apartment building where my mom, decades before, told me my second father had moved after their divorce. I hadn't seen or spoken to him in over forty years. "Wow. What a really weird thing," I thought. Out of curiosity, I took out my phone and googled his name to find out when he'd died (as he was much older than my mother, almost fifteen years). But I couldn't believe what I found: astonishingly, he was still listed at the same address, in his mid-nineties, apparently alive.

I looked up, out the window, at the building, counting upwards the number of floors that matched the address listing, to a dark window where a dim television was just barely visible, its shifting images illuminating the corner of a room. Was he possibly, actually, really in there? Could I really just walk over, into the lobby, take the elevator up to that floor and knock on the door, and he'd be there? What would I say? What would I do?

HERE WE GO WITH OUR OWN EXECRABLE SIMULACRUM

MAD FOLD-IN

MAD Magazine has two principal modes: First, sardonic brain-scorn, a child's first garden of sarcasm and critique (Hey, these products, fads & political ideals I'm being sold are a total rip-off!). Second, a pre-teen body-horror revulsion at the humiliations of the human animal (sexual embarrassment, stubbed-toes & death are all coming for me too!). Jaffee's Fold-In likes to have it both ways.

FOLD PAGE OVER LIKE THIS!

A▶ FOLD THIS SECTION OVER LEFT ◀B FOLD BACK SO "A" MEETS "B"

AGAIN AND AGAIN, IN THE FOLD-INS, SOME TIMELY THESIS MOCKING CONTEMPORARY LIFE IS REVEALED AS HIDING AN UNDERLYING WORLDVIEW OF HORROR :(DEFORMED BODIES, MACHINE FORMS CONSISTING OF MEAT & DEATH HIDING IN LIFE. THIS EXPRESSES AN ODD MIX OF MORBID FEAR AND CAN-DO OPTIMISM: JAFFE'S LIFE COMPANIONS ALONG WITH A MIGHTY CRAZY FAMILY LIFE THAT HE HAD TO GRIN AND BEAR. SUCH TRAUMA TENDS TO DROP INTO YOUNG LIVES WITHOUT WARNING AND ALSO TO RE-TURN THROUGH DECADES AND PROVIDE AN ARTIST'S LEXICON ORGANIZING THEIR SIGNATURE CONTRIBUTION AND ENFOLD-ING THEIR PERSONA IN A STYLE.

contributors

NATHAN ABRAMS is a professor of film at Bangor University in Wales. He is a founding co-editor of *Jewish Film and New Media: An International Journal* as well as the author of *The New Jew in Film: Exploring Jewishness and Judaism in Contemporary Cinema*, and *Stanley Kubrick: New York Jewish Intellectual*. He is co-author of *Eyes Wide Shut: Stanley Kubrick and the Making of His Final Film* and *Kubrick: An Odyssey*.

BONNIE ALTUCHER grew up in New York City and has also lived in Paris. Her essay "How My Worst Date Ever Became My Best" was featured in *The New York Times*'s "Modern Love" series and was adapted as an episode of the Amazon series *Modern Love Tokyo*. An excerpt of her memoir-in-progress was published in the online journal *Statorec* in 2022. Her fiction reviews have appeared in *Electric Literature*, and excerpts from *Autonomy*, a novel are currently online in *Cleaver* and *The American in Italia*. She was awarded a Mac-Dowell fellowship, among other residency fellowships. She lives in Brooklyn.

MAX ANDERSSON started drawing comics around age four. His first comic was silent and ended with the protagonist being blown to pieces by dynamite in his pants. Later he learned the alphabet and subsequently created books such as *Pixy* and *Death and Candy*, as well as several short films. His stories of tractor children, intoxicated fetuses, homeless houses, and softhearted guns have been translated into twenty languages, and his images, objects, and installations have been shown in exhibitions around the world. Andersson and Helena Ahonen's documentary feature film *Tito on Ice*, a spin-off of the graphic novel *Bosnian Flat Dog* by Andersson and his colleague Lars Sjunnesson, was awarded the Grand Prize at the Ottawa International Animation Festival in 2013. His latest graphic novel, *The Excavation*, is an autobiographical family murder mystery that took eighteen years to complete. Andersson currently lives and works on the island of Öland.

MICHAEL BENSON's work focuses on the intersection of art and science. As artist and author he has staged a series of large-scale shows of digitally reconstructed planetary landscape photography in major museums internationally. His most recent book is *Space Odyssey: Stanley Kubrick, Arthur C. Clarke, and the Making of a Masterpiece*. Benson has contributed to many publications, including *The New Yorker*, *The New York Times*, *The Washington Post*, *The Atlantic*, and *Rolling Stone*. He is currently using SEM technologies (scanning electron microscope) to focus on natural design at submillimeter scales for a book and exhibition project titled *Nanocosmos*, which he is realizing at the Canadian Museum of Nature in Ottawa. Michael Benson is a Fellow of the New York Institute of the Humanities, a Weizmann Institute Advocate for Curiosity, and a recent Visiting Scholar at the MIT Media Lab.

SARAH BOXER, a writer, cartoonist, and critic, is the author of *In the Floyd Archives,* a graphic novel spoofing Freud's case histories, and its sequel, *Mother May I?*, a comic lightly based on the works of Melanie Klein and D. W. Winnicott. From 1989 to 2006 Boxer worked at *The New York Times*, where she was, at various points, a photography critic, a Web critic, an arts reporter, and an editor at the *Book Review*. Her essays and criticism have been published in *The Atlantic*, *The New York Review of Books*, *The Comics Journal*, and in numerous anthologies, including *The Peanuts Papers* (Library of America), *Rereading America*, and *The Best American Comics Criticism.* She is the editor of the anthology *Ultimate Blogs* and has drawn two Shakespearean Tragic-Comics: *Hamlet: Prince of Pigs* and *Anchovius Caesar: The Decomposition of a Romaine Salad.*

DANIEL BRONSTEIN teaches in the departments of Jewish Studies and Sociology at Hunter College. Following his ordination at the Hebrew Union College–Jewish Institute of Religion in 1996, Rabbi Bronstein went on to earn his doctorate in Jewish history at the Jewish Theological Seminary of America. His dissertation, "Torah in the Trenches: The Rabbi Chaplains of World War II, 1940–1946," examined intra-Jewish relations in the context of world war and the Holocaust. Bronstein has published on topics including Jewish humor, Jewish foodways, and theology and has edited and contributed articles to the *CCAR Journal, Forward,* and other publications. He has also been a contributor to the *Cambridge Dictionary of Jewish Religion, History and Culture, Jews and American Popular Culture, Jewish Theology in Our Time,* and *Visualizing Jewish Narrative: Jews and Comics and Graphic Novels.*

ROZ CHAST's cartoons have appeared regularly in *The New Yorker* since 1978, before paper and pens were invented. She drew on flat rocks with burnt twigs. She has published several collections of cartoons and illustrated children's books. Her graphic memoir about her parents' declining years, *Can't We Talk About Something More Pleasant?*, was the winner of numerous awards, including the National Book Critics Circle Award and the Kirkus Prize. In 2018, she became the first woman to be inducted into the Harvey Hall of Fame. Her most recent book is about dreams and is called *I Must Be Dreaming.* She now draws on paper with a pen and sometimes uses an Apple Pencil and iPad.

IVAN COHEN is a writer of comic books, prose, and animation best known for cocreating DC Comics's nonbinary superhero "Kid Quick" in 2020. His book projects include the best-selling graphic-novel adaptation of 2021's *Space Jam: A New Legacy, The Batman and Scooby-Doo Mysteries* comic book series, and the film adaptation *Batman Returns: One Dark Christmas Eve—The Illustrated Holiday Classic.* He has also produced documentaries for PBS and Warner Bros.; edited comic books for DC Comics and NPR's *Planet Money,* written about pop culture for outlets including *Esquire,*

Vulture.com, and *Time Out New York*; and contributed to *MAD*'s online joke feed as part of a last grasp at relevance (whether his or the magazine's, who knows for sure?). A graduate of Stuyvesant High School in New York City and Northwestern University, Cohen lives in Harlem with his wife and their son.

R. CRUMB, author of numerous comic works, is one of the pioneers of underground comics. His books include *Kafka, The Complete Crumb Comics* (17 volumes), *The R. Crumb Sketchbook* (10 volumes), *R. Crumb Draws the Blues, The Book of Mr. Natural, The Book of Genesis Illustrated by R. Crumb,* and many more. Born in Philadelphia, he lives in the south of France with his wife, the artist Aline Kominsky-Crumb.

MARY FLEENER has spent much of her life in the Los Angeles area. She attended Cal State Long Beach as a printmaking major and began, in 1984, to self-publish mini comics; she was also published in anthologies such as *Twisted Sisters* and *Weirdo*. Her first solo comic, *Hoodoo*, was a tribute to Zora Neale Hurston, who inspired her to do autobiographical comics. The collection *Life of the Party* was published by Fantagraphics in 1994. *Billie the Bee*, a young adult book, came out in 2018, and she is currently working on a new graphic "bar band" memoir called *The Happy Hour*.

DREW FRIEDMAN's illustrations and comics have appeared in *RAW, Weirdo, Heavy Metal, National Lampoon, SPY, MAD, The New Yorker, The New York Times*, and many other publications. Friedman is the author and artist behind fifteen books and anthologies, the latest being *Schtick Figures*. In 2014, the Society of Illustrators in Manhattan hosted a main gallery showing of Friedman's *Old Jewish Comedians* illustrations. The Billy Ireland Cartoon Library & Museum at Ohio State University held an exhibition of all of the artwork created for his book *All the Presidents* in 2019. A documentary about his life and work, *Drew Friedman: Vermeer of the Borscht Belt*, was released in 2024. The artist's portrait of William M. Gaines, along with portraits of other *MAD* greats, is available as a print at www.drewfriedman.net.

Leah Garrett is the Larry A. and Klara Silverstein Chair and Director of Jewish Studies at Hunter College, CUNY. She has published five books; her most recent, *X-Troop: The Secret Jewish Commandos of World War Two* (2022), was a best seller in the U.K. and was translated into several languages. Her *Young Lions: How Jewish Authors Reinvented the American War Novel* won the 2017 Jordan Schnitzer Book Award for modern Jewish history and was a finalist for the National Jewish Book Award. She is currently working on a new book titled *The Angels of Iwo Jima: The Untold Story of the American Combat Nurses in the Final Battles of World War Two*.

Adam Gopnik is a staff writer at *The New Yorker*; he has written for the magazine since 1986. He has three National Magazine Awards, for essays and for criticism, and also a George Polk Award for Magazine Reporting. In 2013, Gopnik was awarded the medal of Chevalier of the Order of Arts and Letters. The author of numerous best-selling books, including *Paris to the Moon*, he lives in New York City.

David Hajdu is a professor at the Columbia Journalism School and the music critic for *The Nation*. His many books include *The Ten-Cent Plague: The Great Comic Book Scare and How It Changed America* and *A Revolution in Three Acts*, a history of vaudeville in graphic-novel form. While in high school, he drew illustrations for his local newspaper, *The Easton Express*, in a vain, failed attempt to emulate Mort Drucker.

Grady Hendrix is the author of many novels, including *Horrorstör* (about a haunted IKEA*), My Best Friend's Exorcism, We Sold Our Souls, The Southern Book Club's Guide to Slaying Vampires,* and *The Final Girl Support Group*. His *Paperbacks from Hell* is a history of the horror paperback boom of the 1970s and 1980s. A cofounder of the New York Asian Film Festival, he was a regular film critic for the New York *Sun*. His writing has appeared in, among other publications, *Playboy, Slate, The Village Voice,* the *New York Post, Film Comment,* and *Variety*.

FRANK JACOBS (1929–2021) wrote for *MAD* from 1957 to 2014 and contributed more content to the magazine than any other writer. He was the chief author of *MAD*'s song and poetry parodies, which he called his "hysterical light verse." Jacobs invented several new genres, including phony obituaries and do-it-yourself newspaper stories. He also wrote *Alvin Steadfast on Vernacular Island*, a comical boys' book illustrated by Edward Gorey.

TIM KREIDER is the author of two essay collections, *We Learn Nothing* and *I Wrote This Book Because I Love You*, and three collections of cartoons: *The Pain—When Will It End?*, *Why Do They Kill Me?*, and *Twilight of the Assholes*. He's contributed to *The New York Times,* thenewyorker.com, *The Atlantic, Film Quarterly,* and lots of other publications. His essay "A Man and His Cat" was included in *The Best American Essays 2015*. He teaches at Sarah Lawrence College. He should probably be working on his next book right now.

PETER KUPER's illustrations and comics have appeared in newspapers and magazines around the world. He has been a regular contributor to *The New Yorker, The New York Times, The Nation,* and *MAD*, writing and illustrating *Spy vs Spy* for twenty-six years. The cofounder and co-editor of *World War 3 Illustrated*, a political graphics magazine, he has produced more than two dozen books, including *Ruins* (winner of the 2016 Eisner Award) and adaptations of many of Franz Kafka's works into comics, including *The Metamorphosis* and *Kafkaesque* (winner of a National Cartoonists Society award in 2018 for best graphic novel). He was the recipient of the 2020–21 Cullman Fellowship at the New York Public Library. He has lectured and exhibited his work in the U.S. and abroad and teaches courses on graphic novels at Harvard University. He is currently working on a graphic-novel history of insects.

LIEL LEIBOVITZ is editor at large for *Tablet* magazine and the cohost of its popular podcast, *Unorthodox*. He is the author or co-author of several books, including, most recently, *How the Talmud Can Change Your Life: Surprisingly Modern Advice from a Very Old Book*. He holds a PhD in video games from Columbia University, but his real formative education came earlier in life, when he learned from Alfred E. Neuman that you can be on the right track and still get hit by a train.

JONATHAN LETHEM and **MARK ALLEN** live in Claremont, California, where they still fold any paper that comes within reach, hoping for something magic to happen.

DAVID MIKICS has written, among other books, *Stanley Kubrick: American Filmmaker*, *Bellow's People*, and *Slow Reading in a Hurried Age*. He teaches in the Honors College at the University of Houston, where he is John and Rebecca Moores Professor of English. Mikics is also a regular columnist for *Tablet* magazine. A Guggenheim Fellow, he has been reading *MAD* since he was in short pants. He lives in Brooklyn and Houston with his wife and son.

GEOFFREY O'BRIEN was born in New York City in 1948. His books, which encompassing memoir, cultural history, and criticism, include *Hardboiled America*; *Dream Time: Chapters from the Sixties*; *The Phantom Empire*; *Castaways of the Image Planet*; *Sonata for Jukebox*; *The Fall of the House of Walworth*; *Stolen Glimpses, Captive Shadows: Writing on Film 2002–2012*; *Where Did Poetry Come From: Some Early Encounters*; and *Arabian Nights of 1934*. He has published ten collections of poetry, among them *The Blue Hill*, *Who Goes There*, and *Went Like It Came*. An editor at Library of America for twenty-five years, he retired as editor in chief in 2017. His writing on film, theater, music, and literature has appeared frequently in *The New York Review of Books*, *Film Comment*, *Artforum*, *The Village Voice*, and other periodicals.

RACHEL SHTEIR is the author of, most recently, *Betty Friedan: Magnificent Disrupter*. Her other books are *The Steal: A Cultural History of Shoplifting*, *Gypsy: The Art of the Tease*, and *Striptease: The Untold History of the Girlie Show* (winner of the Theatre Library Association's George Freedley

Memorial Award). Her work has appeared in many magazines and newspapers, including *The Wall Street Journal* and *The New York Times*. A six-time Yaddo residency recipient and the head of Dramaturgy/Dramatic Criticism at The Theatre School at DePaul University, she holds a DFA in Dramaturgy and Dramatic Criticism from the Yale School of Drama and a BA in Near Eastern Languages and Civilizations from the University of Chicago.

R. SIKORYAK is the creator of the graphic novels *Constitution Illustrated, Masterpiece Comics, Terms and Conditions*, and *The Unquotable Trump.* He illustrated the comic books that appear in Tom Hanks's novel *The Making of Another Major Motion Picture Masterpiece.* His comics and illustrations have been published in *The New Yorker, The New York Times Book Review, The Onion,* and *MAD.* He teaches illustration at Parsons School of Design, and he presents his live comics performance series, Carousel, around the United States and Canada.

ART SPIEGELMAN is the author of the Pulitzer Prize–winning graphic memoir *Maus: A Survivor's Tale.* His most recent book is, with Robert Coover, *Street Cop.*

CLIFFORD THOMPSON's books include *What It Is: Race, Family, and One Thinking Black Man's Blues* (2019) and the graphic novel *Big Man and the Little Men* (2022), which he wrote and illustrated. His essays and reviews have appeared in *The Washington Post, The Wall Street Journal, The Village Voice, Best American Essays*, the *Pushcart Prize Anthology, The Times Literary Supplement, Commonweal*, and *The Threepenny Review*, among other publications. Thompson has taught creative nonfiction writing at Sarah Lawrence College, the Bennington Writing Seminars, New York University, and the Vermont College of Fine Arts. A painter, he is a member of Blue Mountain Gallery in New York City. Thompson was born and raised in Washington, DC, graduated from Oberlin College, and lives with his wife in Brooklyn, where they raised their two kids.

CHRIS WARE is the author of *Jimmy Corrigan—The Smartest Kid on Earth* and *Building Stories*. A regular contributor of comic strips and more than thirty covers to *The New Yorker*, Ware has had his work exhibited at the Hammer Museum in Los Angeles, the MCA Chicago, and the Whitney Museum of American Art, as well as in regular exhibitions at the Galerie Martel in Paris and Adam Baumgold Gallery in New York. *Rusty Brown, Part I* was selected as one of 2019's Best 100 Books of the Year by *The New York Times*. A solo retrospective of his work, presented at the Centre Pompidou in Paris in 2022 and the Cartoonmuseum in Basel in 2023, will continue to tour Europe through 2025.

MARY-LOU WEISMAN was educated at Bryn Mawr College and Brandeis University and began her writing career as a journalist, primarily an essayist, for *The New York Times*, with her work being nationally syndicated. Other essays, feature articles, and film and book reviews have appeared in *Vogue*, *The New Republic*, *Newsweek*, and *The Atlantic*, among other magazines. Her books include *Playing House in Provence: How Two Americans Became a Little Bit French*, *Al Jaffee's Mad Life*, *Traveling While Married*, *My Middle-Aged Baby Book: A Place to Write Down All the Things You'll Soon Forget*, and *Intensive Care: A Family Love Story*. She has taught personal essay and memoir writing at The New School, the Tisch School of Dramatic Arts at New York University, and Manhattanville College. Weisman is a member of Phi Beta Kappa, the Authors Guild, and PEN.

SOURCES and Acknowledgments

Most but not all of the contributions in this volume are published here for the first time. The selections listed below have previously been published and are reprinted here from the following sources:

Nathan Abrams, "*MAD*'s Jewish America." Versions of sections of this essay have been published in the following publications: "You Don't Have to Be Jewish to Be Mad . . . but It Helps," *Haaretz*, November 13, 2013. https://www .haaretz.com/jewish/2013-11-13/ty-article/.premium/you-dont-have-to-be -jewish-to-be-mad-but-it-helps/0000017f-dbe9-d3ff-a7ff-fbe9d29b0000; and "A Secular Talmud: the Jewish Sensibility of *Mad* Magazine," *Studies in American Humor* 30 (2014): 111–22. Copyright © Nathan Abrams. Reprinted with permission.

Daniel Bronstein, "Brueghel of the Bronx." First published as "Converting Schmaltz into Chicken Fat: Will Elder and the Judaization of American Comedy," in Derek Parker Royal (ed.), *Visualizing Jewish Narratives: Jewish Comics and Graphic Novels* (London: Bloomsbury, 2016), pp. 129–40. Copyright © Daniel Bronstein. Reprinted with permission.

Leah Garrett, "Jaffee in Yiddish." *Forward*, February 21, 2016. Copyright © 2016 by Leah Garrett. Reprinted with permission.

Grady Hendrix, "Cahiers of Ciné*MAD*." *Film Comment,* March–April 2013. Copyright © 2013 by Grady Hendrix. Reprinted with permission of the author.

Frank Jacobs, "A Preface to Gaines." From *The MAD World of William M. Gaines* (New York: Lyle Stuart, 1972). Copyright © 1972 by Frank Jacobs.

Tim Kreider, "The World According to *MAD Magazine*." *The New York Times*, July 12, 2019. Copyright © 2019 by Tim Kreider. Reprinted with permission.

Peter Kuper, "H. Kurtzman." Monte Beauchamp (ed.), *Masterful Marks: Cartoonists Who Changed the World* (New York: Simon & Schuster, 2014). Copyright © 2014 by Peter Kuper. Reprinted with permission.

Geoffrey O'Brien, "Stark Raving *MAD*." *Castaways of the Image Planet: Movies, Show Business, Public Spectacle* (Washington, DC: Counterpoint, 2002). The essay was originally published in *The Village Voice*, October 1, 1989. Copyright © Geoffrey O'Brien. Reprinted with permission of the author.

Art Spiegelman, "*MAD* Love." *Breakdowns: Portrait of the Artist as a Young %@&*!* by Art Spiegelman, copyright © 1972, 1973, 1974, 1975, 1976, 1977, 2005, 2006, 2007, and 2008 by Art Spiegelman. Used by permission of Pantheon Books, an imprint of the Knopf Doubleday Publishing Group, a division of Penguin Random House LLC and Viking, an imprint of Penguin Books Limited. All rights reserved.

THIS BOOK is set in 11 point Warnock, a font designed by Robert Slimbach. First issued in 2000, it is named after Adobe's cofounder John Warnock. The chapter titles are set in Pokerface Regular, designed by Jim Ford; the instances of the word "Mad" within the titles use MADFONT by Harold Lohner, who was inspired by the original logo created by Harvey Kurtzman for the magazine. Author names are set in Franklin Gothic No. 2, developed in the early years of the twentieth century by designer Morris Fuller Benton of American Type Founders. The running heads are set in Proxima Nova, designed by Mark Simonson in 1994.

The paper is acid-free and exceeds the requirements for permanence established by the American National Standards Institute.

Text design and composition by
Gopa & Ted2, Inc., Albuquerque, NM.
Printing and binding by Lakeside Book Company.